The Orange Riots

The Orange Riots

Irish Political Violence in New York City, 1870 and 1871

MICHAEL A. GORDON

Cornell University Press *Ithaca and London*

First printing, Cornell Paperbacks, 2009

First published 1993 by Cornell University Press.
First Printing, Cornell Paperbacks, 2009
International Standard Book Number 0-8014-2754-1 (cloth)
International Standard Book Number 0-8014-8034-5 (paper)
Library of Congress Catalog Card Number 93-9847

Printed in the United States of America

Librarians: Library of Congress cataloging information appears on the last page of the book.

♾ The paper in this book meets the minimum requirements of the American National Standard for Information Sciences—Permanence of Paper for Printed Library Materials, ANSI Z39.48-1984.

For Michele

Contents

Maps, Figure, and Illustrations

MAPS

FIGURE

ILLUSTRATIONS

Tables

Preface

I became interested in the Orange riots while conducting research on Irish working-class thought and behavior in Gilded Age New York City. What struck me at first about these riots was the great opportunity they provided to learn more about the perceptions of Irish workers. Crises like riots, strikes, depressions, and political upheavals have often sparked much public comment by diverse citizens in the form of resolutions, letters to editors, speeches, newspaper interviews, pamphlets, poems, ballads, demonstrations, and other forms of public discourse. As George Rudé and many other students of social disorder have amply demonstrated, however calamitous such events may have been at the time—and the Orange riots surely were—the confrontations and the commentary they provoked give historians access to the thoughts, concerns, and activities of people who in quieter times remain "hidden" from our view.

The July 12 riots are no exception. As I studied these events, it became clear that responses to the clashes in New York in 1870 and 1871 revealed much about Irish-American sensibilities and the activities of such Irish-American groups as the Fenian Brotherhood and the Ancient Order of Hibernians. But as I studied the views and activities of the Orangemen and their supporters, I became interested in the class dimensions of this violence and not just in Irish working-class thought and behavior. Many Irish Catholics viewed

Orangemen as surrogates for wealthy Protestant New Yorkers and nativists whom they believed threatened to oppress them as industrial workers and to subvert republicanism—much as the Irish had been oppressed under Protestant ascendancy as peasants in Ireland. Their class opponents viewed Irish Catholics as debased papal agents and claimed that *they* threatened republican institutions. The contending class views shaped the public debate that surrounded these riots and help to explain their causes and consequences.

It is difficult to write about such violence. We capture a moment in people's lives in which their passion and anger and concern lead them to consider—and in some cases to take—violent action, overlooking the many other facets of their lives in which they express their thoughts and reveal their gentleness, caring, and humor. By focusing just on their hostility, we learn only a little about who they are. Even so, what we do learn is valuable. Irish Catholic comment about the riots was passionate and infused with historical references that reveal much about Irish historical consciousness. Comments by other participants were equally pointed. I have tried to help the contending sides re-create their debate in this book by including lengthy excerpts from their arguments instead of paraphrasing their remarks and reducing their intensity. By so doing, I have enabled long-forgotten or ignored people to be heard as they expressed their often-eloquent and compelling concerns about their lives and the future of their nation.

For related reasons, I also have analyzed the riot events in considerable detail. It is important to explain what actually happened (as much as the sources allow) in order to understand how and why such violence occurred, to compare our findings with the accounts of contemporaries and other historians, and to assess motivation and culpability. Moreover, a detailed analysis helps us to visualize more clearly the social space in which people lived, worked, and attended to their daily affairs. For example, details about meetings of various Irish-American nationalist and fraternal groups on the eve of the 1871 violence suggest that some Irish Catholics were determined to prevent an Orange celebration. But information about their meeting places and addresses helps to define the world shaped by such workers: we know not just that they perhaps planned to attack Orangemen but that they belonged to flourishing Irish-American nationalist and benevolent groups that were important in their lives and that they discussed public affairs at their workplaces and homes, on streetcorners, in saloons, and elsewhere. Finally, a detailed analysis of the riots helps to restore a time dimension to events that preoccupied thousands of New Yorkers for days. A brief summary could not capture even the salient elements that contributed to the frenzy in Elm Park and the fright on Eighth Avenue. In short, I have dwelled at length on the details of these riots in hopes of conveying the complexity of the drama that unfolded in New York streets in 1870 and 1871.

A brief word about sources. Studies of other riots in New York City by Paul Weinbaum, Paul A. Gilje, Adrian Cook, and Iver Bernstein have made use of such indispensable sources as police, court, and hospital records, coroner's reports, and state and federal military records. I was able to locate only a few such sources for the 1870 and 1871 riots. Much important information is missing. I especially regret not finding more police and court documents, the records of New York's infamous Eighty-fourth Regiment, and membership lists and other records of local Orange lodges, the American Protestant Association (APA), and the Ancient Order of Hibernians. City records would have yielded more details about the identities of people who were arrested, killed, and injured. Muster rolls and membership lists would have helped me construct a social profile of local Irish groups, troops, and nativist organizations and to test allegations made by many Irish Catholics after the 1871 violence that members of the Eighty-fourth belonged to the APA. The absence of such sources forced me to rely on local newspapers, which published details about the riots, its victims, and the arrested, as well as the official military reports and the coroner's findings. Because most newspaper reporting of the time was anti-Catholic, relying so heavily on such sources is risky. I have tried to substantiate accounts as best I could. In some cases, I have quoted newspaper accounts of events, even when I could not substantiate them, not to relinquish interpretive authority to the papers but rather to reveal the papers' class and ethnic biases.

It is a pleasure to thank in print the many people who have helped me over the years. I much appreciate the help of conscientious staff members of the University of Rochester Library's microfilm and interlibrary loan departments, Indiana University's microforms department, and the University of Wisconsin-Milwaukee's interlibrary loan department. I also thank the staffs of the American Irish Historical

Society, the New York Public Library, the New-York Historical Society Library, and especially Thomas J. Dunnings, Jr., the society's curator of manuscripts. Years ago, Herbert D. Roistacher, then Chief Clerk, Criminal Branch, of the New York State Supreme Court's First Judicial District, and Sidney Barkan, then a clerk in Roistacher's office, tried to help me locate pertinent riot records that were housed amid the falling plaster in Boss Tweed's old courthouse in downtown Manhattan (they have since been moved, and the building has been restored). Idilio Garcia-Peña and Evelyn Gonzalez also diligently searched for court records and other sources in New York's Municipal Archives and Records Center. Both shared my frustration in not finding more.

I also thank Arthur J. Hughes of St. Francis College in Brooklyn; John Concannon, the Ancient Order of Hibernians' National Historian; and Walter C. Wilson, Supreme Grand Secretary of the Loyal Orange Institution of the United States of America, for their help in locating needed sources. I am grateful for generous research support provided by the University of Wisconsin-Milwaukee Graduate School and Mark Levine, Director of the University of Wisconsin-Milwaukee Urban Studies Programs.

Many relatives, friends, and colleagues have contributed support, encouragement, and comments. It would take many pages to thank them individually, so a general acknowledgment must suffice. I hope I have told each of them how much they have meant. Yet a few deserve special notice. Robert H. Wiebe first sparked my interest in history, at Northwestern University, and has continued his encouragement ever since. Over the years, John O'Brien, David F. Noble, Virginia Shaw, Jerry Lembcke, and especially Paula J. Gordon have read and commented on my work and helped in other ways. I am especially grateful to Douglas V. Shaw and Kerby Miller, who made excellent suggestions for revising an earlier version of this book and from whose own work I have learned much, and to my colleagues Margo Anderson, Michael Dintenfass, and Carole Shammas. A special note of thanks is due to Roger Haydon, my editor at Cornell University Press, for his interest, encouragement, and sound advice, and to Janet Mais for her excellent copy editing.

Like so many others, I regret that Herbert G. Gutman and Edward Magdol are no longer alive to share their intelligence, spirit, and humor with us. I was fortunate that they took so much of their time to share these and other qualities with me while they were alive. I think of them often, as I do of my father, the late Ben W. Gordon, who would have loved to see this book in print.

My father and mother, Edith Simon Gordon, always supported and encouraged my studies. Like their parents, Michael and Rachel Gordon and William and Lena Simon, they also provided a setting that eventually kindled my interest in the history of immigrants. My father and grandparents emigrated from Lithuania, but I have often thought of them and my mother as I studied the lives of other immigrants and their families.

Finally, my wife, Michele Sumara, has been an excellent copy editor and a patient and understanding comrade. Her love and encouragement have helped to sustain me and this project as we both adjusted to the arrival of our daughter, Isabel, and the birth of our son, Samuel, within a year. Michele and our friend, Sophie, have doggedly seen to it that this book was finished.

MICHAEL A. GORDON

Milwaukee, Wisconsin

Abbreviations

Evening Post	*New York Evening Post*
Herald	*New York Herald*
Freemen's Journal	*New York Freemen's Journal and Catholic Register*
Star	*New York Star*
Sun	*The Sun*
Times	*New York Times*
Tribune	*New York Daily Tribune*
World	*The World*

The Orange Riots

1 / Contending Visions

Violent clashes between Irish Catholics and Protestants tore New York City apart in 1870 and again in 1871. On July 12 in both years, members of the Loyal Orange Institution paraded through the streets celebrating the victory of Prince William of Orange over King James II at the Battle of the Boyne in 1690. Outraged Irish Catholic objections to these public commemorations of Protestant ascendancy left the nation scarred by some of the deadliest violence in its history. Eight people were killed and many were injured in the 1870 melee in and around Elm Park at Ninety-second Street and Ninth Avenue.

The violence was worse in 1871. News of an impending Orange parade down Twenty-eighth Street to Cooper Union on the Lower East Side forced a crisis on the city's Democratic leaders: Irish Catholics demanded that officials ban the parade, while wealthy Protestants insisted that Orangemen should have "equal rights" and public protection. The furor coincided with the first newspaper disclosures in early July of how William Marcy "Boss" Tweed and his Democratic cronies had defrauded the city of millions of dollars. Worried that a riot might hasten the collapse of Democratic control, Mayor A. Oakey Hall ordered police superintendent James J. Kelso to ban the Orangemen's parade, but he was overruled by Democratic governor John T. Hoffman, who called out the National Guard to protect Orangemen.

On July 12, guardsmen and hundreds of police tried to prevent another riot. Crowds along Eighth Avenue below Twenty-ninth Street pelted parading Orangemen and their guards with bricks and paving stones. Suddenly, members of the Eighty-fourth National Guard Regiment panicked and opened fire along the east side of the street. The shooting and other violence caused more than sixty deaths and one hundred injuries. The riots both reflected and added to the city's seething ethnic and class divisions that had exploded eight years before into the horrific draft riots. Those divisions, the 1871 riot, and the Tweed Ring's corruption led wealthy New Yorkers and nativists to forge a reform coalition that soon forced local Democrats from power.

Contemporaries and historians of these riots have focused on the 1871 violence because of the great loss of life and the impetus it gave to city reform movements that had begun even before the exposures of fraud by the ring. Although the memoirs and studies are useful, no one has yet analyzed the riots in detail or explored the motives and beliefs of the participants. This neglect has led to some distortions about Irish thought and behavior and about the riots themselves.

Disgusted contemporaries claimed that the riots merely reflected how Tammany Hall had turned over the city to the "wild Irish." One notable example is found in Joel Tyler Headley's *The Great Riots of New York, 1712–1873*, first published in 1873 at the peak of the city's early reform movement. Dedicated to the "Metropolitan Police" for their "Unwavering Fidelity and Courage in the Past," Headley's book discussed eleven "Great Riots" but focused on the 1863 draft riots that left 119 dead and scores injured. A Know-Nothing New York State senator and secretary of state in the 1850s, Headley's politics changed little over twenty years. He believed his book provided "a sort of moral history of the vast, ignorant, turbulent class which is one of the distinguishing features of a great city" and hoped it would encourage New York to adopt policies "to protect itself from that which to-day constitutes its greatest danger—*mob violence*." He attributed the "Orange Riots" to "old religious feuds." His 1870 account was taken almost verbatim from the New York *World*; the 1871 analysis came from the *Tribune*. So did much of the contents of a sensational anonymous pamphlet published shortly after the 1871 riot, called *Civil Rights: The Hibernian Riot and the "Insurrection of the Capitalists."* Intended to rally the city's wealthy Protestants to overthrow Tweed, the pamphlet claimed that the Eighth Avenue riot revealed once again that "the criminal weakness and vacillation of the authorities have caused the peace of the city to be broken and its streets to be filled with blood." Some of Headley's contemporaries shared the view that the crowds of Irish Catholics that surged through city streets on July 12 were composed of the "dangerous classes" that, as a police chief later put it, were bent on "wiping the thoroughfares with the bodies of the paraders."[1]

Studies by Gustavus Myers, Denis Tilden Lynch, and Florence Gibson have perpetuated the view that frenzied Irish Catholics had Tammany Hall and the city by the throat. For such observers, the crowds that tried to attack Orangemen remain, in George Rudé's words, "a disembodied abstraction and not . . . an aggregate of men and women of flesh and blood." Even Thomas N. Brown's otherwise fine study of Irish-American nationalism, and Adrian Cook's meticulous analysis of the 1863 draft riots, treated the riots superficially. Brown cited the "Orange-Green riots" only to illustrate how "a legacy of divisive hatred and violence" made it difficult for nationalist leaders to build unity here. Cook blamed the riots on the "ancient hatred" between Irish Catholics and Protestants. And though Christopher D. McGimpsey and William Casey have studied the riots in more detail, they too have accepted the conventional view that religious hatred ignited the violence.[2]

1. Joel Tyler Headley, *The Great Riots of New York, 1712–1873* (1873; rpt. New York: Bobbs-Merrill, 1970), 5, 17, 19–20, 289, and chap. 21. On Headley, see p. xv in the "Introduction" to the 1970 edition by Thomas Rose and James Rodgers; and Thomas J. Curran, "Seward and the Know Nothings," *New-York Historical Society Quarterly* 51 (April 1967): 141–60. For Headley's sources, see the *World*, July 13, 1870, and *Tribune*, July 13, 1871. See also *Civil Rights: The Hibernian Riot and the "Insurrection of the Capitalists." A History of Important Events in New York in the Midsummer of 1871* (New York: Baker and Goodwin, 1871), 25. Contemporaries: Matthew P. Breen (former state legislator and reform Democrat), *Thirty Years of New York Politics Up-to-Date* (New York: Author, 1899), 370–71; Augustine E. Costello (former police captain), *Our Police Protectors: A History of the New York Police* (1885; rpt. Montclair, N.J.: Patterson Smith, 1972), 244–45; and George W. Walling, *Recollections of a New York Chief of Police* (New York: Caxton Book Concern, 1887), 154–55. On the draft riots, see Adrian Cook, *The Armies of the Streets: The New York City Draft Riots of 1863* (Lexington: University Press of Kentucky, 1974), 194–95.

2. Gustavus Myers, *History of Bigotry in the United States*, ed. and rev. Henry M. Christman (1943; rpt. New York: Putnam's, Capricorn, 1960), 156; Denis Tilden Lynch, *"Boss" Tweed: The Story of a Grim Generation* (New York: Garden City Books, Blue Ribbon, 1927), 366–69, and *The Wild Seventies* (New York: Appleton-Century, 1941), 99–106; Florence E. Gibson, *The Attitudes of the New York Irish toward State and National Affairs, 1848–1892* (New York: Columbia University Press, 1951), 245–49; George Rudé,

Other historians have uncritically cited these disturbances as examples of "negative" violence, "religious and ethnic violence," or "urban" violence.[3] Still others rightly have stressed the riots' impact on city politics. The 1871 riot, in particular, "shocked New York and revived the Know-Nothing attitudes of the 1850s and the nativist fears of the draft riots," Alexander B. Callow observed in his study of Boss Tweed. To the reformers, "no other single event so well illustrated the tie between Tammany Hall and the Irish Catholic voter. The cry for 'clean government' now emitted the voice of nativism."[4]

A closer examination of the Boyne Day riots substantiates their political importance. As Chapters 3 and 6 reveal, the riots were enmeshed in the political uproar surrounding the financial crisis and graft of Tweed's regime. They contributed to the reshaping of local politics in the years that followed by helping to spark the great reform movement, led by the famous Committee of Seventy, that toppled Tweed's Ring and swept most Democrats from office. They also sparked a nativist revival that was often allied with reform efforts.

This book gives due weight to the central political role of the riots, but it also reveals much else that previous works have missed about their causes and meaning. Although it is important to observe Rudé's admonition that "in looking for motives [in a crowd's behavior] we must . . . not be so subtle or devious as to ignore the overt or primary intentions," the riots did not stem from religious hatred alone.

The Crowd in History (New York: Wiley, 1964), 9; Thomas N. Brown, *Irish-American Nationalism, 1870–1890* (Philadelphia: Lippincott, 1966), xvii; Cook, *Armies of the Streets*, 19–29 passim; Christopher D. McGimpsey, "Internal Ethnic Friction: Orange and Green in Nineteenth-Century New York, 1868–1872," *Immigrants and Minorities* 1 (1982): 39–59; William Casey, "The Orange Riots in New York City, 1870–1871" (Master's thesis, St. Francis College, Brooklyn, 1968).

3. See Richard Maxwell Brown, "Historical Patterns of Violence in America," in *Violence in America: Historical and Comparative Perspectives*, ed. Hugh Davis Graham and Ted Robert Gurr (New York: Bantam, 1969), 45, 53–54, 79n; and Richard Hofstadter and Michael Wallace, eds., *American Violence: A Documentary History* (New York: Random House, Vintage, 1970), 321–24.

4. David Montgomery, *Beyond Equality: Labor and The Radical Republicans, 1862–1872* (New York: Random House, Vintage, 1967), chap. 9, esp. 377–78; Jerome Mushkat, *The Reconstruction of the New York Democracy, 1861–1874* (Rutherford, N.J.: Fairleigh Dickinson University Press, 1981), 177–78; Iver Bernstein, *The New York City Draft Riots: Their Significance for American Society and Politics in the Age of the Civil War* (New York: Oxford University Press, 1990), 229–33; Alexander B. Callow, *The Tweed Ring* (New York: Oxford University Press, 1965), 263–65.

Nor do they resemble the pattern of "ritualistic" violence which Gregory Kealey has found in Toronto, where Irish Catholics and Orangemen regularly clashed on St. Patrick's Day and July 12 between 1867 and 1892.[5]

The New York riots derive more closely from conditions that sparked the draft riots, in which, as Iver Bernstein argues, Irish Catholics attacked the city's Protestant Republican elite and its "black cultural and political clientele."[6] Although the Orange riots did not involve race issues, I argue they did stem from contending visions of the nation's past, present, and future, just as in many ways the draft riots did. Irish workers and many middle-class Irish allies believed that the Orangemen symbolized the oppression they had known in Ireland and that Orange principles would help to subvert republicanism and "Anglo-Saxonize" America at the same time that industrialization was causing class lines to harden. Supporters of the Orangemen, believing it was the Irish Catholics who threatened republicanism, attempted to reassert the values they believed should govern social relationships as immigrants like the Irish challenged their class authority.

Irish workers' fears about the impact of Orangeism on America were shaped by experiences in Ireland and America, by republican traditions in both countries, and by personal and collective memories of this heritage. While not all Irish immigrants shared the same experiences, deprivation was a common force that drove some 1.8 million villagers, tenant farmers, farm laborers, small craftsmen, and others from Ireland to England, Scotland, Wales, and the United States in the decade after 1845 alone. Between 1849 and 1882, almost 3.4 million left Erin's shores. Of these, 15 percent had been evicted from their holdings. But hundreds of thousands more did not wait for bailiffs or sheriffs to appear with eviction writs. Along with many urban workers, they evicted themselves—an act that did not reflect resignation as much as it did a conscious decision to seek a better life outside Ireland. Yet, as Kerby Miller has so brilliantly argued, because they had been forced to seek life elsewhere, Irish

5. Rudé, *Crowd in History*, 217; Gregory S. Kealey, "The Orange Order in Toronto: Religious Riot and the Working Class," in *Essays in Canadian Working Class History*, ed. Kealey and Peter Warrian (Toronto: McClelland and Stewart, 1976), 13–34.

6. Bernstein, *Draft Riots*, 232.

immigrants of all classes came to think of themselves as exiles, and they blamed England for every misfortune they and Ireland had suffered.[7]

Part of the ambiguity and ambivalence in Irish-American thought about life in America can be attributed to the different worlds the Irish left and entered, and the time barrier they crossed between those worlds. As an anonymous but probably middle-class Irishman wrote of his fellow immigrants sometime before 1850, "We are a primitive people, wandering wildly in a strange land, the Nineteenth Century." The Irish were hardly "primitive"; but to premodern or preindustrial people, nineteenth-century industrializing America might have seemed "strange" in both its promise of opportunity and its resemblance to a society that, in their communalism, dependency, and conservatism, they had already rejected in Ireland as they came to associate "modernism" with the ills of Protestant ascendancy and commercialism. Many Irish immigrants adjusted to their adopted country and took advantage of opportunities to improve their lives. But as Miller argues, even successful Irish immigrants remained "remarkably estranged from the dominant culture" of the nation, as "Irish-Americans of all ranks and generations" suffered from "an almost institutionalized homesickness" and "often sensed urban-industrial America's moral and human inadequacies for men and women shaped by customs and values attuned to older, less overtly competitive life-styles."[8]

For this reason, newly arriving Irish immigrants in the 1840s might be expected to have shared with other city workers the disdain for competitive capitalism and inequality in America that had formed the core of artisan republicanism and the ideological force of New York's labor movement since early in the century. For decades, native-born artisans had fought to preserve the egalitarian promise of the American Revolution, and artisan independence in the workshop

7. Robert E. Kennedy, Jr., *The Irish: Emigration, Marriage, and Fertility* (Berkeley and Los Angeles: University of California Press, 1973), 30–31, 42–43. Kerby Miller, *Emigrants and Exiles: Ireland and the Irish Exodus to North America* (New York: Oxford University Press, 1985), 3–8, 102–21, 454–62. I made a similar but much less fully developed argument in the introduction to my dissertation, "Studies in Irish and Irish-American Thought and Behavior in Gilded Age New York City" (University of Rochester, 1977). Some of my arguments and material from that study are included here.

8. "Primitive people," quoted in George Potter, *To the Golden Door: The Story of the Irish in Ireland and America* (1960; rpt. Westport, Conn.: Greenwood, 1973), 597; Miller, *Emigrants and Exiles*, 115–28, 427–35, 493 (quote).

and in society. As Sean Wilentz has argued, artisans were threatened by capitalist affronts to their status and to their vision "of a democratic society that balanced individual rights with communal responsibilities" in which hard work and the pursuit of happiness were "undertaken not for personal gain alone but for the public good."[9]

Despite the plausible affinity between Irish sentiments and American artisan republicanism, Irish republicanism, as we shall see, generally was enmeshed in Irish nationalist movements (which did sometimes include rural and urban social reform efforts) and not in the political and social worlds of New York artisans. It took years for Irish exiles to convert their hatred of the corrupting power of Protestant ascendancy and English commercialism in Ireland into a critique of how Anglo-Saxon influences in America threatened the promise and opportunity that many Irish eventually came to identify with republicanism here. This conversion was a complex process involving the creation of an Irish working class; the influence of American and Irish republican traditions; the permutations of artisan republicanism in the 1830s and after; nativism; politics; and the draft riots.

Irish exiles helped to change the composition of New York's working classes. By 1855, 72 percent of the city's work force was foreign born. The Irish formed nearly 30 percent of the city's population and 44.5 percent of all its foreign-born. By 1860, the 204,000 Irish-born residents of New York City constituted 53 percent of all foreign-born inhabitants and 24 percent of the total city population. While the number of Irish residents remained about the same over the next three decades, increased immigration from other countries and population growth among second- and third-generation immigrant families caused a decline in the ratio of Irish-born residents to overall population of from 21 percent in 1870 to just 12.5 percent in 1890.[10]

The Irish and other immigrants entered city life just as the industrial revolution was helping to erode traditional artisanal authority.

9. Sean Wilentz, *Chants Democratic: New York City and the Rise of the American Working Class, 1788–1850* (New York: Oxford University Press, 1984), chap. 2 and pp. 95 (quote), 244–45. In *The Working People of Philadelphia, 1800–1850* (Philadelphia: Temple University Press, 1980), Bruce Laurie argues that republicanism had different meanings for workers and others, but generally "it implied a belief in (white, male) equality of opportunity and freedom from arbitrary rule, or much rule at all, and a justification of action in pursuit of these ideals" (81–82).

10. Ira Rosenwaike, *Population History of New York City* (Syracuse, N.Y.: Syracuse University Press, 1972), 42, 67.

They replaced native-born workers in jobs that had been based in the crafts, and they quickly assumed newly created industrial jobs. Arriving with few skills, the Irish settled into jobs as day laborers, servants, laundresses, stonecutters, and small shopkeepers. By 1855, nearly 85 percent of the city's Irish immigrants were wage workers. They accounted for 87 percent of all foreign-born laborers, 74 percent of domestic servants, 60 percent of women in the needle trades, 65 percent of all stonecutters, and 61 percent of bricklayers. They were important in the tailoring, shoemaking, glass-cutting, rag carpet weaving, and metalworking trades. Most immigrant boatmen, longshoremen, watermen, and ferrymen were Irish born. These trends continued through the Civil War. Lawrence Costello has found that by 1870 the Irish were still "the city's main source of unskilled and semi-skilled labor." By then, the Irish had become the main source of muscle for Tweed's ambitious plans to develop roads and buildings in northern Manhattan.[11]

As the Irish moved into New York's neighborhoods and jobs, they also quickly became part of city labor affairs. Irish-dominated societies of laborers, longshoremen, and quarrymen became large organizations whose members marched in the annual St. Patrick's Day parades and often won major strikes. The predominantly Irish Laborers' Union Benevolent Society claimed six thousand members by 1850 and was clearly the city's largest union. Irish shoemakers were prominent in their union, and by the late 1860s nearly every officer in the unions of laborers, coopers, longshoremen, plasterers, journeyman horseshoers, derrickmen, quarrymen and in some bricklayers' locals was Irish.[12]

The Irish also helped to change working-class culture. Richard Stott has shown how a separate "working-class way of life" had developed by 1860 which in some ways was adapted from Old World cul-

11. Robert Ernst, *Immigrant Life in New York City, 1825–1863* (New York: King's Crown, 1949), 67–71, 73–74, 85–97, 214–17; Amy Bridges, *A City in the Republic: Antebellum New York and the Origins of Machine Politics* (1984; rpt. Ithaca, N.Y.: Cornell University Press, 1987), 56; Carol Groneman Pernicone, "The 'Bloody Ould Sixth': A Social Analysis of a New York City Working Class Community in the Mid-Nineteenth Century" (Ph.D. diss., University of Rochester, 1977), 152–62; Laurence C. Costello, "The New York City Labor Movement, 1861–1873" (Ph.D. diss., Columbia University, 1967), 116–22, 122 (quote). For a discussion of Tweed's role as city empire builder, see Seymour J. Mandelbaum, *Boss Tweed's New York* (New York: Wiley, 1965), chap. 7.

12. Wilentz, *Chants Democratic*, 352–53; Costello, "New York City Labor Movement," 99–100.

ture. In boardinghouses and saloons, and throughout the largely Irish First, Fourth, and Sixth wards in lower Manhattan, Irish immigrants forged a separate ethnic enclave and cultural identity. They debated local politics and neighborhood concerns, treated each other to vast quantities of lager beer and other spirits as they smoked and argued in barrooms, and played billiards and other working-class games—all in communal settings that mirrored Irish rural and urban drinking places and pastimes. They flocked to local theaters in search of inexpensive, realistic sketches of their past and present lives. Many joined volunteer fire companies, which functioned as ethnic social clubs, and sometimes fought pitched battles with rival groups for the right to service their own neighborhoods. The Irish also adapted and developed their customary fighting matches at local fairs in Ireland into a consuming passion for pugilism that was shared by many other city workers by the 1850s. Enmeshed in working-class culture was a code of egalitarianism that was evident in the widespread impulse toward rowdyism among young workers and in the "fair fight" in pugilism and which added a cultural component to egalitarian ideas that stemmed from republicanism.[13]

Other forms of violence much different from the localized brawls that emerged among Irish and other immigrant subcultures helped transform the nature of traditional artisan crowd behavior into a new style of urban, working-class political opposition that figured in the Orange riots as well. Much of the New York City crowd violence in the half-century after the Revolution was informed by republican values and directed against both governments and citizens who violated "communal morality." While this strain of republicanism continued to shape labor affairs and sparked strikes in the 1830s and 1850s, Irish violence also was often aimed at defending Irish subculture against insults to Irish nationality, encroachments by other immigrants and blacks, and middle-class reform efforts. As early as 1799, for example, enraged Irish Catholics on the Lower East Side

13. Richard B. Stott, *Workers in the Metropolis: Class, Ethnicity, and Youth in Antebellum New York City* (Ithaca, N.Y.: Cornell University Press, 1990), 205 and chap. 8; Wilentz, *Chants Democratic*, 5. On theater, see Peter George Buckley, "To the Opera House: Culture and Society in New York City, 1820–1860" (Ph.D. diss., State University of New York at Stony Brook, 1984). On fire departments, see Stephen F. Ginsberg, "Fire Protection in New York City, 1800–1842" (Ph.D. diss., New York University, 1968); and Richard Boyd Calhoun, "From Community to Metropolis: Fire Protection in New York City, 1790–1875" (Ph.D. diss., Columbia University, 1973).

attacked native-born Americans who had paraded through the neighborhood on St. Patrick's Day bearing insulting effigies of the glorious saint which were dubbed "Paddies." Related violence erupted on St. Patrick's Day in 1802, and on Christmas Day in 1806, when the Irish heard rumors that a vigilante group called Highbinders planned to tear down a Catholic Church on Barclay Street.[14]

In 1849 a crowd of irate workers tried to prevent the renowned English actor William Macready from completing a performance of Macbeth at the city's opulent Astor Place Opera House. Militia muskets and other violence left thirty-one dead. In 1855 and 1863, Irish longshoremen beat away blacks in efforts to keep the docks all white (and all Irish) and to prevent black strikebreakers from taking their jobs. In July 1857, six weeks of gang feuding between a Sixth Ward Irish group called the "Dead Rabbits," who often campaigned for Democrats, and a nativist counterpart, the "Bowery Boys," exploded in a riot that left twelve dead and involved nearly one thousand people, including members of the unpopular Metropolitan Police force, which had been created by anti–home-rule Republican state legislators to wrest control of the police from city Democratic patronage. Irish as well as German protesters also objected to a new temperance law that regulated the sale of liquor. As Paul Weinbaum notes, both groups believed that, in the police and temperance laws, the legislature had tried "to disrupt their ways of life." Amid the severe depression the following November, desperate Irish and other workers fed up with Mayor Fernando Wood's inability to provide public relief sought to defend their lives in other ways. In a boistrous demonstration on Wall Street on November 6, they demanded that bankers provide businesses with funds to create jobs. Five days later they sparked a bread riot against the inflated price of a daily staple.[15]

14. Paul A. Gilje, *The Road to Mobocracy: Popular Disorder in New York City, 1763–1864* (Chapel Hill: University of North Carolina Press, 1987), 287 (quote), 129–33. See also Wilentz, *Chants Democratic*, 5.

15. On the Astor Place riot, see Wilentz, *Chants Democratic*, 358–59; Richard Moody, *The Astor Place Riot* (Bloomington: Indiana University Press, 1958); and Bruce A. McConachie, "'The Theater of the Mob': Melodrama and Preindustrial Riots in Antebellum New York," in *Theater for Working Class Audiences in the United States, 1830–1980*, ed. McConachie and Daniel Friedman (Westport, Conn.: Greenwood, 1985). See also Bernstein, *New York City Draft Riots*, 119–20, on longshoremen. On the 1857 riots, see Paul Weinbaum, "Temperance, Politics, and the New York City Riots of 1857," *New-York Historical Society Quarterly* 59 (July 1975), 246–70, 265 (quote); James F. Richardson, *Mayor Fernando Wood: A Political Biography* (Kent, Ohio: Kent State University Press, 1990),

Some of the most dramatic expressions of Irish workers' efforts to defend and extend their class and ethnic interests occurred in the draft and Orange riots. Important ideological and political changes shaped these confrontations. While the old native-born artisan element that had infused republicanism into the labor movement was largely gone by the Civil War, egalitarian values remained central to charges by labor unions and workingmen's parties in the 1850s and 1860s that capitalism was immoral because it both created wage slavery and monopoly and degraded virtue, independence, and freedom.[16]

Other variants of republicanism also derived from the disintegration of the early nineteenth-century artisan workshop and world as capitalism and factories changed the physical and social landscape of America. These versions shaped a contending capitalist ideology. A split in the republican tradition, and between masters and journeymen, emerged in the 1830s. Masters who joined the ranks of rising entrepreneurs became estranged from the workshop communalism and the Revolutionary legacy of radical republicanism. Increasingly they shared with merchants and other commercial interests the belief that republicanism justified unfettered competition and would lead to widespread economic and social mobility. Workers, capitalists, and others developed contending visions of republicanism that shaped class relations down to the Orange riots and beyond, as, in Wilentz's words, "men of different backgrounds and conflicting social views—eastern bankers and western yeomen, slaveholders and abolitionists, evangelicals and infidels—came to judge themselves and each other by their adduced adherence to republican principles."[17]

Protestant evangelicalism of the 1820s and 1830s contributed a spiritual component to republican capitalism by preaching that human will, not divine power, could create order and virtue. By so doing, it provided entrepreneurs with a powerful inspiration to achieve work discipline and maintain social control during the early stages of industrialization. Many northern merchants and industrialists who embraced both revivalism and republicanism combined their zeal for individualism and competition with efforts to achieve

---

69–78; and Joshua Brown, "The 'Dead-Rabbit'–Bowery Boy Riot: An Analysis of the Antebellum New York Gang" (Master's thesis, Columbia University, 1976).

16. Bernstein, *Draft Riots*, 79–85; Stott, *Workers in the Metropolis*, 212; Bridges, *City in the Republic*, 113–14, 121–22; Wilentz, *Chants Democratic*, 89–95, 372–83; and esp. the discussion in Montgomery, *Beyond Equality*.

17. Wilentz, *Chants Democratic*, chap. 2 and pp. 61 (quote)–63, 303.

social order by supporting moral legislation, penitentiaries, asylums, and religious instruction in schools. In that way, they hoped to preserve a "culturally homogenous social order" against perceived foreign and domestic threats to republicanism.[18]

Such concerns sparked a nativist uprising in the 1840s and 1850s led by professionals and merchants steeped in evangelical republicanism. The upsurge stemmed from proposals by Whig governor William H. Seward and others for state funding of Catholic schools, but nativists also complained that city Democrats squandered money on jobs for the immoral, poor, and criminal Irish whom the nativists believed were not fit for citizenship in a Protestant republic. These wealthy businessmen had abandoned their traditional roles of political leadership to the new city bosses by the 1850s, but they occupied a central place in the city's nativist reform movement as guardians of Protestant Anglo-Saxon stock and values.[19]

Many native-born mechanics in New York supported the reform movement. Believing that immigrant labor enabled employers to reorganize work, causing the loss of their social and political status, they flocked into such nativist groups as the Order of United Americans, the Order of United American Mechanics, the Order of the Star Spangled Banner, and the American Protestant Association (APA). They voted for candidates of Samuel F. B. Morse's Native American Democratic Association in the 1830s, the American Republican party in the 1840s, and the Know-Nothing party in 1854–56. Such groups represented a cross-class political alliance of those who believed that foreigners in general and especially Irish Catholics were beholden to Rome and not to republican government. The alliance elected a city government in 1844 under Mayor James Harper, the publishing magnate and former artisan printer, but it broke apart in succeeding years, after Whigs withdrew support and as industrial-

18. Paul Johnson, *A Shopkeeper's Millennium: Society and Revivals in Rochester, New York, 1815–1837* (New York: Hill and Wang, 1978), 138. See also Wilentz, *Chants Democratic*, 96, 303–5; Bridges, *City in the Republic*, 21; the discussion in Bruce Laurie, *Artisans into Workers: Labor in Nineteenth-Century America* (New York: Farrar, Straus and Giroux, Noonday, 1990), 52–54; and Laurie's *Working People of Philadelphia*, 82 (quote).

19. Bridges, *City in the Republic*, 29–31, 85–88, 115–16; Wilentz, *Chants Democratic*, 315. On the school issue, see Ira M. Leonard, "New York City Politics, 1841–1844: Nativism and Reform" (Ph.D. diss., New York University, 1965), 98–194; and Diane Ravitch, *The Great School Wars: A History of the New York City Public Schools* (1974; rpt. New York: Basic Books, 1988), chaps. 4, 5 passim.

ization forced workers into such anticapitalist labor organizations as the New York Industrial Congress of the early 1850s.[20]

The Democrats and Tammany Hall successfully capitalized on nativist efforts to taint and exclude the Irish by rooting their organization in the saloons, gang life, pugilism, and other elements of Irish working-class neighborhood culture; by championing Irish freedoms in New York and in Ireland; and by channeling Irish working-class discontent into a political program that attacked nativism, addressed Irish needs for jobs and fears of black job competition, and opposed Republican-sponsored reform efforts. As important, they eventually made way for Irish working-class spokesmen like Mike Walsh, the Irish-born Protestant veteran of the 1798 Irish rebellion, and "honest" John Kelly, who would take over from Tweed as Tammany boss in the 1870s and build a disciplined political organization. The tough-nosed Walsh had to fight his way into Tammany in the 1840s, but once there, his republican-inspired attacks on capitalist excesses helped the organization develop strong ties to his ardent Irish working-class supporters. By so doing, Walsh and other working-class politicians also helped to provide the important base on which Tweed built his coalition of workers, merchants, real estate developers, and immigrant manufacturers and saloon keepers after the Civil War.[21]

But local politics could not contain or channel all Irish working-class discontent. Throughout the 1850s and the Civil War, the Irish increasingly came to understand that although Democrats offered them some protection from nativist and reformer attacks, provided jobs, and addressed local concerns, they could not protect them from the social dislocations caused by industrialization and unchecked competition. Boilermakers, blacksmiths, longshoremen, common laborers, and industrial workers alike believed that their employers and the Republicans tried to reform their work lives and transform their communities. They feared that state Republicans would wrest political control of community life, while the national party's plans

20. Bridges, *City in the Republic*, 83–84, 88–98, 115–16; Wilentz, *Chants Democratic*, 315–24.

21. Bridges, *City in the Republic*, chaps. 6, 7 and pp. 146–49; Stott, *Workers in the Metropolis*, 235–40; Wilentz, *Chants Democratic*, 327–35; Bernstein, *New York City Draft Riots*, 195–224; Robert Ernst, "The One and Only Mike Walsh," *New-York Historical Society Quarterly* 36 (July 1952): 43–65; Callow, *Tweed Ring*, chaps. 1, 2.

for emancipation would send thousands of blacks north to take their jobs. Once the war broke out, many Irish Catholic workers especially believed that their Republican bosses were urging them to give up their jobs and enlist to help fight a Republican war, and the Republican draft eventually made that commitment compulsory.[22]

Irish Catholic immigrants were also alarmed by the pretensions of such wealthy, Protestant, nationalistic groups as the city's Union League Club. Formed in early 1863 by city merchants, the club aided wounded soldiers and counteracted local Copperhead sentiment. But as Iver Bernstein notes, many Union Leaguers also "hoped to create a 'true American aristocracy' which would adapt the cultural authority of the British elite to the distinctive social and political conditions of American democracy."[23]

From the outset the Union League's activities were guided by the beliefs that uncivilized immigrants and politicians threatened to destroy republican government and that prominent men with ancestors in colonial stock had retreated from public life. This view became especially urgent in the early 1870s as the club turned its attention from war and reconstruction to city reform. In his 1871 presidential address, for example, William J. Hoppin reminded more than one thousand members that the club's original objectives were "to elevate and uphold popular faith in republican government; to dignify politics as a pursuit of study; to reawaken a practical interest in public affairs in those who have become discouraged; and to enforce a sense of sacred obligation inherent in citizenship." Once, "it was taken for granted" that the "best men" would govern, and now "the classes which have the most leisure and the most intelligence" had to reassert their rightful claim as defenders of republican values.[24]

The vision of republicanism espoused by such wealthy New Yorkers was a variant of the same strain that had shaped artisan republicanism earlier in the century. But by 1860, many elites had combined republicanism with capitalist and evangelical values into a justification of a new social order that made no room for Irish workers with a different culture and vision of republicanism. These contending views, together with Irish beliefs that Republican war-

22. Bernstein, *Draft Riots*, 78, 112–24, 162–89.

23. Ibid., 159.

24. Will Irwin, Earl C. May, and Joseph Hotchkiss, *A History of the Union League Club of New York City* (New York: Dodd, Mead, 1952), 2–11, 20–21, 62; *Tribune*, February 10, 1871 (quote).

time policies threatened their livelihoods and communities, are what touched off the draft riots.

Not all Irish Catholic workers rioted or opposed the Union cause. Though often racists and usually loyal Democrats, thousands eagerly joined such distinguished Union regiments as New York's famous Sixty-ninth, which throughout the war carried both the Stars and Stripes and an Irish flag that had been sewn in Tipperary. Many of the most ardent Irish soldiers were industrial workers and members of the Irish Republican Brotherhood. Formed in New York in 1857, the Fenians, as they were known, were a secret revolutionary body, with branches in Ireland, that aimed at liberating the homeland by force. Racked by factional disputes and embarrassed by disastrous, desperate raids on Canada in 1866 and 1870 and on Ireland itself in 1867, the Fenians nevertheless remained an important presence in the city's Irish-American nationalist and political affairs down to 1870. Members drilled regularly, were courted by Tammany Hall and Radical Republicans alike, marched in annual St. Patrick's Day parades, and provided an important ideological link between Irish nationalist egalitarianism and Irish working-class republican sentiments.[25]

By 1870, many other Irish groups besides the Fenians drew upon similar sources of Irish sentiment. In only twenty-five years after the great famine migration from Ireland began, the Irish had become a dominant force in Tweed's efforts to build both a political machine and an expanding metropolis. They also had created a vibrant subculture that nourished bristling Irish-American nationalist activities. Turnouts at annual St. Patrick's Day festivities suggest how eagerly the Irish took part in Irish activities. Impressive celebrations occurred every year after the Civil War to the year of the Elm Park riot in 1870. In 1871 an estimated thirty to sixty thousand people paraded through the city's slushy streets in what one reporter described as "a soft, slippery, black slime, the worst kind of mud." The day began with church services, but the focus of festivities was the gigantic afternoon parade down Second Avenue to City Hall, where Mayor A. Oakey Hall, bedecked "in a new suit of green and black striped cassimere," and common council members, each wearing "green kid

25. William D'Arcy, *The Fenian Movement in the United States, 1858–1886* (Washington, D.C.: Catholic University of America Press, 1947), chaps. 1–7 passim; Miller, *Emigrants and Exiles*, 335–36; John T. Ridge, *The St. Patrick's Day Parade in New York* (New York: St. Patrick's Day Parade Committee, 1988), 37–45.

gloves and sprigs of shamrock in their button-holes," viewed the two-hour procession. From there the parade moved up Broadway to Union Square, then over to Seventh Avenue and up to Twenty-third Street, then back across to First Avenue and down to Cooper Union.[26]

The procession reflected a cross-section of the city's Irish Catholic groups. Led, ironically, by police and city officials who less than four months later would deploy forces to protect Orangemen, the parade included the Irish Sixty-ninth Regiment, two companies of other regiments, and five hundred members of the Legion of St. Patrick, all led by their own bands. Next came two Fenian companies, seventeen divisions of the Ancient Order of Hibernians (each with its own band), three sections of the Quarrymen's United Protective Society and one of the Longshoremen's Union Benevolent Society, eighteen temperance groups, various benevolent societies, the Weehawken Trap Block Makers, and a team of Irish bagpipers. In all, some fifty bands blared Irish tunes to the delight of crowds along the way. A giant bust of Daniel O'Connell, the Catholic "Liberator," brought roars from onlookers as it was wheeled down the street. But the highlight of the day was the appearance of sixteen men, some as tall as six-foot-seven, dressed as gallowglasses, the legendary sixteenth-century Irish foot soldiers who accompanied Ulster's Prince Shane O'Neil on his visit to impress Queen Elizabeth with Irish prowess and strength. Carrying huge battle-axes and broad shields, they were dressed "in saffron tinted cloaks, long green waistcoats, saffron-colored tights, sandals, and gilt leathern helmets." That evening, as Irish workers continued their celebrations in saloons, noncommissioned officers of the Sixty-ninth enjoyed a grand ball in Irving Hall, while more well-to-do Irish crowded into Steinway Hall for a concert by Rosa d'Erina to help raise funds for a church in Armagh. Elsewhere, Irish "swells" who belonged to the Knights of St. Patrick and the Friendly Sons of St. Patrick dined at banquets and toasted Ireland, France, New York, St. Patrick, "The Bench," and each other, far into the night.[27]

Of those in the parade, the organization that figured most prominently in the events surrounding the 1871 violence (it played no role in 1870) was the Ancient Order of Hibernians (AOH). Although the

26. See *Times*, March 18, 1865–70; *Irish-American*, March 26, 1870; *World*, March 18, 1871 ("mud"); and *Sun*, March 18, 1871 (clothes).

27. *World* and *Sun*, March 18, 1871; *Irish World*, March 25, 1871 (quotes).

AOH was formed in New York in 1836, it originated in responses by secret rural and urban Ribbon societies to Protestant ascendancy and the restrictions of the Penal Laws in late eighteenth-century Ireland and to the formation of the Orange order in 1795. According to one historian of the order, the society had its urban roots in a mid-eighteenth-century Dublin group called the Ancient and Most Benevolent Order of the Friendly Brothers of St. Patrick. But it and the Ribbon societies were more directly tied to the Defender movement that spread outward from Ulster in the 1780s and 1790s to address problems arising from land competition and to challenge attacks by such Protestant groups as the Peep-O'-Day Boys. The first Defender bands were much influenced by French republicanism and Thomas Paine's *Rights of Man*. They at first included Protestant and Catholic alike, but in time the movement became mostly Catholic and urban. In Dublin, a Defender center, journeymen weavers formed the core of its membership. In 1796, the Defenders merged with the revolutionary United Irishmen, whose members also embraced French and American republicanism.[28]

The collapse of the United Irishmen and the rising of 1798 sent many insurrectionaries into such clandestine groups as the Ribbonmen, whose name apparently derived from Ulster faction-fights in which men wore ribbons to distinguish themselves from enemies. Drawing its strength from disaffected cottiers and farm laborers, urban workers and small shopkeepers, the Ribbon movement based its organizational structure on the Defenders and United Irishmen and provided a link between the republican nationalist movement of the 1790s and the nationalist Young Ireland upsurge of the 1840s. Staunchly Catholic and nationalistic and ostensibly concerned just with religious issues like the tithing of Catholics to support Prot-

28. John O'Dea, *History of the Ancient Order of Hibernians and Ladies Auxiliary* (Philadelphia: Keystone Printing, 1923), 1:423; Miller, *Emigrants and Exiles*, 69. On Defenders, see Tom Garvin, "Defenders, Ribbonmen, and Others: Underground Political Networks in Pre-Famine Ireland," *Past and Present*, no. 96 (1982): 138–43; and Robert Kee, *The Green Flag: A History of Irish Nationalism* (London: Weidenfeld and Nicolson, 1972), 68–74. On United Irishmen, see Kee, *Green Flag*, 74–131; J. L. McCracken, "The United Irishmen," in *Secret Societies in Ireland*, ed. T. Desmond Williams (Dublin: Gill and Macmillan, 1973), chap. 6; James S. Donnelly, "Propagating the Cause of the United Irishmen," *Studies* 69 (Spring 1990): 5–23; and John A. Murphy, "The Influence of America on Irish Nationalism," in *America and Ireland, 1776–1976: The American Identity and the Irish Connection*, ed. David N. Doyle and Owen D. Edwards (Westport, Conn.: Greenwood, 1980), 105–15.

estant ascendancy, the Ribbonmen also protested against land evictions, falling grain prices, urban labor issues, and the effects of the subsequent changeover from farming to pasturing in prefamine Ireland. They also remained bitterly opposed to Orangemen, who had helped to squelch Defenders in 1798. For the Ribbonmen, injustice was rooted in Protestant ascendancy. Organizing themselves into such groups as the Patriotic Association of the Shamrock and the Irish Sons of Freedom, Ribbon societies clearly maintained links with the republican tradition of 1798. Their members drank toasts to "The Rights of Man," "The Memory of Washington," and "No King."[29]

The Ribbonmen developed an Irish Catholic political consciousness that eventually linked specific local economic grievances to Irish nationalist sentiments. Indeed, many had fought Orangemen as Defenders in the 1790s, resisted the odious Penal Laws, and later joined Daniel O'Connell's drive for Catholic emancipation in the 1820s. According to M. R. Beames, the Ribbonmen "were the only organized section of the Irish Catholic community that expected Irish independence to be achieved by rebellion and violence." As Britain stepped up its efforts to wipe out the Ribbonmen, members changed their name in 1825 to the St. Patrick Fraternal Society, even though they remained popularly known as Ribbonmen. The society's object was "to promote Friendship, Unity, and True Christian Charity, by raising and supporting a stock or fund of money for aiding and assisting its members when out of employment, and for no other purpose whatsoever." After authorities broke up the Dublin center in 1839, Ribbonism apparently became more centered in the north and west of Ireland and focused more on rural issues than nationalistic ones.[30]

Another, if more remote, source of inherited Irish republican values was rooted in the agrarian terrorism practiced by the secret, oath-bound societies of Whiteboys and the like that erupted throughout parts of Ireland from the late eighteenth century down to the famine. These strictly rural groups bore some resemblance to the

29. See Joseph Lee, "The Ribbonmen," in Williams, *Secret Societies in Ireland*, 26–35; Galen Broeker, *Rural Disorder and Police Reform in Ireland, 1812–1836* (London: Routledge and Kegan Paul, 1970), 8–15; Miller, *Emigrants and Exiles*, 60–61 (faction-fights), 68–69; M. R. Beames, "The Ribbon Societies: Lower-Class Nationalism in Pre-Famine Ireland," *Past and Present*, no. 97 (1982): 128–32, 137 (toasts); Tom Garvin, *The Evolution of Irish Nationalist Politics* (Dublin: Gill and Macmillan, 1981).

30. Garvin, "Defenders, Ribbonmen, and Others," 148–52; Beames, "Ribbon Societies," 128–37, 141 (quote); O'Dea, *Ancient Order of Hibernians*, vol. 2, chaps. 30–34 and pp. 768, 773 (object of St. Patrick Fraternal Society).

Ribbon societies, but they were more social and economic than sectarian and nationalist. Although Whiteboy grievances differed from region to region and year to year, most focused on immediate local concerns like taxes, evictions, rents, and tithes. The protests were clearly political because they stemmed from English domination. But they also were what Kerby Miller calls reactive and conservative, because generally "the secret societies sought to maintain what they regarded as traditional patterns of socioeconomic relations in the face of an expanding free market in land and labor." Nationalism and republicanism seem not to have shaped the consciousness of these rural societies, but in the South, at least, egalitarian principles of freedom and equality *were* embedded in the oaths and rituals of these organizations. Moreover, the small tenant farmers, artisans, and laborers who attacked landlord dwellings and assassinated enemies were not motivated by revenge as much as they were by justice—an important element of republican values.[31]

Rural and urban groups that sought justice and liberty swept throughout Ireland and into the collective experience and memory of Irish people. Irish immigrants brought one such group with them to New York shortly after Ribbonmen had changed their name to the St. Patrick Fraternal Society. In 1836, some society members in New York, together with other Irish immigrants with similar sensibilities and traditions dating to the Defenders, received a charter from their counterparts in Ireland for a fraternal and burial society for Irish Catholics "of good and moral character." Members had to be Irish Roman Catholics and devoted to objectives identical to those of the parent organization. The society grew quickly in New York, began calling itself the "Ancient Order of Hibernians" by 1838, and was chartered by New York State in 1853. It spread elsewhere by tapping the economic and social grievances of canal and railroad laborers, and the nationalistic sentiments of workers everywhere, forming, as George Potter put it, "the nexus, among the early Catholic Irish emigrants, between the United States and Ireland."[32]

31. M. R. Beames, "Rural Conflict in Pre-Famine Ireland: Peasant Assassinations in Tipperary, 1837–1847," *Past and Present*, no. 81 (1978): 75–91, and *Peasants and Power: The Whiteboy Movements and Their Control in Pre-Famine Ireland* (New York: St. Martin's, 1983), 145–48 passim; Miller, *Emigrants and Exiles*, 61–69, 62 (quote); James S. Donnelly, Jr., "The Whiteboy Movement," *Irish Historical Studies* 21 (March 1978): 20–54; Maureen Wall, "The Whiteboys," in Williams, *Secret Societies in Ireland*, chap. 2.

32. See O'Dea, *Ancient Order of Hibernians* 2:884–86, 992, 995; Wayne G. Broehl, Jr.,

Those important ties helped the AOH to grow. By 1860 the order had at least twenty-four divisions in New York with some six thousand members. Membership declined during the Civil War, but by 1871 the Hibernians again managed sick and death benefits for thousands of members and continued to promote "Friendship, Unity, and Christian Charity" wherever it thrived. "We practice friendship in assisting each other to the best of our power," one member explained in 1874, quoting the AOH's Preamble; "unity in uniting together for mutual support in sickness or distress; and true Christian charity by doing to each other and to all the world as we would wish to be done by." These ideals may have appealed to a broad segment of New York's immigrant Irish Catholic community, but as the order acknowledged in 1876, "the majority" of its members "belong[ed] to the working classes." Because AOH members, like their Ribbon analogues, were concerned with social and economic justice, not just nationalist issues, many became embroiled throughout the decade in such bitter labor wars as the notorious Molly Maguire struggles against Pennsylvania coal operators. Others combined social reform with Irish-American nationalism. By the 1880s, for example, many were inclined to favor the Irish National Land League, with its reform programs, over the Fenians and other strictly nationalist groups. But in 1883, AOH members readily joined other Irish organizations in scuttling the Land League in favor of the more conservative programs of the newly formed Irish National League.[33]

Many AOH members and other Irish Catholics knew of the links between the AOH and Ribbonism, and Orangeism and its precursors. A few knew that history well. "The society [AOH] . . . had its origin in Ireland at the time when the very right of existence was a 'privilege' to Catholics," Edward Larkin wrote in 1874, "and when they held their faith at the sacrifice of all material interests." A year earlier, Brooklyn AOH brother James O'Donnell had reminded *Irish*

The Molly Maguires (Cambridge: Harvard University Press, 1964), 32–38; Potter, *To the Golden Door*, 61 (quote), 327–36, 574.

33. For a painstaking reconstruction of AOH history between the 1820s and 1870s, see the AOH's publication by John T. Ridge, *Erin's Sons in America: The Ancient Order of Hibernians* (New York: AOH, 1986), 9–36, 16 (the 1876 quote). See also Timothy McCarthy (Franklin Furnace, N.J., June 22, 1874) to *Irish World*, July 4, 1874; and Broehl, *Molly Maguires*. On the AOH and the Land League, see John O'Leary, *Recollections of Fenians and Fenianism* (London: Downey, 1896), 1:111–12; and Brown, *Irish-American Nationalism*, 155.

World readers that "the A. O. is the counterpart of an organization which came into existence in the latter part of the eighteenth century, called the Ribbonmen or White Boys." The groups formed because the Protestant Peep-O'-Day Boys had intimidated Catholics and helped to enforce "the penal statutes of Queen Anne against the Catholics of Ireland." O'Donnell said Ribbonmen protected "the helpless and innocent" from vicious midnight attacks against "some poor Catholic" in which "their first act would be to rob the house if there was anything valuable in it, then if he had a daughter, drag her out of bed and defile her person; if the father attempted to offer any assistance to his child, he would be dragged out of his house and hanged to the first tree they would meet."[34]

Such secret, Protestant, anti-Catholic groups as the Peep-O'-Day Boys evolved into the Orange order (although some of these groups originally were not sectarian). Thus the animosities between Orangemen and the AOH and other Irish Catholics stemmed from the cauldron of Irish Catholic oppression and humiliation that lived in memory down to the 1870s and beyond. Perhaps a late eighteenth-century Orange toast did too. To "the glorious, pious, and immortal memory of the great and good King William," it began,

> not forgetting Oliver Cromwell—who assisted in redeeming us from Popery, slavery, arbitrary power, brass money and wooden shoes. May he never want a Williamite to kick the - - - - of a Jacobite, nor a - - - - - for the bishop of Cork. And he that won't drink this, whether he be priest, bishop, deacon, bellows-blower, gravedigger, or any other of the fraternity of the clergy, may the north wind blow him to the south, and the west wind blow him to the east. May he have a dark night, a lee shore, a rank storm, and a leaky vessel, to carry him over the river Styx. May the dog Cerbarus make a meal of his - - - - - and Pluto a snuffbox of his skull, and may the devil jump down his throat with a red-hot harrow with every pin tearing out a gut, and blow him with a clean carcass to hell. Amen!

Despite their role in sustaining Protestant ascendancy, the Orangmen's divisiveness led Britain to ban the order in 1825 and in 1836. The Fenian upsurge of the 1860s revived the Orange order and also

34. Edward Larkin (Wheeling, W.Va., May 6, 1874) to *Irish World*, May 24, 1874; James O'Donnell (South Brooklyn, February 26, 1873) to ibid., March 15, 1873.

led to the repeal in 1870 of the Party Processions Act of 1850, which had outlawed parades that might provoke sectarian clashes.[35]

Ulster immigrants brought the Orange order to New York in the early 1820s. By 1824 the order was strong enough to prick the Irish Catholic temper by parading all day on July 12 with orange and purple flags through a community of Irish Catholic weavers in Greenwich Village, apparently obeying the order's injunction to celebrate its most glorious victory, but also, as one of the order's official historians has noted, to show "strength in places where [they] thought it would do most good. Where you could 'walk' you were dominant and other things followed." A brawl erupted. At the ensuing trial, the celebrated United Irishman Thomas Addis Emmet successfully defended the Irish Catholic attackers by demonstrating a long history of anti-Catholicism in the city.[36]

After the order was dissolved in Britain in 1836, its American members apparently retained their Orange identity, but they did so as members of the American Protestant Association, the Order of United Americans, and other nativist groups. In the 1850s these organizations sponsored annual Washington's Birthday parades in New York which attracted the membership of the No Surrender and the Excelsior Orange lodges under APA banners, as well as A. Oakey Hall and John C. Helme, who were to be mayor and police captain in 1870–71. In 1870 an APA member recalled that in 1856 the APA had even "adopted the regalia of the old Orangemen." Despite its name, as Rowland Berthoff has noted, the APA clearly "was known as an Ulsterman's order," although its "officers felt obliged to avow its independence of the Orangeism of Ireland."[37]

35. See Hereward Senior, *Orangeism in Ireland and Britain, 1795–1836* (London: Routledge and Kegan Paul, 1966), chaps. 1, 4, 10, 11, and for a convenient summary, "The Early Orange Order, 1795–1870," in Williams, *Secret Societies in Ireland*, 36–45; Aiken McClelland, "The Later Orange Order," in ibid., 126–37; Miller, *Emigrants and Exiles*, 230–34; Peter Gibbon, *The Origin of Ulster Unionism: The Formation of Popular Protestant Politics and Ideology in Nineteenth-Century Ireland* (Manchester: Manchester University Press, 1975); David W. Miller, "The Armagh Troubles, 1784–1795," in *Irish Peasants: Violence and Political Unrest, 1780–1914*, ed. Samuel Clark and James S. Donnelly, Jr. (Madison: University of Wisconsin Press, 1983), chap. 4; and O'Dea, *Ancient Order of Hibernians* 2:529 (Orange toast).

36. Gilje, *Road to Mobocracy*, 134–37; *Irish World*, July 22, 1871; Samuel Ernest Long, *A Brief History of the Loyal Orange Institution of the United States of America* (n.p.: Orange Institution, 1979), 2. The order to parade is quoted in Tony Gray, *No Surrender! The Siege of Londonderry, 1689* (London: MacDonald and Jane's, 1975), 202.

37. Long, *Brief History*, 2; *Irish-American*, July 24, 1869. For coverage of Washington's birthday celebrations, see *Times*, February 23, 1852–56, February 24, 1857, and February

Separate Orange lodges appeared in New York in 1867. In 1868, more than one hundred members of lodge Nos. 339 and 1042 met on Sunday, July 12, at Military Hall, marched to church services, and reassembled at picnics the next day. In 1869, Orangemen paraded from their lodge rooms at 193 Bowery up Broadway to Union Square and then took the Courtlandt Street ferry to New Jersey for an afternoon picnic. Along the way, a man knocked down an Orangeman in Chatham Street and stole his orange sash, while elsewhere a woman, whom the *Sun* called a "red-haired bawd," hurled a brick at an Orangeman and a potato at police. Irish Catholic tempers burned while the Orangemen were away. The Irish considered why they should permit city streets to be filled with the strains of "Croppies Lie Down," "Protestant Boys," and "Boyne Water" and made plans to welcome Orangemen home when they returned that evening. A "crowd of men and boys, armed with clubs and stones," attacked Orangemen at their lodge rooms, injured John Mehaney severely, and were chased away by the police.[38]

The following year, the Grand Lodge of Ireland chartered the American Supreme Grand Lodge of the Loyal Orange Institution of the United States. The order grew steadily from just 4 lodges in 1868, to 43 in 1872, and to 120 by 1875. It claimed upward of ten thousand members by 1873. Apparently the American Orangemen had been affiliated with the Grand Lodge of England but sought the Irish affiliation, and then independent status, after they had been accused of being English agents. John J. Bond, the order's provincial grand secretary and, by 1871, its supreme grand master, emphasized that the order was a strictly American institution. "We are simply a Protestant body who meet for mutual improvement," he explained in 1869. "We are not antagonistic to any creed." Bond said his members took oaths to support the Constitution, that the order's proceedings were patterned after the Masons, and that "we celebrate the 12th of July as being the anniversary of civil and religious liberty achieved in Ireland for all nations; as much for Roman Catholics as for Protestants."[39]

23, 1858–60. See also "An A.P.A." (New York, August 12, 1870) to *Star*, August 13, 1870; and Rowland T. Berthoff, *British Immigrants in Industrial America, 1790–1950* (Cambridge: Harvard University Press, 1953), 190.

38. Berthoff, *British Immigrants*, 191; *Times* and *Sun*, July 13, 1868; *Sun*, July 13, 1869; *Times*, July 13, 1869 (quote).

39. Long, *Brief History*, 2–3. On previous affiliations, see Berthoff, *British Immigrants*, 191; and the interview with Supreme Grand Master John J. Bond in *Star*, July 9, 1871.

Bond's statement read history one way. Irish Catholics understood that history differently. Both understandings had been shaped by actual experiences in Ireland, and by the immigrant experience in America. For Irish exiles who believed they had been evicted from their homeland because of Orange complicity in English oppression, Bond's claim that Orangemen celebrated "civil and religious liberty" for all must have sounded incredible indeed. The collective memories of Irish exiles shaped their belief that Bond's words masked plans to transform the nation into another Ireland.

An important element of the collective memory and the exile motif merits further discussion because of its importance in shaping Irish Catholic opposition to the Orangemen: the Irish Catholics hated Anglo Saxons. They believed that England had tried to "Anglo-Saxonize" Irish culture in order to destroy the foundation of Irish nationality. "Almost with the advent of my youthful reasoning powers," A. McMahon wrote to the *Irish World* in 1874, "I was taught to listen, at my father's knee, with feelings of wonder and awe, to the history of sorrows traced in the blood-stained records of the past; how Erin's children, butchered, starved, and ground by the iron heel of the robber Saxon, till worn and broken, the decimated remnant fled their homes and country, to find peace and a grave in foreign lands—and still the extermination goes on!" "Will you kindly allow me to expose a flagrant act of injustice perpetrated in the town of Tipperary, by Leopold Cust, (*In*)-Justice of the Peace, agent for the absentee landlord Smith Barry?" another *Irish World* reader asked in 1876. The writer said his father and many other older people had recently been evicted from houses they had lived in for over fifty years. A brother, who furnished details of the eviction in a letter, had added, "'Our father . . . must now leave at the bidding of an agent of one of the descendants of the robbers who came over with Cromwell, supported by British law.'" The writer then placed himself and the eviction in a historical context:

> Pious England of "the Open Bible," know you not that mid the turmoil of the elements and the thunder of Sinai, God declared: "Thou shalt not steal!" and yet you legalize the plunder of God's

---

See also Bond (n.p., n.d.) to *Sun*, July 23, 1869; and Supreme Grand [Orange] Lodge of the United States, *Report of the Proceedings of the Annual Meeting, July 11th and 12th, 1872* (n.p., n.d.), 10, 14, and *Report of the Sixth Annual Session of the Most Worshipful Supreme Grand Order Lodge of the United States of America . . . (1875)* (n.p., n.d.), 6–9.

> poor, turn adrift from their homes, endeared by so many memories, the venerable sire, weeping matron, and innocent babe. Hypocritical, canting England, whose every step is traced by oppression and plunder, whose dominion is upheld by blasphemy of the Most High, thank God here in this Republic from which you were driven a hundred years ago, a free press can tear off the Mokanna mask which veils your tyranny, and show you to be, with all your virtuous pretense, the incarnation of plunder, atrocity, and fraud. Tipperary, fruitful mothers of "Rebels," shall the absentee and his agent continue to waste in riot the bloody sweat of thy children?[40]

The Irish viewed themselves as a people who had been oppressed for centuries by Anglo-Saxon conquerors whose most visible surrogates were British troops and land agents. Those who left Ireland still identified themselves with a national experience that included this image of Anglo-Saxon oppression. But for them, the "Saxon yoke" had never stilled a fervent hope for individual and national liberation which was transmitted through generations, telescoping past injustices and incidents of resistance into the present, and placing responsibilities for nationhood and reform upon the Irish in Ireland and America. "I am not an Anglo-Saxon," began William Collins's poem for the *Irish World*.

> Out upon the very name!
> It tells of fraud and treachery,
> Of perfidy and shame;
> It tells of wrong and outrage,
> Of slavery and crime,
> Of deeds the foulest, blackest
> Upon the page of time.
> A Name the darkest, meanest,
> That earth has ever known,
> O! I'm not an Anglo-Saxon,
> I am Irish blood and bone.[41]

40. A. McMahon (n.p., December 24, 1874) to *Irish World*, January 2, 1875; "Tipperary" (New York, June 20, 1876) to ibid., July 8, 1876.

41. William Collins, "I Am Not an Anglo-Saxon," *Irish World*, June 6, 1874. See also Patrick Carpenter, "Ye Rebels of Our Land," ibid., February 21, 1874; "Fenian's Song," in *Stephen's Fenian Songster* (New York, 1866); and James E. Larkin, "Wrongs of Ould Ireland" (1881), in *Delaney's Irish Song Book No.* 2, in boxes 273 and 271, Starr Music Collection, Lilly Library, Indiana University.

This collective memory stemmed first from actual or perceived experiences, then from forms of oral and written history, like songs and poems, and from folklore, customs, and traditions, which transformed real or perceived experiences into recollection. Thousands of popular songs especially reflected common experiences and contributed much to immigrants' historical consciousness. They could be found in homes, union meetings, saloons, at outings, and especially at Irish-American nationalist assemblies.[42]

Such sources contributed to a collective Irish-American memory that fused with republicanism in interpreting the Orange presence in political, not religious, ways. For Irish Catholics, the Battle of the Boyne and Protestant ascendancy were transforming events linked to Anglo-Saxon oppression. This collective memory dwelled on past oppression and the possible impact of Orangeism on America's future. Past and present thereby fused into an Irish vision of terrifying consequences and became the analogue to what David Blight has called "an abolitionist memory" of the Civil War for Frederick Douglass. Just as Douglass sought "to forge memory into action" in order to "save the legacy of the Civil War for blacks—freedom, citizenship, suffrage, and dignity,"[43] so too did memories of Orange and Anglo-Saxon oppression form a source of knowledge for Irish Catholics who sought to realize the promise of republicanism.

42. See Douglas Gilbert, *Lost Chords: The Diverting Story of American Popular Songs* (Garden City, N.Y.: Doubleday, 1942), 40–41, 199 passim; Charles Hamm, *Yesterdays: Popular Songs in America* (New York: Norton, 1979); and Vera Brodsky Lawrence, *Strong on Music: The Musical Scene in the Days of George Templeton Strong, 1836–1875, vol. 1, Resonances* (New York: Oxford University Press, 1988). See also Richard Stott's discussion in *Workers in the Metropolis*, 265–69.

43. David W. Blight, "'For Something beyond the Battlefield': Frederick Douglass and the Memory of the Civil War," *Journal of American History* 75 (March 1989): 1158, 1174. For some useful discussions of collective memory, see Maurice Halbwachs, *The Collective Memory* (1951; rpt. New York: Harper and Row, 1980); and Popular Memory Group, "Popular Memory: Theory, Politics, Method," in *Making Histories: Studies in History Writing and Politics*, ed. Richard Johnson et al. (Minneapolis: University of Minnesota Press, 1982), 205–52.

2 / The Elm Park Riot

Elm Park was located between Ninety-first and Ninety-second streets and Ninth and Tenth avenues not far from Broadway, then called Western Boulevard. Carved from a historic colonial estate that once belonged to Charles Ward Apthrop, a King's Council member, "Elmwood" was maintained by a succession of wealthy New Yorkers until the grounds were converted to a dance and picnic resort in 1860. "Elmwood" became "Elm Park." It flourished for nearly thirty years before succumbing to area growth and the need for a new church. St. Agnes's Chapel brought "respectability" back to the once fashionable site.

In the three decades after the Civil War, the bursts of development that eventually consumed Elm Park also expanded the city far past Columbus Circle at Fifty-ninth Street (once the unofficial northern boundary of Manhattan settlement), where Broadway ended and Western Boulevard began, to beyond 155th Street. But in the early years of this development, few could have imagined the fashionable apartment buildings, mansions, and hotels the city's enormous new Central Park would attract to the area by the end of the century. A *Herald* reporter found no evidence of such possibilities as he toured the Boulevard in 1876, the year Central Park and the Boulevard were completed. For several blocks above Fifty-ninth Street along the western edge of Central Park, he saw "itinerant vendors of old rubbish or merchants in ordinary trudg[ing] along the great highway in small carts drawn by mongrel teams of dogs and goats. From neighboring saloons, as well as from dirty entry ways, a shabby troop of men and children issue." Such persons often lived in shanties atop deep cliffs on either side of the Boulevard. In one area, the reporter saw "ragged urchins and half-starved dogs and goats rolling together" near a muddy pool. Near One Hundredth Street a man plowed his small field as his son led a cow to pasture down the Boulevard.[1]

Many people living that far north seldom traveled downtown. The Boulevard soon changed all that and much more. By the late 1890s, the area surrounding Central Park was distinctly urban, while just to the north old estates, summer retreats, and isolated pockets of jerry-built shanties and frame houses still dotted the avenues. Photographs taken of the Boulevard itself in the late summer of 1900, looking north from Seventy-second and Seventy-third streets, suggest what looks "like the heart of some smaller metropolis." Adolescent elm trees, perhaps forty feet tall, line both sides of the street and, with plants and gaslights, form a parkway down the center. Streetcar tracks and seasoned buildings line either side of the parkway. Horse-drawn carriages and commercial trucks blur by. On the west side of the Boulevard near Seventy-second Street, men unload a Grieme Coal Company wagon in front of the partially vine-covered Rutgers Presbyterian Church. Yet amid this settled scene, there is clear evidence of still more growth just a block north: a construction crane is perched atop a five-story skeleton of the eventually elegant Ansonia Apartment House. Because all this development blurred the distinction between the urban character of Broadway in lower Manhattan and its more bucolic nature to the north, in 1899 the city formally linked the two roads by changing "Western Boulevard" to "Broadway."[2]

The development of northern Manhattan provided jobs to countless city workers. In the steamy summer of 1870, thousands of men

1. Maxwell F. Marcuse, *This Was New York! A Nostalgic Picture of Gotham in the Gaslight Era*, rev. ed. (New York: LIM Press, 1969), 136–53, 163–80, and chaps. 4, 9, 11, 13–15 passim; Harper S. Mott, *New York of Yesterday: A Descriptive Narrative of Bloomingdale* (New York: Putnam's, 1908), 13–16; "The Central Park," *Appleton's Journal*, June 18, 1870, 691; *Herald*, April 6, 1870. See also "Across the Harlem," *Harper's Weekly* 26 (November 18, 1882): 728, 731; and Ian R. Stewart, "Central Park, 1851–1871: Urbanization and Environmental Planning in New York City" (Ph.D. diss., Cornell University, 1973), chaps. 3, 4, 6.

2. Mary Black, *Old New York in Early Photographs, 1853–1901* (New York: Dover, 1973), 188 (quote), 189, and chap. 12 passim; Marcuse, *This Was New York*, 136.

were busily employed on various public works jobs. Some worked in Central Park, which had opened to the public just after the Civil War. Others laid Croton Aqueduct pipelines in Fifty-ninth Street near Eighth Avenue and elsewhere (see Map 1). Still others worked on the extensions of Sixth and Seventh avenues above 145th Street. Perhaps the most sizable crew of laborers worked on the 150-foot-wide Boulevard. Construction on the Boulevard had begun in 1868, and by early 1870 a five-mile roadbed had been laid from Fifty-ninth Street and Eighth Avenue to 155th Street. The Boulevard eventually connected with Sixth and Seventh avenues (also then under construction) at 145th Street and then crossed to the Harlem River, its northern boundary.[3]

The new road projects were supervised by the Central Park commissioners, whose already busy duties had been expanded by Radical Republican lawmakers just after the war. Since 1857, when plans for Central Park had begun to materialize, commissioners had been appointed by the governor. Under the "Tweed Charter," which became law on April 6, 1870, however, the commissioners' responsibilities were transferred to the Department of Public Works, whose four board members were appointed by Mayor Hall. Tweed became head of the Department of Public Works. Tammany Hall thus controlled hefty budgets for public works programs, while Tweed himself supplied patronage jobs to hundreds of political cronies and gave jobs to thousands of laborers on the roads, quarries, and other city projects.[4]

"Holy water"

Unlike Tweed and his friends, who received fat salaries for little work, laborers and quarrymen who carved out parks and streets had no access to easy lives. Despite claims by a *Times* reporter in October 1870 that men working on one park gently prodded the ground with their pickaxes "as if it were hallowed,"[5] the work was tough, hot, dirty, and bought families little. Many laborers apparently lived near

3. Mott, *New York of Yesterday*, 228–32, 237, 438; *Sun*, January 3, 1870; *Herald*, April 6, 1876.

4. *Herald*, April 6, 1870; *Times*, May 29 and June 2, 1869; Charles F. Wingate, "An Episode in Municipal Government," *North American Review* 121 (July 1875): 114–24; Alexander B. Callow, *The Tweed Ring* (New York: Oxford University Press, 1965), 126–29, 236; and Marcuse, *This Was New York*, 133.

5. *Times*, October 11, 1870, quoted in Callow, *Tweed Ring*, 129; see also 128–31 for a discussion of patronage in Tweed's department.

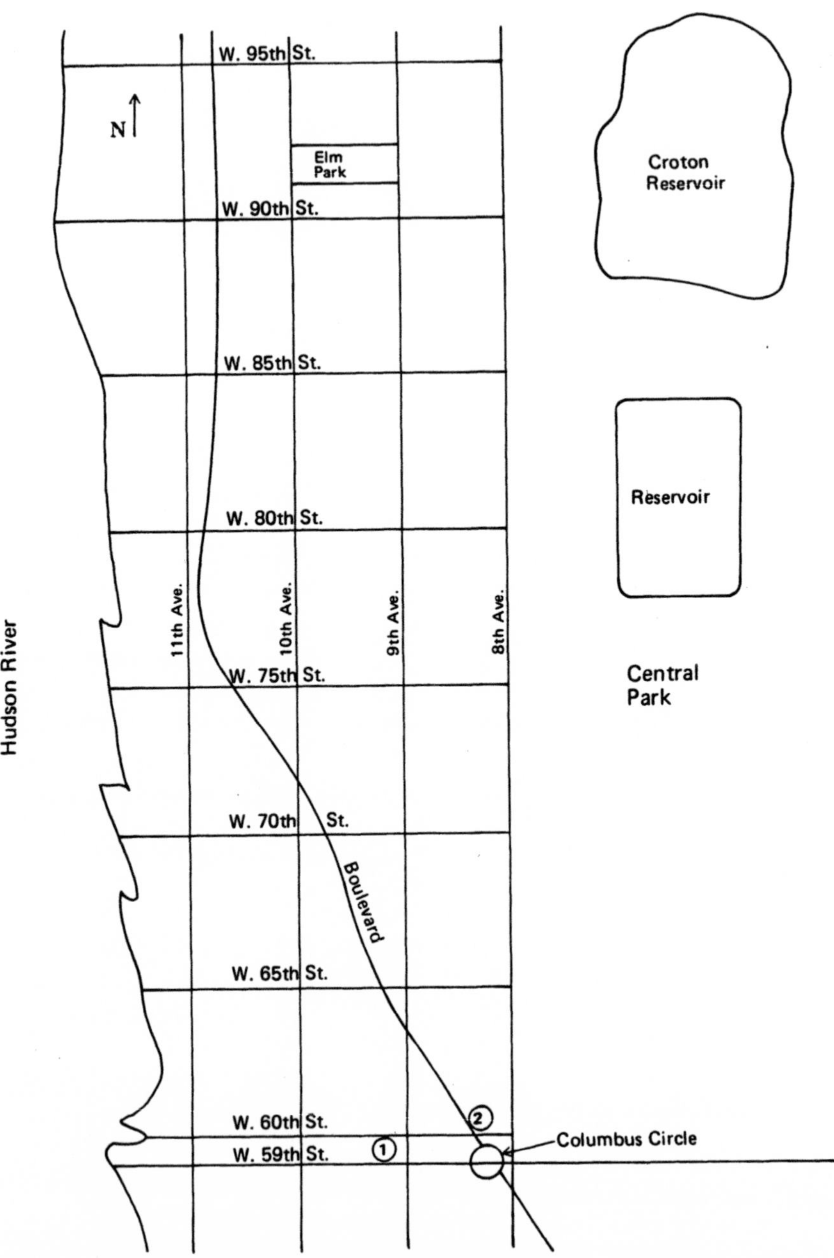

MAP 1. Manhattan, Fifty-ninth to Ninety-fifth streets, west of Central Park. (1) Church of St. Paul's, (2) workers laying section of Croton Aqueduct.

their jobs. Daniel Bernard Crowley, for example, lived with his wife and several children in Bloomingdale (West of Central Park) near Sixty-eighth or Sixty-ninth Street. Born in Ireland, he was about forty years old and worked on the new road. Quarryman William Kane lived on Third Avenue in Yorkville (east of Central Park). Thirty-one, he had emigrated to New York from Ireland in 1857 and also had a family. Patrick Kane, another Irish immigrant, resided somewhere west of Central Park between Ninth and Tenth avenues near his Boulevard job. James Brady was a more youthful Boulevard wage earner. Born in this country to Irish immigrants, the teenager was a tool carrier whose job was the main source of income for his family. The Brady's "small shanty" rested in a hollow near Sixty-third Street and Eighth Avenue.

On the morning of July 12, 1870, these and other workers left home for their jobs. Elsewhere, Charles Brady sought a new job that day to help support his wife and four children. The young unemployed marble polisher lived at Fifty-Third Street and Eleventh Avenue. And sixty-year-old Patrick Brady, about whom little is known, undoubtedly also joined the early morning trek to work. By that night the three Bradys and Crowley were dead. Patrick and William Kane died the next day. All were victims of the Elm Park riot.

Two other victims, twenty-four-year-old John Gardiner and thirty-one-year-old Francis Wood, lived elsewhere in the city. In New York just three years, Gardiner shared quarters with a married sister and her family on West Thirty-seventh Street. He died at Bellevue Hospital on July 14. Another native of Ireland, Wood worked at the Brooklyn Navy Yards and lived with his wife and four children on East Ninth Street. He died on July 13. Both were Orangemen.[6]

Gardiner and Wood apparently took a day off from work to join as many as twenty-five hundred members of the Orange society and the American Protestant Association and their families in celebrating Boyne Day. The sponsor of the parade and Elm Park picnic, the APA, had advertised its plans for weeks and invited lodges in nearby cities to attend. The procession stepped off from Cooper Union at ten in the morning. It included members of Enniskillen Lodge No. 29, the Gideon Lodge, the Prince of Orange Lodge No. 339, and an

6. See Appendix A. Additional information on James Brady was supplied a year later in an interview with a boss quarryman who remembered the Brady family's plight and the boy's death; see *Herald*, July 11, 1871.

Orange branch from Newark. Some in line carried banners reading "Boyne," "Aughrim," and "Derry." The *Tribune* noted that these were "names odious to Irishmen, who can only see in them the humiliation of their race and the overthrow of their nationality." Many also wore orange sashes, ribbons, and other Orange symbols immediately identifiable to the thousands who watched the procession as it moved up Broadway toward Elm Park.[7]

The Orangemen were boisterous. Their loud voices and shouts joined with small bands playing "Protestant Boys," "Croppies, Lie Down," "Battle of the Boyne," and "Boyne Water." The songs celebrated earlier repression of Catholics and recalled specific acts of Protestant torture. "Battle of the Boyne" urged:

> Come, let us all, with heart and voice,
> Applaud our lives' defender,
> Who at the Boyne his valor showed,
> And made his foe surrender.
> To God above the praise we'll give,
> Both now and ever after,
> And bless the glorious memory
> Of King William that crossed the water.

In the broadside "Boyne Water," Orangemen sang:

> So praise God, all true Protestants and I
> will say no further,
> But had the Papists gained the day, there
> would have been open murder.
> Although King James and many more were ne'er
> that way inclined,
> It was not in their power to stop what the
> rabble they designed.[8]

"Croppies, Lie Down" celebrated the 1798 rebellion in which the Crown's military in Ulster tortured information from Catholics about United Irishmen activities. Troops flogged some hapless Catholics. They strung up others by one arm so that their feet rested only on a

7. *Times, Sun, World,* and *Tribune,* July 13, 1870.

8. "Battle of the Boyne," *Herald,* July 11, 1871; "The Boyne Water," in William Butler Yeats et al., *Broadsides* (Shannon, 1935).

pointed spike. In some districts they used a pitch-cap. This gruesome device mocked Catholics who cropped their hair short after the fashion of French republicans. Tormentors filled a brown paper cap with hot pitch, splashed it on a Catholic's head, and then ignited it. As the frantic victim tried to tear it off, burning pitch ran into his eyes and down his face, and chunks of hair and scalp peeled off. The reference to "water" in this song may have referred to the pitch:

Water, water,
Holy water;
Sprinkle the Catholics, every one;
We'll cut them asunder,
And make them lie under.
The Protestant boys will carry the gun.
(Chorus). Croppies, lie down;
Croppies, lie down;
We'll make all the Catholic Croppies
lie down.

Part of another verse warned:

Oh, Croppies, ye'd better be quiet and still
Ye shan't have your liberty, do what ye will,
As long as salt water is found in the deep
Our foot on the neck of the Croppie we'll keep.

This song was so provocative that a year later, New York's Prince of Orange district master James W. Gauld told hired bands not to play the tune in that year's parade, "as that was made the pretext for the assault last year."[9]

Irish Catholics responded to these insults soon after the parade began. As the column passed Fourth Street with banners flying and bands blaring, "some two hundred" Irish laborers quickly assembled and followed it, shouting curses and "vowing vengeance on the processionists." Yet no violence immediately occurred there or even farther up Broadway at Twenty-third Street, where Protestants reportedly taunted more laborers with jeers and faction tunes. A local

9. Verses in *Tribune*, July 10, 1871, and Robert Kee, *The Green Flag: A History of Irish Nationalism* (London: Weidenfeld and Nicolson, 1972), 97–98; James W. Gauld (n.p., n.d.), to *Evening Post*, July 12, 1871.

priest, who defended the Orangemen's right to parade, later said his parishioners told him that Orangemen had shouted "To hell with the Pope" and waved Orange flags in their faces.[10]

At Fifty-ninth Street and Eighth Avenue, laborers laying a Croton water main quit work as the parade passed on its way to Ninth Avenue and urged nearby Boulevard laborers to join them in following Orangemen to Elm Park. From Fifty-ninth Street, the parade evidently turned north into Ninth Avenue and either moved directly to the park or picked up the Boulevard again at Sixty-fifth Street. (The new road cut diagonally northwest from Fifty-ninth Street and Eighth Avenue to Seventy-fifth Street before running parallel to Tenth and Eleventh avenues.) Whatever the Orangemen's exact route, they passed on or near the Boulevard, where "many of the Irish citizens of the upper wards were working."[11]

Three accounts refer to a striking incident at Fifty-ninth Street and Ninth Avenue which must have further incensed Irish Catholics. Vicar-General William Staars told a *Sun* reporter that a person "assured me" that Orangemen "had made threats of demolishing the windows of the Church of St. Paul as they passed." The *Herald* discovered that Orangemen, "in addition to inflammatory flags and music and jeers, . . . fired into Father Hecker's church" at that same location. Although these accounts differ, a third source suggests that whatever actually occurred, many Irish Catholics *believed* a shot had been fired into the church and that that perception alone may have provoked the assault at Elm Park. Moreover, this source demonstrates how the St. Paul incident, real or rumored, added to other unsettled historical scores. Almost a year later—on July 10, 1871—a *Herald* reporter asked a Boulevard laborer, "who confessed himself a Hibernian, and was the principal spokesman of the crowd [of workers]," why he objected to the upcoming Orange parade *that* year. He replied:

> Because when they are allowed to parade they don't know how to conduct themselves. They were allowed to show themselves three years in succession, and no notice was taken of them until last year, when they could not pass the Catholic Church in Fifty-ninth-street without firing into it. That was the cause of the riot last year. The Catholics were quietly at work along the Boulevard, and there

10. *World*, July 13, 1870 (quote); *Sun*, July 16, 1870; *Herald*, July 13, 1870 (quote).
11. *Herald*, July 13, 14, 1870.

> was no intention to attack them until the word was passed along the works that they had fired into the chapel; then men quit work and followed them. So whatever happens they brought it on themselves. Americans forget how they treated us when they had the power, and forced us to say mass in the ditches, and they would do so again. If they got the upper hand in this city a dog could not live under them.[12]

If Orangemen did fire on the church, Irish Catholics apparently did not respond immediately. But Orange taunts and tunes continued. Police at the Thirty-first Precinct station in One Hundredth Street told the *Sun* that workers from Sixty-ninth Street to the park were outraged by the songs and "insulting language" and that many quit work to follow the parade. According to the *Tribune*, after a shouting match erupted just above Eighty-third Street, "the whole body of Boulevard men, as if by common and preconcerted action, quitted work, and, each carrying whatever tools he was working with, . . . went in a body toward Elm Park."[13]

"a sense of duty"

If, as the *Times* reported, the parade "was followed by an excited crowd of men, seemingly all Irish laborers, who uttered sundry threats against the excursionists," it is clear these men did not accept the provocation and immediately tear after Orange throats. As word spread among construction crews and neighborhoods about the parade and the incident at St. Paul's Church, a potential army of thousands could have been mobilized for attacks. Yet Catholics did not begin to invade the park until at least two hours after the picnic began, and estimates by witnesses put Catholic strength at between three hundred and one thousand.[14]

Why, then, did so relatively few Catholics try to storm the park gates and attack those honoring "King William of Glorious Memory?" And what accounts for the delay between half past one, when the

12. *Sun*, July 16, 1870; *Herald*, July 14, 1870, and July 11, 1871.

13. *Sun*, July 14, 1870; *Tribune*, July 13, 1870.

14. *Times*, *World*, and *Tribune*, July 13, 1870; *Sun*, July 13, 14, 1870; *Herald*, July 14, 20, 1870.

picnic began, and the arrival of laborers at about half past three?[15] There are several possible explanations. Press accounts may have exaggerated the provocations and responses to them. Or perhaps the midday heat drew workers into nearby saloons to cool off (although, significantly, no accounts claimed that Catholics had been drinking). Fearing loss of wages and jobs, other workers may have returned to work before festering insults sent them back to Elm Park. Did priests use their influence to delay or lessen an attack? The vicar-general later claimed no priest would countenance an attack, but neither is there any evidence the clergy roamed the streets urging calm.[16]

Perhaps the most plausible explanation for the two-hour delay and the relatively moderate response is related to Fenian concerns and the lack of publicity about the Orange festivities. Embarrassed and frustrated by their failure to capture outposts along the Canadian border the previous spring, and concerned with rebuilding a disciplined and respected military organization, Fenian circles—with many Irish longshoremen and laborers in their ranks—opposed any domestic activities that might discredit their efforts. Members of the Ancient Order of Hibernians, who sometimes drilled with Fenian units, may have been torn between their Fenian allegiances and their Ribbon sentiments. More important, they lacked the time to hold formal meetings to discuss a proper response to Orange insults. (In 1871 such discussions began in early July and continued until July 12.)[17]

The activities of Protestant families early that afternoon are much clearer. Shortly after their one o'clock arrival at the park, between twenty-five hundred and three thousand people listened to Worshipful Grand Master John J. Bond recount the glories of the day they celebrated. A *Herald* reporter in the crowd heard Orangemen make "loud boasts as to their power to repel any attack from Fenians or Catholics." Then everyone left Bond's platform for picnics, dancing at a small pavilion, and shooting matches at Gustave Lenhardt's rifle gallery. Many men kept bartenders Henry Stopleman and Max Movius busy in the park beerhouse until the fighting began.[18]

15. Some Orange families avoided the parade and went straight to the park. Many began arriving between 10:00 and 11:30 A.M. (*Sun*, July 13, 1870); testimony of Frederick Rentz (Elm Park's owner), as reported in *Herald*, July 20, 1870.

16. *Sun*, July 16, 1870.

17. See the discussion of these points in Chapters 3 and 4.

18. *Herald*, July 13, 1870.

By then the Catholics were ready. The *Herald* claimed that "over 400 men" who had quit work at 1:30 P.M. had "armed themselves with handles broken from pickaxes and mallets, with small hand drills, and with a peculiar weapon called a 'flying pike,' . . . a small, pointed iron bar attached to a cord some three yards in length." The paper said they were led by a man named Brophy. The first assault came from the gang of Fifty-ninth Street Croton pipeline workers, whose numbers swelled to some five hundred as they moved up Eighth Avenue. Two Boulevard construction foremen told a July 19 coroner's inquest that much smaller groups had visited their crews. James Hodges claimed fifty or sixty men appeared at 2:55 P.M. with "clubs and sticks" and ordered him to stop work so that laborers could join them at the park. Hodges refused but his men quit work anyway. Only five minutes later, John R. Lawson's laborers left their jobs at 104th and 105th streets to join ten or twelve other men who carried clubs. Elsewhere, police confirmed that at the same time, some one hundred men were seen moving up Eighth Avenue from Eighty-fifth Street. They broke into small groups at Eighty-fifth and Eighty-seventh streets and moved toward the park.[19]

Police were unprepared for the attack. Capt. John C. Helme, a draft riot veteran, later told a coroner's jury that he had gone to Elm Park at two o'clock from his One Hundredth Street station house. An APA member told him he expected no trouble from Catholics until the picnic broke up after dark, but Helme said he advised them to leave by six o'clock to avoid risking travel after dark. Just outside the park at Ninety-second Street, two laborers told Helme that Boulevard workmen were en route to the park. Helme rushed to his station, ordered the precinct's reserves to the park, and telegraphed police superintendent John Jourdan for more help.[20]

These arrangements took precious time. Some 150 police traveled from downtown precincts by coach, and Helme had to wait for them all to arrive before organizing a march to the park. During the interval he received more bad news. The rifle range–keeper Lenhardt sent word that he had learned workers were arming themselves

19. *Herald*, July 14, 1870; testimony of James Hodges and John R. Lawson, coroner's inquest, as reported in *Herald*, July 20, 1870; *Sun*, July 14, 1870.

20. Testimony of John C. Helme, coroner's inquest, as reported in *Herald*, July 20, 1870. The police strength is given in *World*, *Herald*, and *Tribune*, July 13, 1870. On Helme in 1863, see Adrian Cook, *The Armies of the Streets: The New York City Draft Riots of 1863* (Lexington: University Press of Kentucky, 1974), 115–16.

somewhere on Eighth Avenue. Just then a Boulevard foreman appeared saying his men had been forced to join other irate workers who were planning to invade the park.[21]

There is some evidence that the laborers' attack was loosely coordinated. Two reports claimed that thirty "Fenians" used fake identification badges to gain entrance to the park. The *Times* reported that at 3:30 P.M. someone fired a shot, which at once sent thirty workers "to the rear of the dancing shed in the center of the grounds," where they "laid on to the Orangemen with sticks and stones." Yet a *Sun* reporter placed the thirty men inside the beer hall and claimed their shots sent Orangemen screaming wildly in all directions for escape. Bartenders Movius and Stopleman did not confirm the *Sun* story in their inquest testimony, but they did report much fighting inside the beer hall and some shooting outside.[22]

It seems unlikely that Irish Catholics secretly entered the park and suddenly started shooting. If they had, surely more deaths would have occurred—something the anti–Irish Catholic press would have emphasized with much relish. Nor is there evidence that the attackers were Fenians or members of the AOH or other Irish nationalist organizations, as some papers charged.[23]

What seems most plausible is that at 3:30 P.M. some fifty laborers rounded the corner of Ninety-second Street and Eighth Avenue and made their way to the front of the park a block away. At the same time, up to four hundred more appeared in back of the buildings at the southeast corner of the park at Ninetieth Street and Ninth Avenue. Many wore red, white, and blue flannel clothes, dirtied from long hours of Boulevard work. Both groups threw large paving stones inside while others tried either to scale park fences or break them down. A few shots rang out, although witnesses disagreed about which side fired first. Detective James Connor, attached to Helme's precinct, believed the firing began inside, but he did not know if the laborers provoked it. Park owner Frederick Rentz testified that at 3:30 P.M. he was looking after some cattle in a shed when he suddenly saw people dashing in all directions. One passing customer

21. *Sun* and *World*, July 13, 1870; *Tribune*, July 14, 1870.

22. *Times* and *Sun*, July 13, 1870; testimony of Max Movius and Henry Stopleman, coroner's inquest, as reported in *Herald*, July 20, 1870.

23. *Times*, July 13, 1870.

told Rentz that people outside the gates were throwing stones and shooting at those inside.[24]

The battle at the park fences lasted but a few minutes. Hurling epithets, small rocks, and chunks of paving stones, Catholics yelled, "Down with the Orange," "Avenge your wrongs," and "Down with Irish traitors." One reporter estimated that at the south park railings both sides exchanged from sixty to seventy shots within the first seven minutes. One shot ripped open Daniel B. Crowley's chest as he tried to scale the fence. Someone smashed an instrument over bandleader William Robertson's head. Others clubbed Orangemen John Shields and Samuel Smith as they hurried their families to safety.[25]

Within minutes, vendors closed their shops and refreshment stands. Neighborhood merchants also closed as fighting spilled into nearby streets. Drawing their pistols, knives, and swords, Orangemen and APA members charged laborers who had broken through the fences and rushed to other gates to stand guard. Others charged through a small gate at the southeast corner and fired at laborers there before police pushed them back inside. Still others chased Catholics east on Ninetieth Street across Eighth Avenue into Central Park. There, quarryman William Kane, who had remained at his Boulevard job that afternoon, was on his way through the park to his Third Avenue home. An Orangeman mistook him for an earlier assailant, called him a "Papist," and fired a pistol at him. Kane eluded the shot but was stabbed in the back as he tried to flee. Nearby, Charles Brady, the young unemployed marble polisher, was shot in the chest as he looked for work between Eighth and Ninth avenues near Ninety-second or Ninety-third Street.[26]

By shortly after four o'clock, pitched fighting occurred from Tenth Avenue eastward into Central Park, and from Ninety-fourth to Eighty-second Street. One paper described the brawling as "a war of mutual extermination"; another reported that "men ran about in all directions, some armed with picks, shovels, bludgeons, but the greater part carrying huge cobble stones which they hurled at one

24. *Sun, Tribune, Times,* and *World,* July 13, 1870; *Herald,* July 20, 1870 (Connor and Rentz).

25. *Sun, Times,* and *World,* July 13, 1870; testimony of John C. Helme, as reported in *Herald,* July 20, 1870. See also Appendix A.

26. *Times,* July 13, 1870.

another with demonic ferocity." Reporting on the thirty-minute fight along Eighth Avenue, a third paper claimed there were only two policemen present and that "there were not so many clubs used here as in the woods. The combatants were principally armed with pistols, which they used to great effect."[27]

The most serious injuries occurred on Eighth and Ninth Avenue streetcars, which had glass windows and were protected only by a driver and conductor. The attacks incensed a *Times* reporter, who claimed that "the cars, as they came up, were densely crowded, and the Fenians, mad with rage, rushed upon them, dragged out women by the hair, and whenever an Orangeman stood up to defend them he was ruthlessly collared, knocked down with a bludgeon and hammered on the head by three or four in succession." A *Sun* reporter believed "the Fenians" were "white with rage, and stammering with passion they stopped the horse cars, dragged women out by the hair of their heads, and threw stones among the poor little children." He also suspected that one Orange boy may have been shot (the incident was not corroborated), reported seeing two men beaten with large clubs, and said "Fenians" threw Orangemen to the ground and pelted them with stones.[28]

Catholics reportedly sacked other cars at Ninetieth Street and Ninth Avenue. "Stones and bullets were fired through the windows into the cars literally packed with men, women, and children," the *Tribune* reported, "and the fire was liberally returned from the inside." One woman received a gash on her head from a large stone. Another Ninth Avenue car rider was found wandering aimlessly on Eighth Avenue with a bloody face; a bloodied Orangeman ran into Central Park, where he found refuge in a carriage full of women. At Ninety-second Street, Orangeman Robert Nutt was clubbed as he rode downtown to catch a ferry for his Brooklyn home. At Ninetieth Street, police later found the body of young James Brady, the Boulevard tool carrier. Some said he was killed as he assaulted the cars; others claimed someone crushed his skull as he merely watched from the sidewalk.[29]

27. *World*, *Times*, and *Herald*, July 13, 1870. See also *Tribune*, July 13, 1870; and *Sun*, July 13, 14, 1870.

28. *World*, *Times*, *Sun*, *Herald*, and *Tribune*, July 13, 1870.

29. *Tribune*, *Times*, and *Sun*, July 13, 1870. See also Appendix A.

The assault continued for more than thirty blocks along Eighth Avenue. Car No. 91 conductor Thomas McCracken later told a coroner's jury that his car suddenly filled with passengers just after four o'clock. Nearing Eighty-sixth Street, he noticed another car stopped a block away and ordered his driver to wait until it moved on. McCracken then investigated and found "fifty or sixty men and five or six officers" arguing near the stopped car as a crowd threw stones at it (the *Sun* reported Catholics "fired a volley") and refused to let it pass. McCracken returned to his car but shortly was stopped by the melee. A *Sun* reporter saw two Orangemen take refuge in a nearby house on Eighty-fifth Street. Catholics broke windows and forced the Orangemen back outside, where a fight erupted. Similar scenes and sporadic gunfire were reported farther down the avenue, and the *Times* found it "incomprehensible" that "so few were killed."[30]

Yet deaths and injuries did occur, especially near Fifty-ninth Street and Eighth Avenue, where laborers worked on the Boulevard and on Croton pipeline. There, Irish workers reportedly "burst in the sides of the cars, threw large boulders of rock at," and clubbed, the occupants. Orangeman and APA member Francis Wood was badly beaten and died the next day at Bellevue Hospital. Thomas Burnett, a baker, sustained less severe head injuries, while another rider, Daniel Collins, was shot in the jaw. Brooklyn resident William Ross suffered three head wounds and a broken jaw. Outside the cars, teamster Thomas Murray was in the area looking for work when a "tall, well-dressed man" approached and shouted, "You're one of them, you Papal son of a b - - - -; I'll fix you." The man's first shot hit Murray in the face. When a second misfired, the man beat Murray on the head.[31]

Then, suddenly, a driving rainstorm pierced the late afternoon humidity, broke up the violence, and sent stragglers along Eighth Avenue home. Press accounts do not reveal how Orangemen and their families managed to return home or if further violence occurred later in the day.[32]

Surprisingly, the police made few arrests. John Boyd, Robert

30. Testimony of Thomas McCraken, coroner's inquest, as reported in *Herald*, July 20, 1870; *Sun* and *Times*, July 13, 1870.

31. *World*, July 13, 1870; Appendix A.

32. *Sun*, *World*, and *Herald*, July 13, 1870.

Dawson, Patrick Daly, and Peter O'Brien were charged with disorderly conduct as part "of the assailing party." Boyd, a clerk, apparently had threatened to shoot someone. He and the others were jailed when they failed to make bail. Police justice McQuade dismissed the case against Jacob Pater, who had been arrested for firing a pistol in Elm Park. McQuade reasoned that since Pater was German he was not tied to the dispute. There was one other known arrest. John Murphy charged that Stephen K. Hogenboom shot at him the night of July 12 while Murphy cleaned out a sewer on Sixty-ninth Street. Hogenboom denied the charge and was held for trial. No records of these cases remain, and the press did not report their dispositions.[33]

Little is known about other riot incidents, including the deaths of Patrick Brady and John Gardiner. Sixty-year-old Brady was "shot in the breast and stomach." Gardiner, found injured with an Orange badge on his clothes, died on July 14. He and Francis Wood were the only two Orangemen who died from the violence. (A year later Orange leader James W. Gauld said the Elm Park riot resulted "in the death of two of our number and serious injury of several others.") On July 19, a coroner's jury investigated only six of the eight deaths, took testimony from eight witnesses, and found "that the deceased parties came to their deaths from injuries received at the hands of a person or persons unknown at Elm Park, Ninety-second street and Eighth avenue, July 12, 1870."[34]

Details about injuries are also vague. Those who were clubbed or stoned were treated by police doctors and sent home. The *Tribune* estimated that there were "at least 100" wounded "of whom there is no public record." Some of the more seriously injured went to Bellevue, where during the night, family members and friends sat at their bedsides or stood vigil by hospital gates. Others awaited news in a more traditional way. At Brian Born's One Hundredth Street house "a mock wake was held over an effigy, which was arrayed in a regalia captured from an Orange chief, the head being decorated with Orange lilies and other flowers." The event marked a common loss and

33. See Appendix A.

34. See Appendix A for a complete list of killed and injured. The coroner's inquest was reported in *Herald*, *Sun*, and *Tribune*, July 20, 1870. Jury members (whose occupations were not given) were James McClintock, William Ferdinand, John J. Maloney, John Bach, John Carey, Augustus Tautphaces, Charles Shields, and Justus Roach. See also Gauld (n.p., n.d.) to *Evening Post*, July 12, 1871.

reaffirmed communal values. "The most thrilling expressions of grief were simulated," the *Herald* reported, "varied occasionally by real manifestations of sorrow, as news was brought at the door of the sad condition of the wounded and dying in the neighboring huts."[35]

Despite the absence of important details, the available evidence suggests, first, that the Protestants had more in mind than peacefully celebrating a historic victory. Orangemen and APA members deliberately insulted groups of Irish Catholics along the parade route. Even in the papers most hostile to Irish Catholics, there was no report of Protestant efforts to stifle provocations as they moved through "a district peopled exclusively by Ribbonmen," as "A Citizen" remarked, "and in the midst of a precinct which could furnish only nine policemen to meet a sudden emergency."[36] Moreover, many Protestants carried pistols and other weapons. Perhaps they were armed merely as a precaution. But they also may have tried to provoke an attack to taint Irish Catholics, Catholicism, and Tammany.

Yet why would Irish Protestants knowingly endanger their families by such actions? Perhaps they miscalculated the timing of the attack they hoped to incite, thinking they could send their families ahead to the park while they fought Irish "scum" on the way. Whatever the case, Irish Catholics did not limit their response just to Orange*men*—especially as the fights spread to Eighth Avenue streetcars—although as the *Tribune* noted, "In no case was a policeman attacked by the mob of laborers."[37]

Second, the assaults at the front and rear of Elm Park, and the late-afternoon streetcar attacks, suggest that the Catholic actions were purposeful and may have been loosely coordinated. A *Times* editorial cast such movements another way: "A certain amount of lawless organization there must have been, or the muster of Catholic laborers from the streets works on the route of the procession would have been impracticable." By all accounts, laborers were seen carrying tools and other makeshift weapons—the traditional arsenal of spontaneous working-class fighting. They did not steal or sack shops in the park and along the avenues. Even the *Nation* acknowledged that Catholics acted "under the influence of a sense of duty."[38] Yet for the *Nation*, "duty" meant something sinister and irrational. For Irish

35. Appendix A; *Tribune*, July 13, 14, 1870; *Herald*, July 14, 1870.
36. "A Citizen" (New York, July 13, 1870) to *Tribune*, July 14, 1870.
37. *Tribune*, July 14, 1870.
38. *Times*, July 14, 1870; *Nation* 11 (July 21, 1870): 35.

Catholic laborers, "duty" meant responding to Orange taunts and the historical circumstances that made them so intolerable.

"crapeing things that crape"

Reactions to the violence revealed much about the many worlds of New Yorkers. Women and men crowded police stations and Bellevue to view bodies and inquire after the injured or arrested. An unnamed Boulevard contractor reportedly learned that his workers had assaulted streetcars and fired them all. That evening, friends took Francis Wood's body to his home at 623 East Ninth Street. One paper reported that the body's arrival brought out "an immense crowd of [neighborhood] residents" who threatened "to drag the corpse into the street and offer other indignities to the remains." Police dispersed the crowd and guarded the house throughout the night.[39]

Wood's afternoon funeral procession on July 15 turned into public theater. Five to eight thousand angry people crowded the east side of Tompkins Square and adjoining streets to watch the cortege. Escorted by 600 police, 37 carriages, and 227 members of the No Surrender and Enniskillen lodges wearing mourning badges, the hearse moved up Avenue B to Tenth Street, then over to Bowery and down to the Catherine Street ferry and across to Brooklyn's Green-Wood Cemetery. In Tompkins Square, men and women shouted at the cortege (three men were arrested), while in the Bowery a woman cursed Protestants and the police as she hung from a lamppost. Near Monroe and Catherine streets a man hurled a brick at the hearse and was arrested. That same afternoon, Orangeman John Gardiner was also buried in Green-Wood, but his family held a small private funeral to avoid a public confrontation. An extended community had participated in the funeral of the boy James Brady the day before. After Catholic services in his parents' small hut near Sixty-third Street and Eighth Avenue, a procession, led by a band and fifty carriages, made its way to an undisclosed cemetery. Along the way, one thousand people fell in behind the casket.[40]

Class and nativist sentiments informed other responses to the riot.

39. *World* (quote), *Herald*, and *Tribune*, July 14, 1870.
40. *Herald*, July 15, 1870; *Times*, *Sun*, and *Tribune*, July 16, 1870.

Summarizing discussion about the riot among Irish Catholic opponents on July 13, the *Tribune* claimed in a lead paragraph that "the action of the Catholic Irish in attacking the Orangemen and their families while peaceably enjoying a pic-nic in a garden or park hired for the occasion, their brutal and continued assaults on the helplessly wounded and flying women and children, was condemned in unmeasured terms." The paper's editorial that day convicted all Irish workers for the affair and indicted Tammany Hall for complicity. "The ruffians who have committed this crime belong to the same class which, under the leadership of Mr. William Marcy Tweed has taken possession of this City and State," it glowered. The Tweed Ring sought to create a "general license" for its supporters, and threatened "us with free murder, free drunkenness, and free rioting."[41]

A *Times* reporter believed that "nothing whatever had been done to provoke [the] assault on the part of the Orangemen, except the circumstances of wearing the colors and insignia of their order." It was an important exception, and the reporter omitted much else; yet he concluded that "the attack was premeditated and altogether unwarranted." His editor agreed. "The entire disturbance can only be characterized as brutal and terrible," he wrote on July 13, "and the riot appears to be wholly without provocation, except as was furnished by the clannish hatred of the rioters toward their Protestant fellow countrymen." Pursuing the matter a day later, the paper maintained that "the actual criminality is all on the side of the Irish Catholic mob," but it condemned Orange processions because "badges and ribbons [recalled] to the Irish Catholic mind bitter memories of his native land" and because Orange tunes were "offensive . . . to a class numerous in every large city." The editor even perceptively argued that Orangeism "typifies English supremacy in Ireland" and hence was more "political" than "religious." But while he rejected supporting "a secret order which has no significance anywhere, except as a champion of British connection," he believed "as a society to protect the Protestant religion it might be useful."[42]

41. *Tribune*, July 14, 1870. A similar view was expressed in "The Much-Maligned City of New York," *Harper's Weekly* 14 (July 30, 1870): 483. Others combined attacks on Catholics with criticisms of the police under Democratic rule; see, e.g., "A Citizen" (New York, July 13, 1870) to *Tribune*, July 14, 1870; and that paper's own indictment in the same issue.

42. *Times*, July 13, 14, 1870.

Others who shared such views revealed how the collective memory of the draft riots shaped some responses to the Elm Park brawl. Sometime late Thursday night George Templeton Strong wrote in his diary that the Orangemen "were set upon by a swarm of base and brutal Celts, such as those who burned orphan asylums and got up a Negro massacre in July, 1863" (a reference to the draft riots). He thought it a "pity [that] there were no grapeshot for the assailants." "Execrable Celtic *canaille*!" he exploded. "The gorilla is their superior in muscle and hardly inferior in moral sense." Writing to the *Sun* in defense of the APA, "true American" also resurrected the specter of the draft riot and the APA's origins. Pointing out that "the American Protestant Association was organized at the period when bigots were using their endeavors to prohibit the use of the Holy Bible in the public schools," the writer claimed its members were "native and foreign born citizens" who "do not owe allegiance to any foreign potentates, temporal or spiritual; they are never known to create riots, mob the police, burn orphan asylums, murder defenceless [sic] women and children, or even make a raid on the green flag of the foreign devotees of St. Patrick."[43]

Other readers argued that Orangemen should have the same right to parade on July 12 that Irish Catholics enjoyed on March 17, but some urged abolishing all celebrations except true "American" ones. Nativism permeated such views. "The Irish Catholics are quite willing to get all the privileges and immunities they can," a writer argued, "but in return are not so accommodating." "Americus" believed that "Catholic hatred culminates on the English Protestant, but to-morrow, or when they are strong enough, the American will feel the weight of it." As Catholic power increases, "Americans may . . . have to fight for their principles as did William and his followers on the Boyne." Urging a ban on all Catholic and Protestant celebrations, an Orangeman's daughter nevertheless believed it was important to defend her father's principles by reminding that "Orangeism and Fenianism are but other names for Protestants and Popery" (the choice therefore was clear) and that Orangemen would never attack women and children because "they have the natural instinct of Christian gentlemen, while the other party seem imbued with the nature

43. George Templeton Strong, *The Diary of George Templeton Strong*, vol. 4, *The Post-War Years, 1865–1875*, ed. Allan Nevins and Milton H. Thomas (New York: Macmillan, 1952), 295; "True American" (n.p., n.d.) to *Sun*, July 15, 1870.

of savage beasts." Answering an Irish Catholic who had criticized the Orange banner, "Down with Popery," Edith O'Gorman defended the motto because it meant

> down with oppression and slavery! down with ignorance and degradation! down with idolatry and superstition! down with licentious priests and extortioners! down with bloody inquisitions and gunpowder plots! . . . Catholics display a spirit of tyranny in their efforts to rule America with their motto, down with freedom and liberty! down with free schools and the Bible! down with science and progress! down with intelligence and enlightenment! down and to death with heretics, and all who refuse to believe the Pope infallible! down with independence and free speech!

One anonymous writer closed the issue and his letter with this mocking prayer: "Good Laird deliver us from witches an' warlocks, and crapeing things that crape amang the heather, especially the Wild Irish."[44]

Irish Catholics expressed other concerns. Frustrated and angered because the riot hurt Irish nationalist efforts, *Boston Pilot* editor John Boyle O'Reilly condemned all rioters for "making the name of Irishmen a scoff and a byword this day in America." "Why must we carry, wherever we go, those accursed and contemptible island feuds?" he asked. "Shall we never be shamed into the knowledge of the brazen impudence of allowing our national hatreds to disturb the peace and the safety of the respectable citizens of this country?"[45]

Others challenged O'Reilly and the nativists. Arguing that the APA was "nothing more or less than a branch of the 'Orange Association' of England," one writer pleaded for some understanding of immigrant Irish Catholics. "You left your native land to look for peace, prosperity, and requited toil under the beautiful flag of America," he

44. See, e.g., W.M.L. (n.p., n.d.) and R. W. L'Hommedieu (quote) (Brooklyn, July 14, 1870) to *Sun*, and other letters in this issue; "Americus" (n.p., n.d.) to *Sun*, July 14, 1870; "An Orangemen's [sic] Daughter" (n.p., n.d.) to *Sun*, July 15, 1870; O'Gorman (n.p., July 15, 1870) to *Times*, July 16, 1870—O'Gorman had responded to the letter of "Unprejudiced Irishman" (n.p., n.d.) in *Sun*, July 15, 1870; and "Anonymous" (n.p., n.d.) to *Sun*, July 15, 1870.

45. *Boston Pilot*, July 23, 1870. See also the letter of "Fenian" (Greenpoint, N.Y., July 13, 1870) to *Sun*, July 15, 1870, who denounced those papers that blamed Fenians for the attack. He claimed Fenians had no part in the riot because they were pledged to work for brotherly love.

reminded. "You came here only to find that your old enemy on the hated 12th of July was organized, to pursue you and yours, as of old, to the bitter end,—under a new name, but with old principles. . . . Would you tamely submit?"[46]

"What have [Orange] descendants done for America?" another asked. "They come here, in time of peace, try to make capital out of their religion, and impress the natural liberal American with the threatening danger of Catholicism; that the Irish maidservants on a given night are to murder all their Protestant mistresses; and that the Pope of Rome shall soon be in our midst." He alleged that Orangemen hoped the disruption caused by the Civil War would help England regain its lost colonies. "They have no interests in common with us," he concluded. "They are the most inflexible foes of the Government and its institutions." "Justitia" criticized fellow Catholics for their assaults but said Orangemen "are altogether opposed to our institutions" and are "but a branch of a society that has been for two centuries the bane of their native land. . . . They are and have been opposed to every movement which has for its object the amelioration of a large body of their countrymen."[47]

So for many the issue was political, not religious. Calling Orangemen "the vilest and most ignorant scum of the Irish retainers of landlord oppressors in Ireland," the Catholic *New York Freemen's Journal* claimed Orangeism "is no religious institution at all. It is a foreign political faction, of English institution, in Ireland." The *Irish-American* agreed: "The entire of our northern frontier, today, is settled by the descendants of Irish Catholics, driven from their original homes by the persecution to which they were subjected, not on *religious* but on *political* grounds." Then the paper made two other charges that would appear a year later and which cannot be substantiated. During the Civil War, it argued, "nine out of every ten" Orangemen sought refuge as English citizens in the British Consulate, hoping to escape the draft, while "a little over three years ago" Britain sent agents to New York to establish Orange lodges and foment trouble. "Every 'Orange Lodge' in America is therefore a 'Tory' camp," the editorial concluded, "maintained by men who repudiate

46. "Irish-American Officer" (n.p., n.d.) to *Sun*, July 14, 1870.

47. W.H.G. (n.p., n.d.) to *Star*, July 17, 1870; "Justitia" (n.p., n.d.) to *Sun*, July 15, 1870.

American citizenship, and are always ready to swear allegiance to monarchy and claim British protection."[48]

"to provoke a breach of the peace"

The 1870 riot did not threaten Tammany's power, but the possibility of another imminent riot, and questions about policy governing street demonstrations, forced Mayor Hall to make policy that would create havoc a year later. Many could not understand why police were unable to prevent such confrontations. One New Yorker asked why police superintendent Jourdan, who "knew that a meeting of the two Irish clans was the mixture of fire and powder," did not protect Orangemen. "If the police force under Democratic direction is to be the ally of either of the factions, or in any way is to be instrumental in producing breaches of the peace," he argued, "the people cannot know too soon." Others agreed. No investigation of police actions occurred, but when Orangemen announced plans for another picnic on August 5, the *Times* at once demanded that city authorities protect them. "Irish feuds especially call for repressive measures," the paper said, and "those who attempt to create disorder" must be severely punished, "whether the aggressors be Irish Catholics or Irish Protestants."[49]

Now worried that another riot might crush Tammany, Mayor Hall explained his understanding of city policy on demonstrations in a letter to Jourdan and asked him to discuss his letter with the Police Board. Not made public until a year later, Hall's lengthy letter blamed Orangemen for "the primary and proximate cause of the disturbance that resulted in the loss of life" in 1870. Still supporting the right of assembly, he nonetheless believed "the right becomes limited when there exist valid reasons to believe that the intentions of the processions are not wholly pacific, or that their route of march or method of accessory procedure is calculated to provoke a breach of the peace." Mentioning a state law that "makes it a grave misdemeanor for any person to use threatening or abusive language or gesture in the public streets," Hall recommended

48. *New York Freemen's Journal* and *Irish-American*, July 23, 1870.

49. "A Citizen" (New York, July 13, 1870) to *Tribune*, July 14, 1870; the news story in ibid; see also *Sun* and *Times*, July 13, 14, 1870. *Times*, July 15, 1870.

> that if any procession, sooner or later, or at any time, undertakes to walk through the streets of New York with banners, music, or cries which are unquestionably calculated to provoke a breach of the public peace, you deny to the processionists the claim so to march; and that you arrest, under the special statute, all persons, whether in or out of such procession, who, by cries favorable to the ideas of such procession or hostile to them, violate its letter and spirit. While, at the same time, if any procession is utterly devoid of unnecessary objects or accessories, and peaceable in demeanor, gesture and words, it should, on the other hand, receive police protection in every laudable benevolent, religious, political, scientific or artistic celebration.[50]

Jourdan reportedly showed Hall's letter to the Enniskillen Lodge master that same day (August 4). The man discussed Hall's instructions with other Orangemen and returned the next day to inform Jourdan they had canceled their plans. Yet Irish Catholics knew nothing of these proceedings, and amid "widespread rumors" of an Orange parade that morning, Jourdan learned that uptown quarrymen and other Irish workers had quit work and planned to attack the Orange picnic in Jones Woods. By one o'clock, workers had assembled on Forty-second Street near the Union Depot. From there they moved to Crimmon's quarry at Forty-fifth Street and Second Avenue, where fifty laborers joined the angry march. As many as one hundred more were obtained from construction sites up to Seventy-fifth Street. "Hundreds" of others, "all in the rough garb of laboring life," were seen congregating at Hibernian Hall in Prince Street—the headquarters of the AOH. A police captain who estimated their strength at one thousand said most were from Brooklyn, Jersey City, and Hoboken. He reported seeing many Brooklyn and New York longshoremen waiting for Brooklyn Orangemen to arrive on the Manhattan side of the Catherine Street ferry. One paper claimed those at Hibernian Hall were drunk, but no violence occurred. In the course of the day, ten were arrested (two of them women) for "riotous and disorderly conduct," and one, John Sairey, was jailed for carrying a revolver and much ammunition. Asked by a policeman at Bowery and Delancy streets what he was doing, Sairey reportedly replied he was "going to have some fun at a pic-nic."[51]

50. A. Oakey Hall (New York, August 4, 1870) "to the Superintendent of Police," printed in *Herald*, July 16, 1871.

51. Others arrested besides Sairey were Patrick Kickey, Patrick Green, William Green,

Orangemen made and abandoned another plan for a picnic a week later. Despite the cancellation, a small group of laborers from lower Manhattan joined other Irish Catholics in a house at 130th Street and Tenth Avenue later Sunday night (August 14) to be ready early Monday if Orangemen changed plans and paraded in that area. A neighbor, Francis Rowe, complained to the police that the men had threatened him, and eleven were arrested for disorderly conduct.[52]

Although Orange lodges made no further attempts to parade that year, they continued to attract some attention. At a Jones Woods picnic on August 17—this one attended by some six thousand Irish Catholics—Fenian chief John Savage addressed a festive gathering of St. Patrick's Legion. After rounds of target shooting, Irish jigs, and bowling and billiard matches, Savage told legion members and others that he found it unfortunate Orangemen and Catholics fought in America. The cause of Irish unity was bringing both sides together in Ireland and should here too. Not all agreed; for loud jeers greeted Savage's remarks.[53] Savage and other Fenian leaders, who seemed mostly concerned that Orange and Ribbon clashes hindered Irish nationalist efforts, had much more to lament a year later.

Samuel McClaren, Patrick Murphy, Anne Armstrong, Archibald Armstrong, Bridget Smith, and William Smith (*Times* and *Sun*, August 6, 1870). The disposition of their cases is unknown. One minor incident merits attention. Someone posted a sign somewhere on Third Avenue reading "To Hell with King William and all his clan." An irate German baker tore it down, thinking it referred to "King Frederick William" of Prussia (*Sun*, August 6, 1870).

52. Arrested were Patrick Eagan, Frank Eagan, John (or William) Gilligan, John Dooley, John Rourke, Owen O'Bride, Owen (or William) Kelly, John Hector, Hugh Daily, Thomas Daily (or Dailley), and Martin Doolin (or Doren) (*Times*, August 15, 16, 1870; *Tribune*, August 16, 1870).

53. *Sun*, August 18, 1870.

3 / Portents of Violence

The Elm Park riot rekindled tensions between Irish Catholics and Protestants and helped shape the context of the Eighth Avenue massacre a year later. Other events at home and abroad also sharpened class and ethnic tensions in New York. These developments further convinced Irish Catholics that Orangemen and their wealthy Protestant supporters sought to bar them from full political and social citizenship. Many wealthy men and nativists believed that these events, and especially the Irish Catholic outrage at the impending Orange parade and the Tweed Ring frauds, further justified their efforts to wrest power from those whom they believed had stripped the city of its wealth and moral authority.

George Templeton Strong touched on some of these incidents as he wondered in his diary on June 24, 1871, "what single year has ever witnessed events as startling and as weighty as the ignominious overthrow of France, the destruction of half [of] Paris, the proclamation of the infallibility dogma as *de fide*, and the downfall of the temporal power?"[1] The events Strong alluded to were foreign—France's defeat by Germany, the Paris Commune, Italian unifica-

Note: Unless otherwise indicated, all dates in the footnotes are from the year 1871.

1. George Templeton Strong, *The Diary of George Templeton Strong*, vol. 4, *The Post-War Years, 1865–1875*, ed. Allan Nevins and Milton H. Thomas (New York: Macmillan, 1952), 366.

tion, and the Law of Guarantees, which defined papal-government relations. But they sparked reactions in New York which revealed much about the city's class and ethnic divisions and amplified fractures in city politics.

Such divisions worried *Irish World* editor Patrick Ford. On the same day as Strong's diary entry, Ford focused on problems *at home* as he began a series called "Who and What Are the American People." Insisting that America "is a *political* not a *natural*, nation," and that "the various races are one people only in the political order," Ford attacked the "Anglo-American element," which he believed sought to transform America into a "Saxon" nation. He explained: "This people are not one. In blood, in religion, in traditions, in social and domestic habits, they are many." All except American Indians were recent arrivals, including "Anglo-Americans" who believed they "were *the* American people" and that all other immigrants had to assimilate with them to achieve national unity. Ford was insulted by this idea because it meant that non-Anglo-Americans had to "ignore their own identity and origin" and "become Yankees first, before they can be regarded as Americans." To him, assimilation advocates hoped to give "an Anglicized complexion to [America's] moral, religious, and educational institutions." Ford promised his paper would fight such attempts. "As democrats, we are opposed to any class ascendancy," he wrote, "and as Irish-Americans we are opposed to any race ascendancy."[2]

In many ways, the views of Strong and Ford reflected the beliefs of two large segments of New York's population—one, Irish-American Catholic; the other, Protestant, nativist, and wealthy. By the time each man wrote, many events since the Elm Park riot had probably increased their concerns, and those of like-minded people, about class and ethnic relations and about the future of the city and the nation. Two such events were the Franco-Prussian War and Italian unification. In New York, Germans, Francophobes, and anti-Catholics demonstrated their support for Germany in the weeks after the outbreak of war in July 1870 and jubilantly celebrated France's defeat the following September. One "Native American" asserted that he would not support France because it "is a nation that upholds Popery" and claimed that "this Popish power, and any national Government that upholds it, is doomed by the word and spirit of proph-

2. *Irish World*, June 24.

ecy." This sentiment was shared by the Rev. Albert D. Vail of St. Paul's Methodist Episcopal Church after the war ended in September. He told his congregation that God had started the war to spread Protestantism by destroying those institutions that were based on "superstition." Such sentiments also informed support for a January 12, 1871, meeting at the Academy of Music, called by over 130 wealthy Protestant New Yorkers, who congratulated "the Roman people upon their deliverance from this oppressive [papal] yoke." The city's Irish Catholics, who had sent money and some volunteers to aid France, were stung by the defeat, but in September 1870 they hailed the new Republic at picnics and demonstrations. A Franco-Irish Society raised funds for wounded soldiers. Irish republicanism and Celtic kinship formed the basis for such support. A boisterous September 12 Cooper Union meeting proclaimed that as "Irish men by birth, and citizens of this Democratic Republic, we hail with pleasure and pride the establishment of the Republic among our hereditary friends and allies, the people of France." Calling France "the head of the great Celtic race, of which we Irish are a part," the *Irish World* rejected arguments in the English and Anglo-American press that nations like France and Ireland needed strong monarchies. "We steadfastly affirm that no intelligent people can ever remain long at ease . . . except under [a] Republic," the paper asserted. As for the Italian unity meeting, the *World* perhaps best analyzed the meaning of support for this cause in calling the meeting "an ill-judged and inconsiderate event" that was "a mere Protestant Paean, irritating to Catholic feeling, insolent to fallen power."[3]

Wealthy New Yorkers who found in Italian unity a victory over one form of tyranny were aghast by reports in late March that thanks to the Commune a red flag now wafted over the Hôtel de Ville in Paris. "The capital of a great nation has for the moment allowed itself to sink to the political level of a South American republic," the *Times* lamented. As news of the Commune's activities filled front-page columns almost daily from March to late May, many New Yorkers be-

3. For reactions to the war, see *Times*, July 16 and August 2, 5, 1870; *Tribune*, September 5, 1870; "A Native American" (n.p., n.d.) to *Times*, July 30, 1870; and *Herald*, September 4, 5, 19, 1870 (Vail). On Italian unity, see *Tribune* and *World*, January 6, 13, 14 (Academy quote, *Tribune*, January 13). For Irish responses, see *Tribune*, September 13, 14, 1870; *Irish-American*, September 17, 1870, and February 4; *Times*, September 13, 1870 (Cooper Union); *Sun*, September 14, 1870; and *Irish World*, November 12, 1870, and June 10.

gan to fear that workers everywhere would catch the insurrectionary fever. "The ruling classes had the 'Commune' on the brains," Friedrich Sorge remembered in his August 6 report to the International Workingmen's Association in London on how the Commune shaped reactions to the Orange parade: "Prominent men like Henry Ward Beecher, Wendell Philipps, and others had warned them of the danger they were exposed to even in this country. And it was time to teach the 'dangerous classes,' that the 'order' could & would be saved also in the United States."[4]

Three other important events also helped to shape the context of the 1871 riot. One was Britain's release in January of the famous "Cuba Five" Fenian prisoners (named after the ship that brought them to New York)—Jeremiah O'Donovan Rossa, John Devoy, John McClure, Henry A. Mulleda, and Charles Underwood. Gala receptions welcomed them to the city on January 19. The celebrations increased as other released Fenians arrived in New York in following weeks. Not all New Yorkers were pleased by these festivities. Some, like George Templeton Strong, resented the Irish presence. "All travel in Broadway was suspended for nearly two hours this afternoon," he wrote in his diary on February 9, 1871, "and half the people of New York were subjected to annoyance and inconvenience by an exasperating procession of pediculous Celtic bogtrotters, aldermen, miscellaneous blackguards, justices of the Supreme Court, roughs, deputy sheriffs, hedgepriests, corner-grocery politicians, and the like scum, gathered together in honor of certain Fenians who escaped their desert of hanging at home and have come here to rule Americans." The freed men quickly tried to revive nationalist efforts here by forming a new coalition of temperance, Hibernian, benevolent, and revolutionary groups, which they called the Irish Confederation. Although Rossa sparked friction by telling a Tammany crowd that he would welcome Orange support in Ireland as a gesture of unity, many Irish organizations joined the confederation in a surge of nationalist fervor. The Fenians, however, formally remained aloof until they created a joint directorate with the confederation the following summer.[5]

4. *Times*, March 21 (quote), 24, and daily coverage between March 21 and May 28. On Sorge's letter, see Bernard Cook, "A Report from Friedrich Sorge to the General Council of the I.W.A.: The New York Riot of 1871," *Labor History* 13 (Summer 1972): 415.

5. For a discussion of Fenians, see William D'Arcy, *The Fenian Movement in the United States, 1858–1886* (New York: Catholic University of America Press, 1947), 370–

Another important influence on the riots was the growing effort by wealthy reformers to oust Tweed's government as accounts of fraud and the city's enormous debt surfaced and as worried bondholders pressed for restoration of financial integrity in the spring and summer of 1871. Even before it began publishing accounts of massive fraud in city and county government on July 8, the *New York Times* had harangued "merchants and other influential persons of business and property" to "shake off their sloth, and put their hands to the work of reformation without delay," claiming that in both Paris *and* New York "the so-called 'better classes' have pretty much given up any share in [city] administration." The paper's efforts led to a mass meeting at Cooper Union on April 6, sponsored by the Council of Political Reform, which prefigured the successful nativist, upper-class campaign against the Tweed Ring and the Irish the following fall.[6]

The unsuccessful strikes of uptown quarrymen in May also shaped the context of the riot. Although details are sparse, it appears that on May 1, nonunion men working on the sewers in Eighty-second Street struck to raise their wages from $2.25 a day to the union rate of $2.50. To gain support, they roamed throughout the day from one construction site to another, visiting Boulevard work gangs and sewer and cellar men, adding twos and threes to their ranks and crowds of women and children along the way. Their appearance in Second Avenue led some residents to fear another riot and, remembering Elm Park, police soon arrived. But no serious violence occurred; by late afternoon only two hundred remained on strike; and by the next day the strike was over, apparently because members of the Quarrymen's Protective Society refused to cooperate with nonunion men. Yet later that month, union quarrymen went on strike to raise *their* wages to $2.75 a day.[7]

---

79. See also Strong, *Diary*, 4:345; and *Leader*, January 14, 21 and February 4, 11; *Star*, January 6, 20, 28, 30; *Tribune*, January 21 and February 10; *World*, January 20, 21, February 10; *Sun*, January 21, 23; *Irish World*, January 14, 21, 28 and April 29; and *Irish-American*, March 18, July 10, and October 7, 14, 28.

6. For a discussion of the city's financial condition and fraud disclosures, see Alexander B. Callow, Jr., *The Tweed Ring* (New York: Oxford University Press, 1965), chaps. 16–18; Seymour Mandlebaum, *Boss Tweed's New York* (New York: Wiley, 1965), 77–81; and Edward Dana Durand, *The Finances of New York City* (New York: Macmillan, 1898), 120–45. On the council, see *Times*, April 3, 4, 7. The *Times*'s disclosures appeared on July 8, 20, 22, 26, 29.

7. *Star*, May 2, 3, 24; *World*, May 2, 3.

These events together did not fully shape the context for the drama of July 1871, but they reveal much about—and helped to sharpen—class and ethnic tensions in the city. On July 1, a brief item in the *Tribune* sparked an extraordinary debate that revealed even more about contending visions in New York. These clear but very different visions led many people to assemble along portions of Eighth Avenue on a hot July afternoon in 1871. Most of them and their varied supporters believed the future of America was at stake in this moment of crisis.

The event mentioned in the *Tribune* was the July 12 Orange parade. The paper's notice drew attention to Orange opponents by reporting a prevailing rumor, which "found circulation in one or two papers, that the Roman Catholic secret societies were organizing, arming, and drilling bodies of men, preparatory to a bloody fight with the Orangemen, who hold their annual pic-nic on July 12." Another rumor compounded the horrors New Yorkers might face. "It was also asserted," the paper claimed, "that the members of the [Irish] 69th Regiment would take part in the affray on the side of their Roman Catholic brethren."[8]

In following days, related rumors led many to believe that Irish Catholics would sack the city as they had done in 1863. *Herald* readers who might have missed these accounts or the 1863 parallels could not have escaped the message the paper tried to convey in its July 11 edition. The entire first and last columns were filled with banner headlines that originally had appeared in papers just after the draft riots. In this brilliant stroke, the *Herald* clearly sought to summon the collective memory of frightened New Yorkers for a massive campaign against the Irish and Tammany.

"fearful language"

Rumors and other efforts to shape the public mind fed on preconceived views about the Irish Catholic agenda in America. Orange grand master John J. Bond launched one such effort in a remarkable and brilliant July 1 letter to the *Times*. "As the 12th [of] July approaches," he wrote, "it is desirable to ascertain whether the members of the Loyal Orange Institution, who parade upon that day, shall

8. *Tribune*, July 1.

be protected in their rights as citizens, or whether they shall be murdered for being Protestant citizens who celebrate the anniversary of freedom from priestcraft and the tyranny of King James II." Bond said that police superintendent James J. Kelso had "promised" to "protect" Orangemen on the twelfth, but wondered if there should "not be some positive assurance that the Police themselves shall not be injured while protecting the Orangemen." He claimed that there already had been "threats of vengeance issued by the parties who deny the freedom of the land to every party but themselves, and threatening letters are being received by the Orangemen with hideous coffins, skulls, pistols and death." Orangemen were told that they "have been tried before the Ribbon tribunal and found guilty, crime not stated, and that they are sentenced to death, and that very good advice is given them in the shape of preparation for death." These letters, "written in fearful language," revealed "most wicked minds and intentions" and "a fearful state of society in New-York" in which "Liberty has even taken her seat in 'Rome of the Tyrants.'" Bond asked for support and advice, first from "Protestants, to aid us in maintaining the Protestant freedom our fathers bequeathed us in days gone by," then from "the better portion of the community." He posed two questions. The first asked, "Shall we attempt [to] parade, or shall we not?" Bond answered this in a second question, which also closed his letter: "Is America able to guarantee freedom in peace, law and order to her Protestant citizens and supporters, or is she not?"[9]

Bond's letter combined fear of Irish Catholic riot and murder with nativist sentiments and a plea for safeguarding Constitutional rights. It was clearly political because it linked Catholic pretensions on the twelfth to national safety. American Protestant society, and not just the Orangemen, was threatened. *That* was the issue.

The letter was political in another way. Sometime in late June, two Orangemen had privately informed police commissioner Henry Smith of Orange plans to parade through Irish Catholic wards in lower Manhattan. At Smith's suggestion, the Orangemen had agreed to ask Bond to parade above Fourteenth Street in Eighth and Fifth

9. John J. Bond (n.p., July 1) to *Times*, July 3. Kelso, born in 1835 in the city's seventh ward, rose from patrolman to detective. He replaced John Jourdan on the latter's death on October 17, 1870. See Augustine E. Costello, *Our Police Protectors* (1885; rpt. Montclair, N.J.: Patterson Smith, 1972), 240; *Times*, October 18, 1870; and New York City Police Department, *First Annual Report of the Police Department of the City of New York* (New York: New York Printing, 1873), 7–8.

avenues, where police could better protect them. But Bond had never replied.[10] Now, by calling for assurances that the police would not be harmed while guarding Orangemen, Bond was asking city and state officials to protect police *and* Orangemen by calling out the National Guard. Bond's public statement compounded accumulated grievances against the Tweed Ring as city officials had to contend both with Orange demands and Tammany's Irish Catholic constituents. A dispute about American political society suddenly raised questions about how practical politics could resolve such differences. Whatever it did, the ring could not emerge unscathed. Only a few days after Bond's letter appeared, the *Times* began its disclosures of the ring's corruption. Now, nativists also accused ring leaders of conspiring with Irish Catholics to subvert political institutions by giving them access to government and giving in to their demands.

Bond's letter gave Mayor Hall little room to maneuver. Hall entered politics in the 1850s as district attorney with help from the Mozart Hall faction within Tammany's Democracy, but by 1868 he was fully Tammany's man and its nominee for mayor. Hall cultivated an Irish Catholic following in campaign propaganda by slighting his father's English ancestry in favor of a relative on his mother's side who took part in the regicide of King Charles I. Worried about losing Irish votes for Tammany, Hall first tried to address Bond's appeal privately. On July 6 he sent Bond a carefully worded letter. Noting that Bond clearly expected violence on the twelfth, Hall said that though public demonstrations "have never become matters of public right," they usually were tolerated. Courts warned that groups could not incite violence, as the Orangemen's parade might do. Hall believed Orange celebrations rekindled Old World feuds and weakened American unity. Why, then, should citizens allow the celebration? The mayor asked Bond if "it would not be more politic for you and your friends to forego any popular or public demonstration of the event to which you and they attach so much importance?"[11]

Bond changed his mind four days later. Now convinced that a parade would spark much violence, he told Kelso that Orangemen "have not taken my advice" about canceling the parade, asked district masters to discuss the issue at a July 11 meeting, and ordered lodge

10. *Brooklyn Daily Eagle*, July 12.

11. Jerome Mushkat, *The Reconstruction of the New York Democracy, 1861–1874* (Rutherford, N.J.: Fairleigh Dickinson University Press, 1981), 31; Croswell Bowen, *The Elegant Oakey* (New York: Oxford University Press, 1956), 4, 17, 33–34, 49–50; A. Oakey Hall (New York, July 6) to John J. Bond, printed in *Herald* and *Times*, July 11.

masters to convene special sessions "for the purpose of prayer and admonition to the Brethren and those intending to participate in the procession." Then Bond explained to the public why he now opposed the demonstration: "I have been well informed, that there are between six thousand and seven thousand Catholics under arms [who will] oppose the display." He also cautioned that "Orangemen are prepared, and . . . if they are attacked they will stand their ground and will not show the white feather."[12]

By then the Tweed Ring's leaders fully realized that major violence could lead to their demise. They knew that wealthy residents blamed them for the city's decline since the wealthy had abandoned local governance to the ring and the Irish. A riot would only confirm such views. The prominent New Yorker George William Wright expressed a prevailing upper-class view when on Monday he wrote to his brother, "We are in danger of another uprising of the Popish Irish Wednesday—Forewarned is forearmed sometimes but whether our City or State government can or will put them down is doubtful—They elected all the men who are called upon to operate against them, and I do not believe they will meet the matter fairly."[13]

On July 10, Tweed's old pal Peter Barr Sweeney, who had doled out thousands of jobs as head of the city's parks, convinced Hall and Kelso to issue General Order No. 57 banning the parade. He later told Governor Hoffman that "a version of it [the Order] is in my language," pleaded with the governor not to "give this to the papers as you might ruin *my prospects*," and explained he had urged Kelso's order because he had been "afraid our Police and our Military would have been but infants against the armed host which would have scattered the Orangemen and [President Ulysses S.] Grant would have been put in possession of the City and would be there now!"[14]

12. John J. Bond (Fort Hamilton, N.Y., July 10) to James J. Kelso, printed in *World*, July 17. The *World* did not print the names of the men Bond asked Kelso to contact. See also *Sun*, *Times*, and *World*, July 11.

13. George William Wright (New York, July 10) to "My dear Neeley [Wright]," George W. Wright folder, New-York Historical Society. On changing class rule in New York, see Callow, *Tweed Ring*, 3–6 passim; Iver Bernstein, *The New York City Draft Riots: Their Significance for American Society and Politics in the Age of the Civil War* (New York: Oxford University Press, 1990), esp. chaps. 3–7; and Amy Bridges, *A City in the Republic: Antebellum New York and the Origins of Machine Politics* (1984; rpt. Ithaca, N.Y.: Cornell University Press, 1987).

14. Peter B. Sweeney (New York, July 21) to John T. Hoffman, John T. Hoffman Papers, Personal (Misc.), New York Public Library.

Sweeney, Hall, and Kelso apparently had decided to prohibit the parade much earlier than July 10. Hall later recalled that the order was printed on Saturday, July 8, and that police commissioners had agreed to the idea "prior to that." Hall said he wanted the order published late Tuesday to prevent Orangemen from making alternate plans for a celebration on Wednesday, but the commissioners demanded publication on Monday. Perhaps it was just as well. With the first scent of Tweed Ring frauds wafting from the *Times*, city comptroller Richard "Slippery Dick" Connolly told Hall that it was crucial to hold onto Irish votes for the fall election by publishing the order as soon as possible. Yet it also had to appear that the ring was *not* catering to Irish Catholics. Hence it was the Protestant Kelso, the police superintendent, whose name was affixed to the order.[15]

Kelso's directive put the problem solely in terms of public safety. He said only that he had been advised "not to aid any street celebrations that involve feuds and animosities belonging solely to the history of other countries other than our own, and which experience has proved to endanger the public peace abroad and at home." Worried that a riot might ignite widespread looting by "the lawless and dangerous classes," Kelso ordered police captains to prevent all street demonstrations on July 12 and to arrest those who disturbed the peace.[16]

"predicted riots seldom occur"

Sweeney and others had good reason to fear that swarms of Irish Catholics would overpower Orangemen and their protectors alike. The Ancient Order of Hibernians took the lead in organizing an armed response to the Orangemen. In late June, the AOH began organizing regiments of Hibernian Volunteers, a quasi-military nationalist group similar to the Fenian brigades. Notices claimed vaguely that the AOH planned "a grand target excursion party in July," but it was clear the volunteers fixed July 12 for the outing. On July 8, James Clarkin and Francis O'Hara of AOH No. 17 called

15. *Philadelphia Evening Star*, July 15, rpt. in *Herald*, July 17 (quote); *Herald* and *Times*, July 11; Denis Tilden Lynch, *The Wild Seventies* (New York: Appleton-Century, 1941), 99; Callow, *Tweed Ring*, 34.

16. Kelso's General Order No. 57, dated New York, July 10, appeared in the July 11 editions of the *Herald*, *World*, *Times*, *Tribune*, and *Sun*.

members to a meeting that evening at Constitution Hall "to receive arms and drill for their coming excursion that is to take place in a few days." They invited "all true-hearted Irishmen" to join them. Some fifty men, "nearly all [of whom] had the appearance of working men," appeared at the hall above a saloon at the corner of Twenty-second Street and Third Avenue. Elsewhere, members of AOH No. 21 practiced street drills outside their Washington Hall headquarters at 126th Street and Third Avenue. And the following day, officers of AOH No. 11 ordered members to meet at Constitution Hall "to receive arms and instructions, and make final arrangements for the excursion."[17]

The AOH quickly mobilized an incensed Irish Catholic populace. By July 8, eighteen city branches reportedly had enrolled 2,277 volunteers. Kings County added another 3,000, the St. Columbus Total Abstinence Society contributed 140, and other Irish groups provided 2,500 more, swelling the volunteers' total strength to 7,917. Reports projected a Hibernian Volunteer membership of 15,000 by July 12. Volunteers' activities sent shudders throughout the city. Even a funeral procession carried ominous signs: 3,500 Brooklyn Hibernians accompanied a member's casket to a cemetery on July 9, and the *Sun* wondered if their military-like precision was part of their preparations for an encounter on Wednesday.[18]

Fenian leaders tried to suppress such activities lest a riot hurt Irish-American nationalism. Chairing an Irish Confederation discussion on July 9, police captain Augustine E. Costello urged Fenians and others to ignore Orangemen on July 12. Because the confederation's purpose was "to establish a republican form of government" in Ireland and to eliminate "English rule and tyranny," and because Orangemen were "English plants" who hoped to incite violence and discredit Irish Catholics, Costello asked Fenians not to interfere with the Orangemen, "as it would evidently please England and retard the progress of Irish liberty." Delegates narrowly defeated a resolution that incorporated Costello's plea. The next day, the Fenian exile Henry A. Mulleda told the O'Donovan Rossa Club of the Irish Confederation that an attack on Orangemen amounted to an assault on city government and their adopted country, not on England. Arguing

17. See meeting notices in *Star* classified section, June 29, July 3, 6, 7; see also *World*, July 9 (Clarkin and O'Hara); and *Tribune*, July 10.

18. *Star*, July 8, 9; *World*, July 8; *Sun*, July 8, 11; *Tribune*, July 10; *Evening Post*, July 10.

that Irishmen must accord the same rights to other citizens which they claimed for themselves, Mulleda said the Irish should not dictate who could parade in New York's streets. Club president G. J. Powers agreed, but many in the audience did not. Fenians took stronger action at the quarterly meeting of the Fenian Brotherhood Council on July 11. Apparently still unaware of Kelso's order, the council issued an address to area Fenians about "the contemplated demonstration by a political-religious society in this city to-morrow," reminding members they were obliged to promote peace and love, to liberate Ireland, and not to perpetuate "dead" issues.[19]

Kelso's ban and the Fenian appeals did not stop AOH preparations. On the eve of the parade, AOH No. 3 members argued late into the night at Emmett Hall about what to do if Orangemen ignored Kelso's order. At a steamy AOH No. 4 meeting in Hirsch's Hall in West Houston Street, some one hundred Irish laborers tapped a keg of beer, vowed to fight if the parade occurred, and marched to Hibernian Hall, where they continued discussions with perhaps five hundred others who were there. Outside Kessell's saloon at 475 Pearl Street (the AOH No. 29 headquarters), fifty men conducted short street drills under Capt. Frank Kiernan, a former Civil War officer, before they joined others at Hibernian Hall. And a Brooklyn AOH meeting at 328 Gold Street, attended by "well-dressed laborers and mechanics," decided to go to Manhattan with other Brooklyn and Long Island Hibernians on Wednesday.[20]

Such reports added to the Irish Catholic animosities and to the Tweed Ring's pressures. Rumors in the press did too. Some suggested the AOH had ten thousand members in New York and five thousand in Brooklyn. Thousands more might travel from New Jersey and Philadelphia. And while the *Herald* estimated that one thousand Orangemen and fifteen hundred American Protestant Association members would parade, the *World* reported on July 11 that ten thousand Canadian Orangemen already had arrived in New York. James W. Gauld, district master of New York's Prince of Orange District, told one source that twelve hundred Orangemen would march, another that fifteen hundred Orangemen and fifteen hundred APA members had enrolled in the parade, and still another that both groups would furnish about one thousand participants but that the

19. *World*, July 10 (Costello), 11; *Sun*, July 11; *Herald*, July 12 (Fenians).
20. *Sun*, *World*, and *Herald* (quote), July 11.

APA actually had disavowed the parade. And John J. Bond told the *Sun* on July 11 that "our Society numbers only 500 men, but, with the accessions we expect to receive from the American Protestant Association, we shall turn out about 2,000."[21]

Other rumors added to the city's concerns. According to the *Times*, Fenians and Hibernians were collecting weapons and actively enlisting "thousands" to fight the Orangemen. After interviews with East River longshoremen, a *Herald* reporter claimed that eleven thousand Irish Catholics were ready for battle and reported, "It was plainly to be seen that the various gangs had received instructions from either the officers of their organizations or some of the mysterious chiefs of the movement set on foot to oppose the celebration of the Orangemen." A Broadway gunsmith said that "he sold more revolvers within the past few days than in the previous six months." Police claimed to have confiscated fifty Hibernian muskets stored in a building on Third Avenue between Sixty-third and Sixty-fourth streets. Such rumors led one reporter to Kelso's office with questions about police preparations. "We are ready for anything that comes—no matter how thick or hot it is, we can meet it," he assured, just before banning the parade. Then he added sarcastically, "I don't think there will be any riot; but if there should be it would not break out in many more than fifty places at one time." One person's jest compounded another's fear as the *Herald*'s grapevine supplied information that "if the Hibernians attacked the Orangemen . . . they would do it while the procession is in motion, and at different points, the Hibernians moving in small detachments, within supporting dis-

21. *Tribune* and *World*, July 11; *Herald*, July 11, 12; *Times*, July 10, 11; James W. Gauld (n.p., n.d.) to *Tribune* and *Evening Post*, July 12; *Sun*, July 11, 12. *World*, July 11, listed the following projected Orange lodge turnouts to parade on July 12:

Scofield	151
Prince of Orange	100
Derry Walls	79
Chosen Few	35
No Surrender	41
Enniskillen	88
Washington	145
Washington Lodge	28
Mount Horeb	132
Gideon	141
Joshua	80
Enniskillen True Blues (Elizabeth)	36
Total	1056

tance of each other, with signs and passwords, and without uniforms." As if to verify *this* rumor, an unnamed police official gave the *Tribune* this secret document, which he claimed to have obtained from an AOH member:

ORANGEISM.
1st, 2nd, 3rd, 4th, and 5th, will follow
SLEVEINAMON!
6th, 7th, 8th, and 9th, follow
VINEGAR HILL!
10th, 11th, 12th, 13th, follow
THAT CITY VIOLATED ITS TREATY!
14th, 15th, 16th, 17th, 18th, 19th, 20th, follow
GIANT'S CAUSEWAY!
21, 22, 23, 24, 25, 26, 27, 28, 29, 30, 31, 32, follow
CROPPY LIE DOWN!

The numbers could have referred to Hibernian brigades; the coded names, to points where Orangemen would be attacked or where Hibernians should assemble. "Giant's Causeway," for example, may have meant Broadway; "Croppy Lie Down," Lamartine Hall; and "Vinegar Hill" (a 1798 rebel encampment some eighty miles south of Dublin), perhaps Hibernian Hall.[22]

To the *Sun*, such reports meant that "Hibernians are at the bottom of the trouble" and were "anxious to prevent the Orange display by force, and to shoot down the men in the procession." The paper reported on July 10 that "the number of armed opponents of the Orangemen is estimated at fifteen thousand" and said there was "an understanding among the Hibernians that all are to quit work on Wednesday, and attack the Orangemen at any available point."

Others viewed these movements differently. Giving credence to a seemingly "extravagant" July 10 rumor, the *Herald* told on July 11 of a Republican plot to foment a riot between Irish Catholics and Protestants and then appeal to President Grant for federal troops—a scenario Sweeney had considered in his letter to Hoffman. Explaining

22. *Times*, July 10 (quote), 11, 12; *Herald*, July 10 (Kelso), 11 ("gangs" and "revolvers"), 12 ("Hibernians"); *Tribune*, July 12. On Vinegar Hill, where Catholic rebels executed scores of Protestant Loyalists, see Robert Kee, *The Green Flag; A History of Irish Nationalism* (London: Weidenfeld and Nicolson, 1972), 112–13; and Thomas Pakenham, *The Year of Liberty: The Story of the Great Irish Rebellion of 1798* (London: Hodder and Stoughton, 1969), 256–58.

that "four months ago," Republican agents provocateurs "became members of the Hibernian societies" and eventually persuaded lodges to attack Orangemen on the twelfth, the paper alleged that "2,500 rifles were furnished, officers appointed to command companies, and a regular military organization accomplished." The paper said these secret activities were designed to embarrass Tammany and force them to transfer their control to federal troops. This forfeiture would clearly demonstrate Tammany's inability to govern and would lead to its defeat in the fall elections. The paper found support for its conspiracy theory in a July 10 visit by AOH members to Grant at Long Branch.

No other paper mentioned the Long Branch visit, but much was made of the allegation after July 12. Politics undoubtedly accounted for Republican support of Orangemen before and after the parade. But party considerations did not seem to shape Irish Catholic motives for opposing the Orangemen. As we shall see, their motives stemmed from other concerns. Nor did they affect the views of men like George Templeton Strong. His concerns lay elsewhere. "There is a proclamation of civil war for day after tomorrow," he wrote on July 10. "The lawless, insolent arrogance and intolerance of these homicidal ruffianly popish Celts must be suppressed somehow." And while he agreed with "sagacious old Cyrus Curtiss" that "predicted riots seldom occur," Strong also believed that "if we experience any rumpus, it will be a rather grave one—*a la mode de Paris*. Hundreds of Irish harridans are quite equal to the role of a *petroleuse*," he said. "I remember them in July, 1863."[23]

"a bigoted religious tyranny"

For many, the likely Hibernian assault was but another example of Catholic efforts to dominate America. Kelso's July 10 order intensified such fears, but even before that day, letters, resolutions, and editorials argued that if the city did not protect Orangemen, Irish Catholics would use city government to foster papal designs.

Such views contained several elements. One strain argued that even though Orange demonstrations perpetuated Old World feuds, Orangemen should have the same right to parade on July 12 as Irish

23. Strong, *Diary*, 4:368.

Catholics enjoyed on St. Patrick's Day. A *Times* reader made this point more crudely. "The low Irish Catholics having been allowed to have their parade," he wrote, "the decent Irish should also have theirs." "This is supposed to be a land of liberty," another protested, "and surely to goodness our rights as American citizens are not going to be trampled on by those who have made it the land of their adoption and by many who, by their lawlessness and disrespect of all order, had to leave their own land." Arguing that Boyne Day commemorated "our religious independence" and "the religious freedom of the world," an APA member believed his organization's festivities were more legitimate than March 17 celebrations. Attempts "to put down liberty of conscience" in America always failed, he wrote, "and we claim the right to use it without offence to any one, although our enemies would claim the right to exterminate us." Other APA members thought words alone would not guarantee that right. On July 8, Enniskillen Lodge No. 29 adopted a resolution pledging "to give to our Protestant brethren our support by every means within our power" and to "attend in a full body prepared for any emergency that may arise."[24]

Other themes incorporated nativist fears with arguments for protecting Orangemen's rights. Finding it a "shame and disgrace" that people were "threatened by a crew of vagabonds" forced out of Ireland "because they were not fit to live with civilized people," a writer asked: "Where do you get the murderers, wife-beaters, thieves, and all other vile creatures, but from the party who propose to make a disturbance on the 12th?" Another believed that "we are quietly, and without protest . . . submitting to a bigoted religious tyranny" and that Catholics sought "to control our politics, [so] that the Church may rule the State." And a War of 1812 veteran asked Americans: "What will you say when your children, as they go into the public schools, will have to make the sign of the cross?" Supporting such sentiments, *Times* editor Louis Jennings saw in the various Irish meetings proof that Catholics sought to conquer the city in order "to set up a State Church here, and to drive Protestantism to take shel-

24. S. (New York, July 8) to *Times*, July 10; for similar arguments about St. Patrick's Day, see "Freedom" (n.p., n.d.) to *Herald*, July 10; "Knickerbocker" (n.p., n.d.) to *Times*, July 8; and the editorials and news items in *Herald*, July 10; *Sun* and *Times*, July 8; and *World*, July 9. "Freedom" (n.p., n.d.) to *Herald*, July 10 ("land of liberty"); R. K., APA no. 8 (n.p., n.d.) to *Sun*, July 10; resolution, signed by Worshipful Master George W. Clark, printed in *Sun*, July 10.

ter in holes and corners." He warned the mayor "that the Catholics intend to cut down all the men, women, and children who attempt to march" and said Hall must prevent their deaths.[25]

But what could be done? Many urged Hall to warn rioters they risked being killed by the police and the guard. That way, as one put it, the streets would be cleared "of the scum." Another suggested that "if necessary, fifty to a hundred thousand citizens [could] be called upon as special constables," whereas "Volunteer" proposed that "5,000 American Protestants" turn out to march with their "Protestant Irish brothers."[26]

Others believed that New Yorkers would not be free as long as they voted for "Irish Catholic candidates." Calls for political action completed the critique of Irish Catholics. Class and nativist concerns informed such views. "We are yet strong enough," "Manhattan" wrote on July 10, "if we unite, to decide whether we will be perpetual bondsmen to the Irish or assume the reins of government and let them understand that though they are at liberty to become brethren of our family, they are not at liberty to be the head of it, to the eternal shame of its founders." He was convinced that "decent men" were alarmed and that if only "some well-known, trustworthy individuals" could be found "to issue a call," thousands would rally to the cause "by which our 'scurvy and degraded masters' would soon be displaced." "I do not desire to see a religious war here," said one Orangeman, "and I would say to my Catholic fellow-citizens, the time has not yet come for Irish supremacy in this country. The Americans—and what I term the 'better classes'—of the city—are Protestant and sincerely sympathetic with us." Others took steps at once to form an organization. Groups in New York enlisted members for a Protestant League of America. "The claims of Roman Catholicism are incompatible with civil and religious liberty," a circular proclaimed. The *Evening Post* considered the idea unwise, but it did suggest forming "an organization of honest citizens, whose object shall be to dethrone the sharks, the reckless and corrupt demagogues, who misrule New York, and whose flattery of the mob it is which has brought this last disgrace upon us." It would not be long

25. "A Disgusted Citizen" (n.p., n.d.); "Religious Toleration" (n.p., n.d.); "Old Vet of 1812" (New York, July 11): all to *Times*, July 12; and *Times* editorial, July 10.

26. "A Native Born Protestant" (New York, July 11) to *Times*, July 12; S. (New York, July 8) to *Times*, July 10; "Volunteer" (n.p., n.d.) to *Times*, July 11.

before the "decent," "honest," and "better classes" emerged to lead efforts like the one these writers envisioned.[27]

"Orangemen are very different from Protestants"

Just as many agreed with Bond, so too did many Irish Catholics share Patrick Ford's view that English and Irish Protestants sought to "Anglicize" America, and it worried them. One wrote, "The Irish have such deep-seated national feelings that they can never be brought to look at any question except through an Irish medium."[28] That "medium" involved the way New York's Irish Catholic workers identified their personal histories with a common Irish national history and a common American class experience. This consciousness of shared experiences—a combination of actual events, myth, and memory—led Irish Catholic groups to oppose Orange pretensions in New York. The Irish explained that Orangemen had always opposed Irish freedom and independence. Moreover, the Orangemen had helped to destroy Irish nationality by persecuting Catholics and scoring their religion, by pretentious Irish culture, and by political oppression. They had helped to enslave the Irish and establish class rule. Would they do differently here?

July 12 "celebrates the denigration of a proud nation and a still prouder people," AOH member Michael Madigan told the *World.* "In 1798, when the Irish people were pitch-capped and triangled for doing, or trying to do, what the Americans did in 1776, it was Orangemen who made and used the pitch-caps and whip, and Orange bands that played the music at the bloody massacres of priests, and women, and little children." Another Hibernian explained that "it is a question not of religion, but of Irish nationality, we want to settle. In Ireland the Orangemen fought against the anti-English principles we stood up for." Arguing that the July 12 quarrel was not just a continuation of Old World feuds, a Brooklyn Hibernian said, "We

27. S. (New York, July 8) to *Times*, July 8; "Manhattan" (Harlem, July 10) to *Times*, July 11; "an Orangeman" (New York, July 8) to *Star*, July 9. The circular was printed in the *Tribune*, July 12, and in a slightly different form in the *Times*, July 12; see also *Evening Post*, July 12.

28. "An American Roman Catholic" (New York, July 10) to *Herald*, July 12. It should be noted that the writer was sympathetic to Irish Catholic complaints about Orangemen but was critical of their inability to "examine a question on the basis of reason alone."

only remember what those Orangemen used to do to us when they outnumbered [us] in the North of Ireland, and we know that they only wait to get the American Know Nothings to join them in committing the same outrages on us here, and that's why we are determined to put an end to them before they get strong enough to be as bad as they were in Ireland." In an open letter to Mayor Hall, *Irish Republic* editor Daniel R. Lyddy said, "The question is not, sir, a religious one, and religion has been introduced by the Orangemen for the purpose of securing allies and to deceive the public mind." Orangemen actually celebrated the defeat of "the people of Ireland fighting for their liberty. The Irish Orangemen of William's day took sides with him against their country, as the American Tories ranged themselves with George III against the patriots and heroes of the revolution."[29]

Orangeism threatened republicanism, not just Irish nationality. The *Irish-American* argued that Orangemen did not honor the founder of a national religion, as Irish Catholics honored St. Patrick, but rather the subjugation of one people by another. Others agreed. "It is sufficient to know," Joseph Cullen wrote to the *Sun*, "that the poor misguided Orangeman discards the sacred emblem of his country's nationality, which he in spirit tramples in the dust and proposes parading in honor of being enslaved by a foreign tyrant." *Sunday Democrat* editor D. P. Conyngham insisted that Orangeism and Protestantism were not the same: "Protestantism is a religion of toleration, Christian precepts and charity," whereas "Orangeism is the embodiment of intolerance, bigotry and slavish degradation." "The Irish do not like to see a parade in their midst celebrating their downfall," a County Down native appealed. "It cuts us to the heart to see our most bitter foes parading in our midst; for we know only [that] for Orangemen Ireland would have her place as a free country." He said, "My family and myself had to flee from our native land on account of Orangemen."[30]

Related grievances accompanied arguments that Orangemen would subvert American republicanism. While "J. B." summarized that "republicans, patriots, Christians, do not act as do Orangemen," others resorted to a more elaborate analysis to remind Americans

29. *World* and *Herald*, July 11; Daniel R. Lyddy (n.p., n.d.) to Mayor A. Oakey Hall, printed in *World* and *Star*, July 11, and *Leader*, July 15.

30. *Irish-American*, July 8; Joseph Cullen (New York, July 6) to *Sun*, July 8; D. P. Conyngham (n.p., n.d.) to *Herald*, July 11; "A County Down Man" (n.p., n.d.) to *Herald*, July 10.

that Irish Catholics had done much for the nation. Thomas Robinson wrote that "Irishmen and their descendants are connected with this country from its infancy" and had defended the country in all its wars. But as the County Monaghan native reminded, "the fiercest, most cowardly, and contemptible enemies they had to contend against were the old tories, the ancestors of these very men who claim the protection of the authorities to flaunt their tory colors on the 12th." In interviews, letters, and editorials, New York's Irish repeatedly claimed that Orangemen did not deserve the protection usually accorded citizens because Orangemen, in fact, were *not* United States citizens. Since their oath and obligation required them "to yield allegiance to the very dynasty whose authority the Americans shook off in the Revolutionary era," they were "utterly incompetent and unwilling to ever become citizens of the republic"—a claim Orangemen repeatedly denied.[31]

Another common allegation was that during the Civil War, "when our glorious Union was again in peril," Orangemen claimed they were English subjects and either sought refuge from the draft in the British Consulate or fled to Canada and used it "as an asylum and a base of operations for the Southern rebels." *That* was the time, another Hibernian recalled, when Americans were *not* willing to countenance Orange parades (a claim that cannot be substantiated). Moreover, as Lyddy (and so many others) believed, "in any struggle in the future between England and this republic they would be found arrayed against the republic," and, as the County Monaghan immigrant said, they "would prove themselves worthy representatives of the tories of the Revolution." One anonymous writer thought Americans should remember that the Irish "have always taken the field in [America's] defence, and will do it again"; another reminded that during the Civil War "the foremost in the ranks who were fighting to maintain the liberty and independence of this country were the Irish Catholics of New York and elsewhere." Still another remembered that "the Irishmen who compose the Ancient Order of Hibernians were fighting for 'the Stars and Stripes,' although many of them were poor and had to leave their families to do so, while the

31. J. B. (Brooklyn, July 11) to *Herald*, July 12; Thomas Robinson (n.p., n.d.) and "A County Monaghan Irishman" (n.p., n.d.) to *Herald*, July 11; *Irish American*, July 8 ("yield allegiance"); Lyddy to Hall, in *Star* and *World*, July 11 ("utterly incompetent"). The oath made no such requirements. For the Orange constitution, see *Star*, July 9; *Times*, July 11; and Michael A. Gordon, "Studies in Irish and Irish-American Thought and Behavior in Gilded Age New York City" (Ph.D. diss., University of Rochester, 1977), app. A.

others were seeking to destroy the freedom and liberty which they now invoke." Irish Catholics did not hate Protestants, Irish Confederation secretary and port warden Edward Carey raged, "but Orangemen we do hate and despise for they would plunder us if they had a chance, and we protest against these men, who are not citizens, and who never will be citizens; who ran away from the draft, . . . and we protest against their marching and insulting men who are citizens, and who have fought and bled for this country."[32]

The Orange demand for "equal rights" also was preposterous. As Lyddy put it, "Equal rights with those who have made their homes here, have fought our battles, made our roads and bridges, felled our forests, and contributed millions to our taxes [?]" What stake did Orangemen have in republicanism? One quarryman even claimed that Orangemen were "paid" to "come here playing party tunes and getting up a muss." Similarly, a Brooklyn Hibernian believed that "these fellows are still helping the English government, only in another way. Their dodge now is to disgust the American people with the whole of us, for you must know the English government's hatred of Irishmen didn't stop when they drove us out of our country. They must follow us over here." The APA was no better. The association "is simply the Orange Society made to smell sweetly in American nostrils under an American name." Another observer argued that it was not "proper that three or four hundred fanatics and British tools should be allowed to insult" New York's Irish. He explained that "the English people are tired of their robberies, murders, burnings, &c. They bring a bad name to the government. Send them to America, yet we will protect them; certainly they will get up riots, join the Know Nothings, burn churches. Besides," he continued, "the Irish are getting too powerful; they are a dangerous element against England in case of war."[33]

Two incidents in the Elm Park riot compounded Irish Catholic

32. "A County Monaghan Irishman" to *Herald*, July 11 ("glorious union" and "foremost in the ranks"); Lyddy to Hall, in *Star* and *World*, July 11; "Anonymous" (n.p., n.d.) to *Herald*, July 10; "A Wexford Man of the Town of Newtownbarry" (New York, July 11) to *Herald*, July 12 ("'Stars and Stripes'"); *World*, July 11 (Carey). See also the many interviews in the July 11 *Herald*, which make similar points, as do such other letters as Conyngham to *Herald*, July 11; Patrick Merrigan (New York, July 12) to *Star*, July 4; "An American" (n.p., n.d.) to *Star*, July 7; O. O'R. Y. (New York, July 11) to *Star*, July 11; and John Kelly (Brooklyn, n.d.) to *Star*, July 16.

33. Lyddy to Hall, in *Star* and *World*, July 11; *Herald*, July 10 (Brooklyn Hibernian) and 11 (quarryman); "Anonymous" (n.p., n.d.) to *World*, July 10 ("fanatics").

grievances and suggest that revenge provided another motive for some Irish Catholics. One, mentioned previously, was the shot into the Church of St. Paul. A boss quarryman resurrected the other. "Do you see that house down in the hollow?" he asked a *Herald* reporter near Sixty-fifth Street and Eighth Avenue. "Well, an old man named Brady lives there, and this time last year he had a son, a fine young fellow, who was born in this country, and was the chief support of his family. Last 12th of July he was carrying some tools through the Park, interfering with no one, when he was shot dead by these Orangemen, and that was a pretty hard case."[34]

However important these grievances, the main reason Orangemen were "not entitled to the same privileges and protection in this City as Protestants or Roman Catholics" was their politics, not their religion. "The last refuge of Orangemen is to claim that they celebrate the religious triumph of Irish Protestantism," Lyddy protested to Mayor Hall. Since not all Irish Protestants were Orangemen, he repeated that "this question, then, sir, is not religious, but political, and the contemplated celebration, to our Irish citizens, is a fiend's dance on the grave of their country's liberty by the demented dastards who aided in striking down their national independence." An Irish quarryman insisted to a *Herald* reporter that "this thing has got to be settled—either this is a free country, where no man has got the right to insult us, or it isn't, and we don't intend to put up with the insult." He claimed that "we don't want to interfere with the citizens" but believed that "the authorities ought not to protect a lot of Orangemen, who hate this republic, carrying a dirty old king's flag through the city." A Boulevard foreman told the same reporter that Orangemen "parade their affections for a foreign government under the flag of an English king, and they have no right to demand the protection of the government which they insult and despise." "Orangeism is in reality a political organization, under the guise of religion," P. E. Cornelious said. "It does not follow that, all Orangemen being Protestants, all Protestants are Orangemen." His letter was intended to "impress on the minds of Americans of all religious denominations that it is not on account of their religion that Orangemen are hated by patriotic Irishmen, but on account of their politics."[35]

34. *Herald*, July 11.

35. Conyngham to *Herald*, July 11; Lyddy to Hall in *Star* and *World*, July 11; *Herald*, July 12; P. E. Cornelious (New York, July 10) to *Tribune*, July 10.

Implicit in many of these Irish Catholic views was the republican obligation to accord equal rights to all citizens regardless of their religion. Some, like a Brooklyn Hibernian who attended the July 10 Gold Street meeting, made that view explicit. "We don't interfere with Protestants," he explained. "Protestant schools and church societies march by our doors every day celebrating some anniversary or another, and if anybody interfered with them we'd be the first to come out and protect them. If the Orange societies were purely religious we'd even fight for their right to march here or anywhere else; but they're only an English faction, and our duty as American citizens, to say nothing of our recollections as Irishmen, ought to make us put them down." This anonymous immigrant saw the issue clearly. "Orangemen," he concluded, "are very different from Protestants."[36]

Did Catholics plan "to prevent the Orange display by force, and to shoot down the men in the procession," as the *Sun* charged? The evidence supplied by the Catholics themselves is inconclusive. Some urged others not to prevent the parade because violence would only help England and because American Irish were "on trial." Others, like Lyddy, urged Hall to prohibit the display. If the celebration took place, "citizens will prevent or crush [it], beyond all doubt, perhaps at a terrible cost of blood and crime and outrage." "True," he argued, "the law can always punish lawlessness; it seems the higher wisdom to avoid evoking it." "Are the authorities of New York willing to permit this brand of discord to be deliberately prepared under their eyes, and flung into our midst to enkindle civil strife?" asked the *Irish-American*. "Or will the Mayor and magistry of this city tolerate what would not be permitted in any city in Great Britain or Ireland?" Another Irish Catholic contended that it was not necessary to cancel the parade or even attack its participants. "Orangemen, being opposed to republicanism," he wrote, "any display on their part will only expose them to the contempt of the American people."[37]

Many threatened violence. Interviewed on July 10 as he waited to see the mayor at City Hall, an AOH member said Orangemen merely wanted to "flaunt their partisan banners in our faces" and promised, "They'll rue it this time, if they never did before." The Boulevard foreman, who said there were "between six and eight

36. *Herald*, July 11.

37. *Sun*, July 10; *World*, July 11 ("trial"); Cornelious to *Tribune*, July 10; Lyddy to Hall in the *Star* and *World*, July 11; *Irish-American*, July 1 (quote), 8; Conyngham to *Herald*, July 11.

thousand men" at work on the roads and quarries above Fifty-ninth Street, reminded a reporter that "this isn't England or Scotland or Ireland—it is America." He believed "these old quarrels ought to be left at home" but thought "if there is a row I would say to the men to go and protect their rights." Others along the Boulevard expressed similar views despite a July 10 order by park board president Henry Hilton to fire laborers who quit work on July 12. A quarryman and a Boulevard laborer said Catholics would not repeat their error in 1870 and attack Orangemen unarmed. Asked if his crew would report to work on the twelfth, another laborer replied, "We can't tell you, sir; we don't know ourselves until after the meeting to-night [July 10]. A good deal will depend upon what the quarrymen do. If they quit work we shall be obliged to go along." The militia would not stop them. "There are plenty of workingmen just as smart as the militia," he explained. "Nearly every man of us has been in the army during the war." His Boulevard tour over, the reporter now believed that quarrymen "seem to be the prime movers with the Ancient Order of Hibernians in the present unpleasantness."[38]

Besides these accounts and the ominous reports of AOH drills, there were yet other indications that Catholics would attack Orangemen. Hibernian Michael Madigan maintained that "if Orangemen parade with their banners, scarfs, and colors, playing Orange aires, the insult to the Irish citizens of this city will be so great and deep a one that in my opinion it will be impossible to prevent serious trouble." Surrounded by fellow laborers, another Hibernian promised that if Orangemen appeared, "some of them will never march again." Asked if the Hibernians had many members, he replied, "Yes, but more than the Hibernians will be out; the Fenian Circles, the Longshoremen and a number of other Irish societies will turn out. Last night [July 10] the Quarrymen's Society received orders to hold themselves in readiness." The man was little concerned about police opposition "because they are not very likely to fire on their neighbors."[39]

The many Irish complaints, boasts, and statements must not be allowed to obscure the central Irish Catholic concern. John J. Bond had asked if America would guarantee equal protection to Protestant

38. *Herald*, July 11 (AOH, foreman), 12 (laborers).

39. *World* (Madigan) and *Herald* (Hibernian), July 11.

citizens. To many Irish Catholics the question was just as simple: will America become another Ireland, or will she not?

"a crime against your God and your Country"

Priests tried to discourage Catholics from acts that would further tarnish the Catholic image. Aware of increasing Catholic threats against Orangemen, Archbishop John McCloskey instructed city priests to warn congregations not to meddle with Orangemen. On Saturday, July 8, McCloskey sent aides to half the city's parishes to enlist the aid of local priests. On Sunday, in dedicating a Harlem church addition, McCloskey said he believed Orangemen had sparked "a systematic and combined effort . . . to excite an anti-Catholic movement in the community." While he hoped city officials would ban the parade, if it should occur, McCloskey told Catholics, they should "beware of even going near that Orange procession." "Avoid them as you would any other pests," he ordered. If Irish Catholics should attack Orangemen, "you will commit a crime against your God and your Country."[40]

Many city priests repeated McCloskey's warnings in their Sunday sermons. Some priests understood why their message was not always received well. "The Catholics have much to remember," said St. Andrew's Father Michael Curran. So did he:

> I remember well how my father took part in an election in our part of the old country and a Catholic member was returned; and on his way to town he had to go along a certain road, and there was a great crowd going with him, and a big triumphal arch like was built over the road and the Orangemen put a lot of insulting mottoes and lines on it, and, rather than go under that arch, the member turned his horse and swam across the river, and the Orangemen were so put out when he didn't go under the arch that they threw stones at him and cut him on the head.

Curran concluded that while "there's many a little thing like that to remember," he did not think it "right to bring those differences here to this country." Another priest encountered much resistance. "I made quite a lengthy address at mass yesterday," that St. James

40. *Herald*, July 10 (quote), 11; *Star*, July 10.

priest, Father Farrelly, explained, "taking the ground of the American Constitution." That night, however, he was "surprised" to learn from the church's school committee "that they were indignant at my remarks. It had, they said, always been the same—that the priests were always against the people in asserting their rights, whether in Fenianism or what not."[41]

Other Catholics believed that the priests' efforts would do little good because Catholics seldom paid attention to the clergy's admonitions anyway. One Brooklyn Hibernian said he had heard McCloskey's warning but said, "I know, too, that the Archbishop or his priests never suffered as we did in this business. They know nothing about it." An East River longshoreman agreed. Were the clergy's appeals persuasive? "No, sir, by God!" he replied, "that time's past; it's all very well so long as the parade is conducted quietly, but when that music commences then you'll see hot times." Despite such sentiments, priests still might have had some influence on AOH members who followed clerical instructions closely. Read one way, the following resolution adopted at a July 10 AOH meeting at Hibernian Hall seems like a sarcastic response to clerical dictates. But it also may indicate that the clergy was having some influence on an important Irish group.

> As peaceable and law-abiding citizens, our thanks are due, and are hereby tendered, to the Most Rev. Archbishop and the reverend clergy of this city, for their efforts to preserve the peace of the community, and the good and wholesome advice which they gave their flocks in cautioning them against being drawn into any disturbance of the public peace; and . . . the members of this Society will, by their actions and their behavior, as good and peaceful citizens, show that they appreciate the counsel of their pastors, and will be guarded by them in all things lawful.[42]

41. *Times*, *Herald*, *Sun*, and *World*, July 10; see interviews with priests in *Herald* (Curran and Farrelly), and New York *Express*, July 11, rpt. *Irish-American*, July 22.

42. *Herald*, July 11 (interviews); New York *Express*, July 11, rpt. *Irish-American*, July 22. The resolution was signed by Hugh McCourt (general president), Lawrence Clinton (general secretary), Patrick Campbell (national delegate), and Timothy Darcy (national secretary). Some papers applauded the clergy's efforts, but "Knickerbocker" was outraged. "Pusillanimous, indeed, have we become," he spouted, "if, for the preservation of peace and order in our midst, we are compelled . . . to solicit the interference of the Catholic clergy, through whom the gracious permission of the Irish is sought to be obtained." Few of even the bitterest nativists would have agreed with his solution: "Rather than be so

"Surrender to The Mob"

On Tuesday night, John L. Hall entertained another large audience at Dan Bryant's Opera House on West Twenty-third Street. Responsive to the day's events, Hall improvised a short verse to the tune of "Mable's Waltzes." He sang:

> You ask my opinions of Superintend't Kelso;
> The answer I will not smother—
> Just wrap him up in the American flag,
> And kiss him for his mother.[43]

Other New Yorkers strained to find a hint of humor where Hall saw opportunity for light-hearted ridicule. As the Tweed Ring began to teeter from the fraud disclosures, nativists and ring opponents now viewed Kelso's order as final proof that Tweed and company had to go. Calling Kelso's directive "the surrender order," the *Times* contended that "all the more decent and respectable classes" knew that Hall was behind the parade's cancellation. The decision was proof that "the City authorities . . . dare not disobey the commands of the Irish Catholics," that "they now officially proclaim that the City is absolutely in the hands of the Irish Catholics," and that "it is now decided that Protestants here have only such rights as Catholics choose to accord them." In another editorial, the paper insisted that "the Romish Church has never sought to impose a greater tyranny upon any people than that which our Roman Catholic rulers have now imposed upon us. For the first time, the Irish mob has been officially informed that its word shall be law in this City." Saying the order was a "disgraceful confession" that police would not protect citizens holding peaceful meetings, the *New York Evangelist* wondered, "Are we then to hold the public meetings at the dictation of the Catholic Irish of this city?" In "Surrender to The Mob," a *Tribune* editorial saw city officials capitulating "to a few thousand disorderly foreigners" and believed "the lesson of 1863 has evidently been lost to them." Others also noted the 1863 parallels. "In the riot of 1863 the Government gained a victory over the mob," the *Indepen-*

---

disgraced," he wrote, "let the rabble unroof the City" (Knickerbocker [n.p., n.d.] to *Times*, July 8). See also editorials in *Sun*, July 8; *Herald*, July 10; and *World*, July 11. See Conyngham to *Herald*, July 11; *World* and *Tribune*, July 11.

43. *Sun*, July 12.

dent editorialized on July 12. "But in 1871 this same Irish Catholic mob, which hung negroes [sic] and killed babies and burned orphan asylums, had but to threaten. The City surrendered." Alleging that Kelso's order was "an official denial of our rights" and an "absurdity" that would be "funny" if it were not so serious, the *Herald* demanded that "the spirit which prompted these threats against the Orangemen must be put down." It was "the same spirit which prompted the Paris Commune" and "the draft riots of 1863, inducing men to burn asylums where children were nurtured and hang negroes [sic] to lamp posts. It is the same spirit," it concluded, "which was exhibited at Elm Park last year—the spirit which brooks not freedom of opinion, speech and action in others."[44]

Instead of sternly rebuffing the mob, these views argued that Hall and Kelso had succumbed to "bigoted" political pressures. "The law can forbid or regulate processions," the *Brooklyn Daily Eagle* maintained, "but the mob must not." The *Standard* conceded that Irish Catholics—"a party . . . as brutal in their instincts as they are bigoted in their purposes"—had more power in 1871 than in 1863. That was why city officials were "prompted more to conciliate a powerful political faction at the expense of humiliating the police than by anything else." "They have been terrified by the threats of the Hibernian societies," the *Sun* agreed, "and have bowed their heads. They have virtually submitted to mob rule. They have confessed that the will of a secret organization has more weight with them than the rights of the people." "Let us of the northern states no longer deplore the condition of the South," the *Evening Post* admonished. "We have our Ku-Klux here in New York; but they do not take the time to conceal themselves. Ruffians, carrying muskets and pistols, were seen in the streets of New York last night." Only the *World*, Tammany's *Leader*, and the *Star* supported Kelso. They argued that Catholic leaders had tried to prevent bloodshed while the Orangemen seemed bent on provocation. The Orange parade would be as insulting as a Klan march in front of the Union League Club.[45]

Few appreciated such an analogy. Although the *Herald* reported that "a large number of merchants, bankers and prominent citizens" visited Kelso on Tuesday to thank him for banning the parade, other

44. *Times*, July 11, 12; New York *Evangelist*, July 13; *Tribune*, July 11; *Independent*, July 12, rpt. *Tribune*, July 13; *Herald*, July 11.

45. *Brooklyn Daily Eagle*, July 12; *Standard*, July 11, rpt. *Herald*, July 12; *Sun*, July 11; *Evening Post*, July 11; *World Leader*, *Star*, July 11.

prominent citizens were indignant. Early that morning, members of the Produce Exchange circulated a petition on the exchange floor that supported the Orangemen's right to parade and denounced Kelso. At an afternoon rally, irate speakers condemned city officials and urged exchange members to act to preserve their homes, families, and freedom. By the time a committee returned the next day with a draft resolution, Hoffman had overruled Kelso, so exchange members quickly thanked the governor "for the prompt and efficient manner in which he has relieved the Empire City from the odium of being governed by an irrepressible mob."[46]

Other protests published in city newspapers (the *Times* alone printed two dozen on July 12) all expressed the belief that America was becoming a papal state. The July 12 violence elicited many more such letters, but none surpassed the intensity of nativist fears or better revealed the extent of nativist sentiment than those sparked by Tammany's parade injunction. "Foreigners have had their say and rule long enough," wrote "Law and Order," who claimed a twenty-five-year Democratic affiliation. "The serpent has showed its head, and if fondled will surely sting." He declared it was now "time for Americans to band together in one common cause" and "to elect none to office but Americans . . . who will see that Americans can and shall enjoy the same privileges as foreigners." "Our rights as American citizens," wrote "Star Spangled Banner" "—liberty and freedom—must not be trampled upon by those who have accepted the country as the land of their adoption." "Alas! for the Republic," "K." exclaimed, "if we do not soon force a change and place true Americans to rule us, instead of a foreign mob." Another writer contended that "if Protestants once succumb in this disgraceful manner to the dictation of Papist Irish, our liberties are gone forever." "Are you prepared to surrender your rights?" asked "S." Jesuits, "friends only of ignorance, degradation and superstition," menaced the country, and "S." worried that people would "meekly lay your necks down that you may be trampled over by the Irish Papacy." The merchant Junius W. Seymour thought that Catholics "have us by the throat, controlling the Bench and all political power, our very purse-strings, and now they notify every anti-Catholic that the very streets are un-

46. *Herald*, July 12; *Tribune*, July 12, 13; *Times*, July 13; *Sun*, July 12, 13 (Produce Exchange quote). Members of the resolutions committee were Horatio Reed, Charles J. Hall, John T. Miller, E. O. Lamson, Charles H. Hickock, R. Buchanan, and W. P. Benzel.

der their control, and we must not walk them." "An American" made the point still more strongly. "The denigration of the City is complete," he wrote. "The boast of the Roman Catholics that the City of New York is a Catholic City, is emphatically justified." This writer urged a revival of a nativist party: "The abject submission to the threats of the miserable curs, who, in 1863, achieved an infamous notoriety by the burning of an orphan asylum, the hanging to lampposts of inoffensive blacks, the destruction of our homes, and the maintenance of a reign of terror for three days, cannot fail to fire the American heart, and prompt a concerted action that must wrest the political control from the hands of our betrayers."[47]

More impatient nativists insisted that city officials put down Irish Catholics by force. A Democrat, who said he was ashamed by city officials' behavior, argued that "if the instigators or mobites insist on violating and trampling under foot our laws, we must save our country the disgrace of riots and strikes if nineteen-twentieths of the mobites are killed." Describing himself as "an American citizen," "Equal Rights" believed "the quicker we wipe out from existence the mob who wish to rule here the better and safer it will be for humanity." New Yorkers missed an opportunity to eliminate that element once before. "The attacking party of to-day are the same who laid waste the city during the bloody week of '63," he wrote, "and it is about time it was stopped." Such frustrated, embittered, and hateful writers saw only one solution to the Irish Catholic cancer. "Has it come to this," an anonymous "American" huffed in disgust,

> that as the "Irish Catholics" have sold the most bad whiskey, made the most drunkards, created the most riots, committed the most murders, polled the most votes with the least number of voters, and now hold the most offices and receive the greatest amount of public money, they are now to dictate who shall and who shall not enjoy the liberty of American citizens? . . . The only alternative for all good citizens seems to be this—to form one grand Vigilance Committee and take this matter into their *own* hands. It ought to have been done long ago.[48]

47. "Law and Order" (n.p., n.d.) to *Tribune*, July 12; "Star Spangled Banner" (n.p., n.d.) to *Star*, July 10; K. (Jersey City, July 12) to *Tribune*, July 13; "St. Thomas" (n.p., n.d.) and S. (New York, July 11) to *Times*, July 12; Jno. [sic] W. Seymour (New York, July 11), and "An American" (n.p., n.d.) to *Times*, July 12.

48. "Septuagenarian" (New York, July 11) and "Equal Rights" (New York, July 11) to *Herald*, July 12; "A Sixty-Year-Old-American Citizen" (n.p., n.d.) to *Tribune*, July 12.

"Dogs that bark so loudly seldom bite much"

What of the Orangemen? By July 11, many of them apparently were determined to parade despite Bond's plea to stay at home, but after Kelso's order was issued, they decided not to defy it and risk arrest. Because the Orange constitution required members to observe the Boyne victory each year, various lodges hastily arranged private observances. District Master Gauld was clearly disappointed. "The parade would not have occupied more than two hours," he complained, "and there would not have been more than three thousand men in line, half of whom would have been members of the American Protestant Association." Yet the young American-born printer (his grandparents had come from Scotland) found some consolation: Kelso's order would help Orangemen and damage Tammany. "We are poor men," he explained to a *Sun* reporter:

> We have no men of influence among us. We are not Tammanyites. And for those reasons our rights to walk the streets has [sic] been taken away. That order of Superintendent Kelso's will do us more good than any effort of our own could possibly effect. It will be the making of our organization. We will become a power in the land, and in the future we will be allowed to parade when and where we please. That order has killed the Democratic organization in this State, and it has completely wiped away the influence of Tammany Hall in national politics for all time to come. The whole people are with us. We have reason to rejoice.[49]

Though many Orangemen and APA members agreed with Gauld's assessment, few found "reason to rejoice." At APA meetings in Thirty-fourth and Thirty-fifth streets, angry men denounced the ban and said they would assemble the next morning but would not parade if their leaders opposed it. Snubbed in their attempts to discuss the parade with city authorities, many wondered why Hall and Kelso had waited so long to make their decision. One member said that "during the July riots of 1863, when the authorities called for help, the APA turned out to a man to quell the insurrection, and they feel that they are surely entitled to some consideration for this." But one Orangeman seemed less perturbed. Found in a Bowery saloon by a *World* reporter, he argued that an Orange parade would *not* spark

49. *World, Herald,* July 12; Gauld to *Tribune* and *Evening Post,* July 12; *Sun,* July 12.

violence. "Dogs that bark so loudly," he casually observed, "seldom bite much."[50]

"our feelings shall not be outraged"

Hibernian Hall was the headquarters of the Ancient Order of Hibernians (see Map 2). The first floor housed a saloon; on the second was "a long room, with a low ceiling, furnished with plain wooden benches, [and] a rough floor, through which the nail heads stick up prominently." The heads were "bright and polished" from years of dancing at charity balls and traditional Irish festivities. Despite the rain on Tuesday night, the rooms still were hot and stuffy from the day's swelter, much of it brought in by the hundreds of men who gathered there for an Irish Confederation meeting. To one reporter, the atmosphere was like "a mass meeting of all the smells in Prince street between the North and East Rivers."[51]

At nine o'clock, President Timothy Darcy, Thomas Kerrigan, and Edward L. Carey sat down at a long desk in the center of the room. Other men settled onto the rough wooden benches or huddled on the floor. Kerrigan said they met to discuss Kelso's instructions and to respond to charges that Irish Catholics planned to riot the next day. He and Carey insisted that religion had nothing to do with the convention's quarrel with Orangemen. They said Catholics did not hate Protestants, but Orangemen had caused Catholics much suffering in Ireland and would do so here.

After much debate, the convention adopted a proclamation addressed "To the People of the United States and The Citizens of New York in Particular." The document claimed the press had misled readers about the "motives and objectives" of the various Irish societies. It was necessary "to come before the public in vindication of our character as law-abiding citizens" because "a studied effort has been made" to convince Americans that the societies "are composed of intolerant, bigoted Irishmen, arrayed on religious grounds against their fellow countrymen and ready to assail and persecute them for differences of belief. . . . Nothing could be further from the truth than this assertion." For more than twenty years the convention had

50. *Sun*, *Herald*, and *World* (quotes), July 12.
51. *Sun*, July 12.

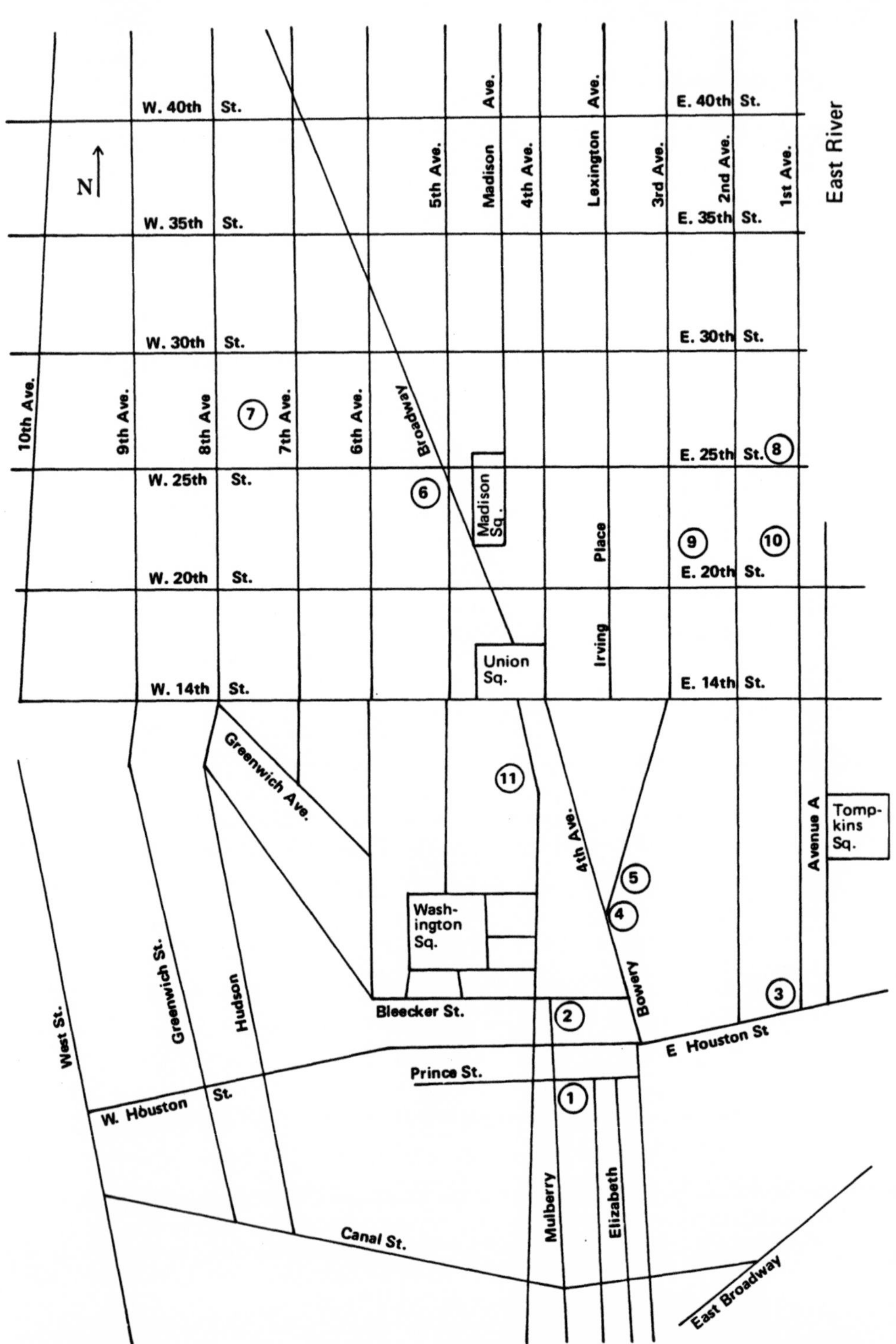

MAP 2. Manhattan, Canal to Fortieth streets. (1) Hibernian Hall, (2) police headquarters, (3) Fenia armory, (4) Cooper Union, (5) Bible House, (6) Fifth Avenue Hotel, (7) Eighth Avenue riot scene, (8 Bellevue Hospital and morgue, (9) Constitution Hall, (10) Eighteenth Precinct police station, (11 Grace Protestant Episcopal Church.

welcomed Irish Protestants, hoping to repair factional Irish disputes. But Orangemen only seemed bent on fostering discord in Ireland and America. "Obedient to the laws of the community of which we are a part," the members emphasized, "we have no desire to evade or curtail the right of any body of our fellow citizens *when properly exercised under the sanction of the authorities*, and as respectable and unoffending citizens we have a right to expect that our rights shall be held inviolable, and that our feelings shall not be outraged wantonly and with impunity under any pretext, however specious."[52]

There were other Irish meetings that night in Constitution Hall and on Broome Street. Details are sparse, but they suggest many Irish Catholics did not believe Kelso's ban was final. The meetings lingered late into the night. And at Hibernian Hall, well after the Irish Confederation had adopted its proclamation, a young reporter brought startling news from his tour of city armories. Rushing upstairs to the officers' desk, he reported that many guard units had already assembled and that some had been issued weapons. The reporter did not explain further, but his information led many delegates to believe that an Orange parade might occur after all. Amid much excitement, they agreed to reconvene at nine o'clock the next morning.[53]

"They will be protected to the fullest extent possible"

Irish Catholics reasonably believed that the arrival of guardsmen meant the Orangemen would parade. Yet what they did not know was that extensive police and military plans for a parade had been made even before July 10. What that young reporter saw as he visited armories late Tuesday night represented the culmination of orders originally intended to strengthen city officials' determination to prevent an unauthorized parade and a riot. By Tuesday, however, the military presence was intended to enforce Governor Hoffman's decision to permit the parade. Like city officials, Hoffman, who in an

52. *Herald*, July 12, 13; *World* and *Sun*, July 12. Printed in the July 12 *Herald*, *World*, *Times*, and *Tribune* (my emphasis), the proclamation was signed by Timothy Darcy (President), Patrick Campbell, Hugh McCourt, Patrick McArdle, William Carroll, Lawrence Clinton, Thomas Kerrigan, Lawrence Langan, Hugh Murray, and Edward L. Carey.

53. *Sun*, July 12; *Herald*, July 13.

1867 public letter had expressed "my most earnest sympathy in the [Fenian] struggle," now risked alienating his Irish Catholic supporters.[54]

Like Hall, Hoffman had been a loyal Tammany man with close ties to Tweed. He was the city's recorder in 1865 when Tweed picked him as Tammany's mayoral candidate. With strong Irish support, Hoffman managed a narrow gubernatorial victory in 1868 against upstate rivals and their supporters who disliked his ties to Tammany and the Irish. As he struggled to wean himself from Tweed in the summer of 1871 to broaden his base of support, Hoffman knew that his handling of the Orange parade could jeopardize his plans and much else.[55]

As it happened, his July 12 "Proclamation" authorizing the parade proved just as controversial as Kelso's order. In the document's first sentence, Hoffman claimed that he had "been only this day appraised, while at the Capitol, of the actual condition of things here [New York City] with reference to the proposed processions to-morrow." Because he believed "that my presence was needed," he went to the city at once. Hoffman later said that he decided to nullify Kelso's order because it would "be regarded as having been made by those in authority in submission to the demand and dictation of those who were not, and as subversive of the equal rights of men of all races, creeds and sentiments to protection, and would tend to permanent strife and bitterness, and to the disturbance of the peace of the State, perhaps, for many years to come."[56]

Many Democratic foes who supported the Orangemen viewed Hoffman's decision as a desperate attempt to repair the damage done by Keslo's order. The *Tribune* claimed that Hoffman had learned of the parade and its political implications while passing through the city on Monday, not Tuesday, and moreover that Gen. James McQuade, inspector general of the militia, had informed Hoffman of Hall's plan to suppress all processions. Claiming to have seen Hoffman on Broadway early *Tuesday* morning before the governor's re-

54. *The Record of John T. Hoffman. His Views on Fenianism. Letter of March 12, 1867* (n.p., n.d.), in Ford Collection, New York Public Library.

55. Jerome Mushkat, *Reconstruction*, 80–81, 131–42, 144, 150, 174–76, 183, 196–98, 238, and *Fernando Wood: A Political Biography* (Kent, Ohio: Kent State University Press, 1990), 156–61, 167–69, 175.

56. *Herald*, July 12; Hoffman, "Annual Message," Albany, January 2, 1872, in *Public Papers of John T. Hoffman, Governor of New York, 1869–70–71–72* (Albany, 1872), 295.

turn to Albany, *Tribune* reader C. S. Smith said he was certain that "two men sent him a telegram about 1:20 o'clock, to Albany, stating that Kelso's proclamation was doing the party immense harm, and suggested that they had better allow a small procession over a short route, under military escort."[57]

When, then, *did* Hoffman first learn that Kelso planned to ban the parade? If McQuade gave him this information on July 10 and if Hoffman did not immediately try to quash the order, Hoffman was implicated in a conspiracy with Tammany officials to float Kelso's ban either to test public sentiment or as a ruse to prevent Orangemen and Irish Catholics from rioting on July 12. The governor would then still have time to take appropriate action if the trial balloon sank.

McQuade stuck by his man. In a long letter to the *Utica Daily Observer*, McQuade answered "unqualifiedly that Governor Hoffman did not learn through me on Monday that Mayor Hall intended to suppress the Orange procession." McQuade explained that he had accompanied Hoffman to New York from Newport early Monday morning. During the coach ride to the Clarendon Hotel, McQuade told Hoffman that fears of violence had increased when the archbishop considered the riot likely enough to admonish Catholics to stay home on the twelfth. Yet McQuade did not believe regular Catholic churchgoers would be influenced by "a few fanatics" and said he was "confident there would be no serious disturbance." Hoffman then told McQuade to look into the matter further and to telegraph him later that afternoon in Albany.[58]

That same morning, Hall visited Maj. Gen. Alexander Shaler, commander of the guard's First Division. In his postriot report, Shaler said Hall told him he would ban the parade that evening. Hall worried that violence might occur anyway and asked Shaler for help. "In order that the police authorities of this city may well be sustained in suppressing a disturbance of the peace," Hall wrote, "I desire you to order out and hold in readiness at their armories for active service three regiments of infantry and one of troop cavalry."[59]

57. *Herald*, July 12; *Tribune*, July 13, 15, 17; C. S. Smith (New York, July 12) to *Tribune*, July 13.

58. Gen. James McQuade (Utica, July 22) to *Utica Daily Observer*, July 23, rpt. *Herald* and *Times*, July 23.

59. A. Oakey Hall (New York, July 10) to Major General Alexander Shaler, Commandant of the First Division, in Shaler's untitled report drafted in the form of a letter to "Sir" (presumably Gov. John T. Hoffman), dated July 19, and printed in the *Herald* (and other

Meanwhile, McQuade had left Hoffman at the Clarendon Hotel and waited to see Kelso at police headquarters. Kelso emerged from a long meeting with police commissioners and told McQuade "that a serious riot was threatened from the collision of the Orange procession, and the so-called target companies of the other side, who were drilling to parade on the same day with the Orangemen." Assured by Kelso that the police and militia were prepared for the emergency, McQuade next learned from Shaler that military orders would not be issued until Tuesday noon. Hall corroborated this information. McQuade then telegraphed Hoffman "that I thought everything was all right."[60]

Unknown to McQuade, Hoffman apparently was already on his way back to New York. Newark resident John Boylan claimed to have informed Hoffman's secretary and the governor himself of Kelso's order at the Capitol on Tuesday afternoon. The secretary, John D. Van Buren, told Boylan neither he nor Hoffman had read the afternoon papers, and denounced the ban. Hoffman left Albany late that afternoon. It is not known if he received McQuade's telegram or any other communications about the parade before departing. But it does seem clear that throughout the day, city authorities became increasingly alarmed by the prospect of violence on Wednesday and may even have anticipated Hoffman's eventual decision to allow the celebration. By late Tuesday afternoon, Kelso had ordered all police captains to report to headquarters at 6:00 A.M. Wednesday with three-fourths of each precinct's available patrolmen. At City Hall, officials frantically prepared strategic maps and bolstered forces in hopes of preventing what many already had accepted as an inevitable bloody clash between Orangemen and Irish Catholics.[61]

Hoffman arrived in New York at ten o'clock and hurried to a Clarendon Hotel conference with Hall, Kelso, and McQuade. No details immediately emerged from this meeting. Yet just after midnight, a carriage hurried along Mulberry Street in a driving rainstorm and pulled up in front of police headquarters. Hall, Kelso,

---

papers) on July 22. The legislation referred to was Section 242 of Chapter 80. Shaler's official published report does not include Hall's letter; see New York State, Adjutant-General's Office, *Annual Report of the Adjutant-General, 1871* (Albany, 1872) (hereafter cited as Shaler's *Report*); for the roster of men on duty on July 12, see p. 26.

60. McQuade's letter in *Herald* and *Times*, July 23.

61. Boylan's account in *World*, July 18; Shaler's *Report* in *Herald*, July 22; *World*, July 12, 13.

Smith, and two detectives hopped out and dashed inside. The men carried important information from the hotel conference. Calling in reporters, they announced that at eleven o'clock Hoffman had issued a proclamation revoking Kelso's order and that Orangemen would be protected if they decided to parade on Wednesday. Following the proclamation's controversial first sentence (that he had "been only this day appraised" of the potential riot on Wednesday), Hoffman stated:

> The order heretofore issued by the police authorities in reference to said processions having been duly revoked, I hereby give notice that any and all bodies of men desiring to assemble and march in peaceable procession in this city to-morrow . . . will be permitted to do so. They will be protected to the fullest extent possible by the military and police authorities. A military and police escort will be furnished to any body of men desiring it, on application to me at my headquarters (which will be at Police Headquarters in this city) at any time during the day.
>
> I warn all persons to abstain from interference with any such assemblage or procession except by authority from me; and I give notice that all the powers of my command, civil, and military, will be used to preserve the public peace and to put down, at all hazards, every attempt at disturbance; and I call upon all citizens, of every race and religion, to unite with me and the local authorities in this determination to preserve the peace and honor of the city and State.

Kelso also sent a brief message to all police captains revoking his order but retaining his instructions for the deployment of police on Wednesday.[62]

Hall had asked Shaler to call up just one cavalry and three infantry regiments. Police Board president Henry Smith had increased that request, and now Hoffman demanded still more. When Shaler finally issued Special Order No. 16 sometime Tuesday night, he ordered twelve infantry regiments, the Washington Gray Troop cavalry, and Batteries G and C—4,266 officers and enlisted men in all—"to assemble at their respective armories, in fatigue dress, fully armed and equipped for active service" at 7:00 A.M. the next morning. "The infantry will be supplied with forty rounds of ammunition," he noted,

62. *Times*, *Herald*, and *Sun*, July 12.

"and the artillery with twenty rounds per gun." Shaler refused to release these specifics to the papers, allowing them to print only the time and place of assembly, the number of rounds per man, and the reason for the call ("in obedience to a requisition from the civil authorities"). But he added that the regiments "have been called upon without regard to nationality or religion." Disclosed in his final report, the particulars revealed that still another increase in troop strength must have been made during the night. Shaler's account indicates that four infantry regiments and a regimental cavalry detachment were added. These 1,061 more men brought total troop strength on duty on July 12 to 5,327. The *Herald* ominously reported that of all the regiments ordered on duty, only the Seventh was trained in "street firing."[63]

"the spirit of assassination"

Sometime during the night the rain stopped, and by six o'clock, when Hoffman returned with Van Buren and McQuade to police headquarters on Mulberry Street, a mid-July sun already had begun to creep over the city. People who milled on Mulberry from Bleeker to Houston were pushed back in small waves as police contingents arrived. The nearly fifteen hundred policemen were divided into three battalions, one each commanded by inspectors Walling, Dilkes, and Jameson. Two companies of the Seventh Regiment were stationed on the upper floors. Numerous omnibuses, parked along Houston and Bleecker streets, would transport them and the police as needed.[64]

Hoffman took charge of these activities from his command post in Kelso's office. He interrupted conferences with aides to explain to a reporter why he had nullified Kelso's order. Hoffman said he believed "it was necessary, not only for the present, but for the future, that whatever lawless element there was in the city of New York should be made to understand at once and finally that there was force enough in the city, military and civil, to assert the power of the authorities and of law, and to preserve peace and order, and to protect the lives and property of the people." He said he believed all

63. *Herald*, July 12; Shaler's *Report* in *Herald*, July 22.
64. *Herald*, *World*, *Times*, *Sun*, and *Tribune*, July 13.

people, regardless of their nationalities, had a stake in protecting the right to assemble and parade.[65]

The *Tribune* and *Times* had made similar but much more acidic arguments. They now claimed that Hoffman's justification was intended to mask a cunning political maneuver. The *Tribune* saw in the governor's actions "a desperate though tardy effort . . . to save the Democratic party of this State" from Tammany embarrassments. It warned Catholics that "ignorant and prejudiced anti-Papists" might believe that because the pope opposed republicanism, Irish Catholic street processions were intended as an affront to the Republic. "Grant that the Catholics *mean* nothing of the sort," it added. Calling the orders of Hoffman and Kelso "A Double Humiliation," the *Times* wondered "whether New-York has more reason to be ashamed of the original order or its precipitate withdrawal." The Tweed Ring's "Catholic supporters," by turns flattered and deceived, were now so confused and angry that blood surely would flow. "This week's work has at least done one thing," the paper asserted. It has "ruined the Democratic schemes for regaining possession of the national Government. The people will never consent to see the liberties of the whole country handed over to the tender mercies of the Irish Catholics." Not all shared that view. W. F. Allen dashed off a quick note to Hoffman that morning thanking him for "your *manly* proclamation," because "I felt that our New York friends had made a mistake which might seemingly affect us and possibly lose us the state this fall."[66]

Few others took time that Wednesday morning to ponder the political implications of Hoffman's surprising order. Most were preoccupied with sensational reports in early papers that suggested their lives and property were in danger. One paper claimed that on Tuesday police had captured "fifty muskets" from Hibernians at a house on Third Avenue between Sixty-third and Sixty-fourth streets. Another maintained that some arms and ammunition had been found at the House of Good Shepherd on East Eighty-ninth Street. Another paper reported that longshoremen were flocking into Fenian and AOH military units. The *Sun* claimed that Boulevard laborers were promising trouble. "Their foreman is said to be Andrews, the leader of the riots of '63," it said. (This was a reference to John U. Andrews,

65. *Sun*, July 13.

66. *Tribune* and *Times*, July 13; W. F. Allen to "My dear Gov." (Fire Island, July 12), in John T. Hoffman folder, New-York Historical Society.

who was tried and convicted in federal court for conspiring to wage war against the government after the riots. He served three years in Sing Sing, returned to New York in 1870, and apparently practiced law—he was not a laborer—until his death in 1883.) Added to these ominous signs was a *Star* interview with an APA member who claimed every APA brother who planned to parade with Orangemen "has provided himself with a six shooter."[67]

All such rumors helped to shape newspaper coverage of July 12 events. The *Sun* claimed that "everybody seemed to feel that the spirit of assassination haunted the city and rode upon the atmosphere." The paper reported that "the rabble which had cowed the Mayor into the surrender of the dearest rights of a free people were jubilant, and bloodthirsty. They swore that they would kill every Orangeman that should appear in the streets, despite the Governor's proclamation." The *Tribune* painted a more sinister picture:

> Sullen groups gathered on the street corners in threatened districts or in the localities where the Irish reside in greatest numbers. Among these groups women were most conspicuous by the vehemence with which they denounced Orangemen. . . . The men generally were gruff and silent, evidently angry that their opportunities had been wrestled from them by the enforced action of the men whom they had made Mayor and Governor. Separate gangs of ruffians, six or eight in number, moved from street to street, eager alike for fight or pillage.

To an equally grave *Times* reporter, "no civilized city" ever witnessed a stranger sight than did New York as the police and militia hurried to an appointed rendezvous. "It was as if a deadly enemy of the Commonwealth was expected at the gates," he continued, "and an alarmed people were making hasty preparations for defense." The analogy was wrong, and the reporter made matters worse. "But when it was considered that the enemy was within the community," he concluded, "every reflecting citizen saw that the crisis was more por-

67. *Herald* and *Tribune*, July 12; "Anonymous" (n.p., n.d.) to *Herald*, July 15; *Sun*, July 12. On Andrews, see Adrian Cook, *The Armies of the Streets: The New York City Draft Riots of 1863* (Lexington: University Press of Kentucky, 1975), 60–61, 184–87, 309 n. 61. See also *Star*, July 12.

tentous than if a foreign fleet were bombarding the City, or a foreign host at its gates."[68]

"In spite of Father Daly"

At 11:05 A.M. a reporter at police headquarters noted that at that moment two photographers were atop the building taking pictures of the crowd below in Mulberry Street. "It is hoped they will be successful," he noted, "as people in alter ages will want to see how the 'old thing' looked on the 12th of July, 1871." Whatever the results, and however interesting the sight, no frozen image could capture the frenzy that culminated in the Eighth Avenue violence that afternoon. Nor can we. Yet thanks to that same reporter's diary, to the notes kept by Shaler and published in his report, and to numerous other accounts, it is possible to reconstruct some of the details, and to sense the tenor of the city, as clocks moved toward a two o'clock Orange parade. From all accounts, it appears that Irish Catholic workers formed the core of Orange opposition; yet there is little evidence of an AOH presence that day—despite their recruiting efforts and military street drills.[69]

6:00 A.M.

The arrival of guardsmen, police, and city officials at police headquarters turned the neighborhood into a military encampment. Almost immediately, police were sent to Forty-second Street near Seventh and Eighth avenues to stop a band of "armed Hibernians" reportedly on its way to Boulevard work areas in search of recruits from labor gangs. By the time police arrived, the men already had marched far up Eighth Avenue, and Mount Morris quarrymen had quit work, marched down to Eighth Avenue and 103d Street, and forced some fifty men working for Jeremiah McCarty to join them. Other quarrymen left their jobs as the work gangs moved downtown.[70]

At 6:30 a Fourth Precinct police detail rushed back to its station in Oak Street in response to a rumor that men were about to attack the nearby Harper's Building in Franklin Square. They stood guard

68. *Sun*, *Tribune*, and *Times*, July 13.
69. *Herald*, July 13.
70. Costello, *Our Police Protectors*, 245; *Sun*, July 13.

there all day. Only five minutes later, Fourteenth Precinct police on Spring Street notified headquarters that a large crowd had gathered in front of Owen Finney's Spring Street liquor store not far from Hibernian Hall. As the crowd cheered, a straw-stuffed effigy of an Orangeman swung from a police telegraph pole. Police cut down the symbol and patrolled the area.[71]

7:00 A.M.

News arrived that men threatened to burn banker Henry A. Heiser's house because Heiser had given Orangemen sanctuary after the Elm Park violence. As troops chased after that rumor, Kelso learned that other men were threatening to torch a house at 623 East Ninth Street, where the APA member Francis Wood had lived before he was killed at Elm Park.[72]

Meanwhile, reporters following the worrisome laborers above Fifty-ninth Street found that after 50–100 laborers learned of Hoffman's order, they spread throughout uptown districts where nearly 900 men worked along the Boulevard. Gathering strength as they marched downtown, the men stopped at Central Park, convinced many of the 1,500 workers there to join them, and then went to Columbus Circle at Fifty-ninth Street. Other workers tried to recruit the 260 men working in Sixth and St. Nicholas avenues, but few left work. In Harlem, a group of 200 was formed from men working on the Seventh Avenue extension, the new district courthouse, and state senator Henry Genet's new house at 128th Street and Sixth Avenue. Others came from repair work on the Third Avenue Railroad, from sewer construction in Fourth Avenue between 122d and 125th streets, and from the Harlem Gas Works. All headed downtown. Near Forty-seventh Street and Tenth Avenue, a street paver sang his song to a *Herald* reporter:

> Me name it is Kelly, the rake,
> An' I don't care a damn about any mon;
> Off I had but a knife in the hat,
> Shure I'd shtick it right into an Orangeman.

71. *Herald*, *Tribune*, *Times*, and *World*, July 13.
72. *World* and *Tribune*, July 13.

Kelly's friend Moriarity then improvised on an old song known to many in Ireland. His updated version commented on priests' efforts to discourage attacks on Orangemen:

> If they mane to do us ill,
> Says the Shan Van Vaugh,
> Shure we'll come from Mackerville,
> Says the Shan Van Vaugh;
> An' march along so gaily,
> Wid' musket an' shillelah,
> In spite of Father Daly
> Says the Shan Van Vaugh.[73]

By 7:30, Kelso and Shaler decided to deploy more forces in midtown and uptown districts in hopes of preventing labor riots along the Boulevard and elsewhere.[74]

8:00 A.M

As these forces spread throughout the city, 250 policemen investigated reports that quarrymen near Central Park were loitering in saloons and picking fights. At 8:15, 250 more police hurried to Twenty-ninth Street and Eighth Avenue to protect Orange meeting rooms in case Orangemen were attacked as they filed into the street for the parade.[75]

9:00 A.M.

Hundreds of workers appeared at police headquarters to confirm Hoffman's decision and then quickly broke into groups and spread word to other parts of the city. Some hurried to a nine o'clock meeting at Hibernian Hall and listened to AOH captain Frank Doyle read Hoffman's proclamation and a list of new volunteers. Then Doyle, a Captain Money, Frank Lenahan, John B. McHugh, and John Maher drafted resolutions expelling all AOH members who failed to appear for the day's military drills and sent word of the new developments to members already at work. Elsewhere, workers reportedly beat

73. *Herald*, July 13.
74. Shaler's *Report* in *Herald*, July 22.
75. Ibid.; *Herald*, *Tribune*, and *Times*, July 13.

1. Orange headquarters at Twenty-ninth Street and Eighth Avenue on the morning of July 12. *Frank Leslie's Illustrated Newspaper*, July 29, 1871. State Historical Society of Wisconsin.

three quarrymen near Forty-sixth Street and Tenth Avenue when they refused to quit work. As two hundred policemen dispersed workers there, some eight hundred longshoremen assembled at the foot of East Houston Street and marched "with arms in their hands" to Bowery and then scattered as other police forces arrived. Despite the great movement of Irish workers, even the *Times* noted that many of them stayed at work throughout the day. And Irish streetcar conductors and Twenty-third Street stone yard workers voted not to leave work and risk being fired.[76]

By 9:30 many Broadway businesses had closed for the day, but worried shopkeepers stood guard inside. Still more concerned merchants closed their windows and shutters from Sixth to Ninth Avenue as surging crowds followed police through the area. In search of disturbances along Eighth Avenue, the police encountered only hostile glares from people on rooftops, in windows, and on lampposts.[77]

Police were busy elsewhere too. They responded to a 9:35 report of rioting in Yorkville and to news that a mob had swept spectators and police off the street at Eighty-third Street and Third Avenue. One account said the police dispersed a "great crowd of rioters" at Eighty-third Street; another reported that they waited for an hour at Thirty-fifth Street and returned to headquarters when they learned the rumors had no substance. Whenever they returned—it may have been as late as eleven o'clock—the police then encountered other large crowds in Eighteenth, Fourteenth, and Eleventh streets. At each point they were jeered and used clubs before moving on.[78]

Meanwhile, in Second and Ninth avenues, amid the slaughterhouses and tenements on Avenues A, B, and C near the Houston Street ferry, the *Herald* reported having seen drunk men preparing weapons. Many of them trudged to police headquarters, denounced Hoffman and the troops, and then were chased down to Bowery Street, where some were arrested. The *Herald* reporter's diary mentions none of this. A 9:45 entry notes only that the streets around headquarters "are completely blocked up by a crowd of every description and nationality," that "a number of Irish laborers are walking up and down Mulberry street," and that police made no attempt to clear the streets because there were "no riotous demonstrations."

76. *Herald* and *Times*, July 13.

77. *Herald*, July 13.

78. Shaler's *Report* in *Herald*, July 22; *Times*, *World*, and *Herald*, July 13.

Another diary entry at 9:55 suggests that officials were more concerned about events elsewhere. "Things are commencing to look serious," the reporter noted. "Dispatches are constantly arriving from different quarters of the city and the officials about the building are flying about like hens with their heads off. Everything and everybody is excited, and a rough time is certainly at hand."[79]

10:00 A.M.

McQuade and other military officers conferred with Shaler. Hoffman assessed alarming reports with Kelso. Shaler said his meeting was interrupted at 10:20 with news that "a large crowd of evil-disposed persons had made a demonstration" at 143d Street and Seventh Avenue "and obliged all the workmen in that neighborhood to quit work and join their party." Other accounts indicate that police in that area reported that Italians and Swiss or German quarrymen on *Ninth* Avenue near 143d Street had been attacked. Whatever the case, Shaler ordered five Seventy-first Regiment companies and the Washington Grays, all stationed at Elm Park, to the scene. Twenty minutes later, when he learned that police had dispersed the crowd, he ordered troops back to the park. Already on their way to 143d Street, guardsmen apparently did not receive Shaler's order for some time and wandered aimlessly through upper wards before finally returning to Elm Park just after noon.[80]

But serious trouble erupted elsewhere. At 10:40, Shaler sent two Seventh Regiment companies to the Fenian armory on Avenue A, where perhaps five hundred armed men from Hibernian Hall were demanding muskets and ammunition from Fenian guards. Eight minutes later, one hundred policemen were sent after fighting broke out there and at the Sixty-ninth Regiment's armory at Essex and Grand—just five blocks south of the Fenian hall. Police stopped the Fenian armory disturbance and confiscated 138 rifles.[81]

Authorities continued to worry about the activities of workers. At the Eighteenth Precinct station on East Twenty-second Street between First and Second avenues, roundsmen reported that crowds of men had infiltrated the precinct and that "another gang of strange

79. *Herald*, July 13.

80. Shaler's *Report* in *Herald*, July 22; *Herald*, *World*, and *Times*, July 13.

81. Shaler's *Report* in *Herald*, July 22; *Herald*, *Times*, and *Sun*, July 13. The armory formerly was used by the Fifty-fifth Regiment (*Tribune*, July 13).

men" had organized all East River longshoremen from Fourteenth to Nineteenth streets. Police also claimed that twenty-five plasterers working at Twenty-second Street and Fifth Avenue, and many Irish workers at the Jackson and Badger Foundry on Fourteenth Street, had all quit work. Fearing widespread class violence, police telegraphed headquarters shortly before eleven o'clock that "large bodies of Irish laboring men . . . were roaming through the ward in [an] extremely threatening manner." Kelso quickly sent 100 policemen to Third Avenue and Nineteenth Street, where they encountered 150 men who had marched down from Constitution Hall and from Dooley's Hall at Twenty-second Street and First Avenue. Papers claimed these were drunk AOH members. "They looked unkempt and desperate," described a *Herald* reporter. Scattered by the police, they reappeared at the precinct station, passing "up and down the station in squads of twenty and thirty." If they were "rioters," as the reporter claimed, he failed to explain why they "did not attempt any violence." Yet their presence alarmed precinct captain John Cameron. His station house had been burned by a mob in 1863. The captain remained at his post throughout the night, leading frequent patrols through his district.[82]

11:00 A.M.

By midmorning, then, the city was rumbling with rumors, squads of troops and police, and angry bands of laborers and longshoremen. Passengers stepping onto all Eighth Avenue streetcars were confronted by wary policemen, stationed on board for the day to prevent riders from leaving the cars where crowds of people gathered. Shoppers on Broadway, Third, Sixth, and Eighth avenues and on Canal and other streets found many stores closed. They still could enter A. T. Stewart's splendid department store at Broadway and Tenth Street, but the spacious rooms were darkened by lowered shutters. In Printing House Square, near Broadway and Ann Street, crowds of people waited for the latest headlines to appear on bulletin boards in front of newspaper offices. Seemingly indifferent Wall Street brokers revealed their concerns in the crass joke of the day: they offered to trade a live Orangemen for a dead rioter. The alarm raised by Hoff-

82. *World* ("strange men," "large bodies"), *Times*, *Herald*, July 13; see also Cook, *Armies of the Streets*, 69–70, 124.

man's startling proclamation and by the first reports of roving, angry laborers was intensified by the arrival of each fresh rumor. In a rare display of discriminate reporting, the *Times* commented that "almost with the speed of wildfire the news traveled down town, and by the time it reached Wall-street it had grown in magnitude, and the news thus reported was that the entire upper portion of the City was in control of the rioters; that the Police had been driven from the ground, and that the military were hastening to the scene to check the mob, which was then on its way down town sweeping everything before them." Later that morning, a "report reached the lower part of the City that the Station-house in 'Mackerville' had been torn down, the wires cut, and the force in charge had been captured and murdered." The paper stressed that these rumors were not true.[83]

One startling report was verified. Shaler said that just after eleven o'clock he learned "that an organized force, formed in companies, having a leader with a drawn sword at their head, was moving down Prince street towards Hibernian Hall," where they planned to distribute weapons. At 11:15, police and troops under Kelso and Shaler trapped the men in Prince Street. They sent Capt. William Copeland with eight hundred policemen up Mulberry to Prince and other police forces up Bowery to Mott. Then Shaler sent the Eighty-fourth Regiment from its Fourth Street armory to support the police. The *Irish World* alone mentioned that as the Eighty-fourth marched to the hall, it was "almost attacked by a mob, they [mob members] exclaiming that the regiment was Orange in feeling and sentiment" and that its regimental banners resembled Orange colors.[84]

A large and angry crowd greeted the police in Prince Street with jeers and stones. According to Eighty-fourth Regiment Colonel Cornelius B. Mitchell, when the crowd rejected Copeland's orders to disperse, Copeland made a "brilliant and successful charge" on men, women, and children in the street and the hall. Blood spotted the street and sidewalk from scalp and face wounds. Storming into Hibernian Hall, police used their weapons indiscriminately. "All those found were clubbed senseless and half killed, some having their skulls fractured," the *Irish World* reported. It also claimed that "about a hundred persons were more or less injured, and no doubt

83. *Tribune*, *Sun*, *Herald*, and *Times*, July 13.

84. Shaler's *Report* in *Herald*, July 22; *Tribune* and *Herald*, July 13; *Irish World*, July 22.

some killed," although these injuries did not appear in casualty reports. Yet all accounts suggest that police clubbed people west into Broom and east into Bowery and that they may have arrested between eighteen and forty, although these great numbers cannot be verified in sparse police records and other sources (see Appendix B). Not all prisoners were "rioters." Patrolmen Thomas O'Grady and Michael Harrison were fired and jailed for criticizing police methods and refusing to fight fellow Irishmen.[85]

With much of the police reserve scrambling after the crowds in Prince Street, police learned at 11:30 that some two hundred armed longshoremen, led by a man waving a sword, had marched from lower Manhattan through Crosby and Houston streets and Broadway to Twenty-eighth Street—only a few blocks from the Orangemen's Lamartine Hall. The reporter's diary noted only that "the police are after them." Alarmed by these reports, by accounts that drunken bands of men roamed the city, and by the incidents at the Fenian armory and Hibernian Hall, Mayor Hall ordered all liquor stores closed. And just before noon, as two Seventh Regiment companies hurried to Houston and Bowery to suppress a fight there, authorities announced that Orangemen would begin their parade at two o'clock at Twenty-ninth Street and Eighth Avenue.[86]

12:00 P.M.

Between noon and two o'clock, groups of people from various parts of the city made their ways through the midday heat to Lamartine Hall. Claiming that the heat was too oppressive, more longshoremen and quarrymen quit for the day. As militia regiments began leaving their armories at 12:30, Orangeman Joseph Barton delivered the final parade route to Hoffman. Concerned by reports that New Jersey Orangemen might join the New York parade, Hoffman told Col. James Fisk, Jr., to stop all Erie ferries and announced at 12:35 that city and state forces would only protect New York Orangemen.[87]

At the same time, some 150 armed longshoremen and laborers formed at Hibernian Hall, stepped onto Broadway from Prince Street, and started north toward Lamartine Hall. The *World* claimed

85. Statement of Mitchell to *World*, July 16; *Irish World*, July 22; *Tribune* and *Herald*, July 13; *Sun*, July 20.

86. *Herald* and *World*, July 13.

87. *Times*, *Sun*, *Herald*, and *World*, July 13.

that many "were armed with clubs extemporized from packingboxes and barrels" and that "they were led by a villainous-looking individual, who wore a long-skirted broadcloth coat and straw hat, and carried an old cavalry sword." Growing more boisterous as it swelled in numbers, the crowd pushed shoppers and others off the street, knocking some down. Just above the Grace Protestant Episcopal Church, near Broadway and West Eleventh Street, a squad of mounted police charged the procession, clubbing and tumbling many people to the ground.[88]

Not all of those who had gathered at Hibernian Hall joined that march. Two hundred police and the Eighty-fourth Regiment hurried to the hall when they learned that fighting had erupted inside. Just after leaving their armory at Broadway and Fourth Street, regiment members encountered an angry crowd of men and scattered them with a blank musket volley. As police rushed to the armory to seize arms left behind, part of the regiment stationed at headquarters used bayonets to fight its way through Mulberry Street, while the armory contingent forced back screaming crowds near Hibernian Hall. By 1:15 or 1:30, the police and troops had reached the Prince Street area, the Grace Church skirmish had ended, and attention focused on Hibernian Hall.

Troops and police found Prince Street packed with people from Mulberry to Mott. Unfortunately, because press coverage was so shaped by class and ethnic bias, it is impossible to know what happened there. For example, in front of the Catholic orphan asylum, just east of Hibernian Hall at Mott Street, one report claimed there were "thieves from the slums of Five Points—recognizable by their demonic countenances and squalid appearances generally," while to the west at Mulberry there was "a dense crowd of Irishmen and Irishwomen of the lowest class." It was a "motley gathering" of "the Hibernians and the constitutional thieves from the Eighth and Sixth Wards." Charged by the police and prodded by troop bayonets, "the cowardly mob broke and ran in all directions, the women and aged hags screamed with terror, and the men who had their heads out of the windows of their houses quickly withdrew them." While the composition and activities of the crowds are murky, what does seem clear is that the police attacked Hibernian Hall, broke down the mas-

88. *World* and *Tribune*, July 13; "A True Irishman" (New York, July 15) to *Star*, July 11.

sive wooden door, and again freely clubbed many of those inside. They beat one hapless longshoreman and tossed another out a window. Women cursed the police, calling them "'spawn of the devil,' 'black-hearted traitors,' 'sons of - - - - - - -,' and so on infinitum." A reporter claimed that "one dirty-looking old Irishwoman, with long dirty gray hair over her shoulders, took up a brick, and flinging it at Captain [Joseph] Petty, cried out, 'Take that, ye black-hearted ould son of - - - - - - ! I know by yer back ye're an Orangeman.'" People threw a few stones at soldiers, and police made several arrests. It was the second assault on the hall that day, but the *Times* called it "The First Outbreak."[89]

The important confrontations between Irish Catholics and others on the morning of July 12 were preliminaries to an even greater confrontation. Like the rumors and bitter arguments before that day, the morning's reports and clashes revealed much about the attitudes of diverse New Yorkers. Many Irish Catholics, Orangemen, and their varied supporters readily made the crucial leap from argument to action. The morning's events transformed complex historical elements into a new reality. Channeled into a few afternoon moments on Eighth Avenue, that new reality was altered yet again.

89. *Times* ("thieves," "motley gathering") and *World* ("dense crowd," "cowardly mob," curses), July 13.

4 / The Eighth Avenue Riot

From the third-story windows of Lamartine Hall on the northwest corner of Twenty-ninth Street and Eighth Avenue, two American flags wafted in the slight breeze of a hot July afternoon. A tea and spice shop occupied the first floor of this simple brick building. Various Orange lodges shared fourth-floor rooms. Clad in Orange regalia, lone figures periodically emerged from the building, silently looked up and down the avenue, and then disappeared back inside. By 1:30 P.M., crowds lined both sides of Eighth Avenue from Twenty-first to Thirty-third Street. Others filled the cross streets from Seventh to Ninth Avenue. Irritated by the commotion and the loss of business, area shopkeepers complained to watchful police, but to no avail. Busy with other concerns, the police had already blocked Eighth Avenue from Twenty-eighth to Thirtieth Street, and Twenty-ninth Street from Ninth to Seventh Avenue.[1]

George Templeton Strong's concerns that same hour led him to another part of the city. Visiting "the Bank for Savings, which I thought might be in danger of molestation, as Bleecker Street was occupied by a hard-looking crowd," he found inside that "all was serene, and the clerks told me the only peculiarity they had noticed

Note: All dates in the footnotes are from the year 1871.

1. *World* and *Tribune*, July 13.

was an unusual deference and civility on the part of their Irish depositors." While strolling back to Eighth Avenue (he arrived too late for the parade), Strong took mental notes of what he saw. "Curious to observe," he later wrote, "how little effect this orgasm of riot and bloodshed produced in side streets. Children were playing on shady spots of sidewalks, ladies in lovely flowing summer robes fanning themselves at parlor windows or on balconies, little tradesmen pursuing their vocations."[2]

Elsewhere tensions simmered. In uptown districts, especially on streetcorners from Sixth to Tenth Avenue, small groups of people stood quietly discussing the morning's events. Many others awaited the latest news in Tompkins Square, in Union Square, and at Tammany Hall. Still others moved downtown from Boulevard areas in groups of three to ten. Brief fights erupted from Thirty-fourth Street to Central Park after some saloons closed, but none apparently resulted from too much or too little drink. In fact, the *Herald* conceded that "very few" of the "rioters" were noticed in saloons at all. Moreover, except for the Eighth Avenue district, the paper observed that "one of the most peculiar features . . . was the entire absence of women. In only very few places were they to be seen, and as one of the gangs of men came along [from uptown areas] one of the party might be noticed dropping his head a little, and almost instantly the women and children would disappear." Another writer found German saloons closed but most Irish ones open on Sixth and Seventh avenues above Twenty-third Street. "The windows were full of women," he added, "and the sidewalks of men. These latter were mostly laboring men, wearing long black coats and dirty white shirts, without waistcoats or collars, and with a general air of expectation and dogged determination."[3]

On Eighth Avenue itself, short city blocks crowded closely together from Twenty-first to Thirty-third Street. A person looking down from a rooftop at Twenty-fourth Street could see the entire avenue between those two points. It was a typically busy mixed residential and commercial neighborhood. "The houses are generally brick, of four stories, with flat roof, and the first story is almost in-

2. George Templeton Strong, *The Diary of George Templeton Strong*, vol. 4, *The Post-War Years, 1865–1875*, ed. Allan Nevins and Milton H. Thomas (New York: Macmillan, 1952), 370.

3. *Herald* and *World*, July 13. On the absence of women, see also *Sun* and *Times*, July 13.

variably a retail shop or saloon or restaurant," described a *Herald* reporter. "The corners are generally liquor stores or lager beer saloons. The street has a dingy, bricky look, and conspicuous by height and whiteness is the great Opera House and Erie Railroad headquarters, at the corner of Twenty-third street." Stores in this neighborhood also sold teas and coffees, cigars, bakery goods, books, candies, jewelry, furniture, hardware, and produce. There were druggists, plumbers, butchers, tinsmiths, painters, undertakers, shoemakers, tailors, basement restaurants, and oyster houses. The proprietors' names suggest the heterogeneity of this community: Abels, Anguin, Cohen, Cregan, Ganz, Geswein, Isaac, Koehler, McDonald, Meagher, O'Gara, O'Shea, Schinkel, Shaw, Toplitz, White.[4]

The larger Eighth Avenue neighborhood was little different. Perhaps as many as fifteen thousand people lived in the area bounded by Seventh and Ninth avenues and Twenty-ninth and Twenty-third streets. A sampling from the 1870 census schedules suggests that Irish-born residents and their families predominated but that sizable numbers of American-born and German and English immigrant families lived there also (see Table 1). Most immigrants evidently married before leaving home. Most of their children were born here. Among this mixed ethnic working-class neighborhood there were carpenters, chairmakers, wheelwrights, masons, sailmakers, dock builders, bootblacks, servants, machinists, laundresses, waiters and cooks, agents and salesmen, a few physicians, and merchants. In spite of the large Irish population, the area contained only one Catholic but seven Protestant churches. Yet ostensibly it was not an area congenial to Orange displays.

"Walk the streets like men"

Clashes soon erupted near Lamartine Hall. Orangemen peered out of the doorway just after one o'clock, causing the now-sizable crowd at Twenty-ninth Street to surge toward police lines there. Police clubbed many to the ground and made some arrests. One of those arrested was Bernard McGinnis, aged thirty-two. Born in Ireland, McGinnis was a reporter for the New York *Star*. Police claimed

4. *Herald*, July 13. The businesses and names are found in the list of riot damage reports in Appendix B and in my "Studies in Irish and Irish-American Thought and Behavior in Gilded Age New York City" (Ph.D. diss., University of Rochester, 1977), 219–24.

Table 1. Birthplace of Eighth Avenue area residents: A sampling from the 1870 census schedules

	Number	Percentage
Aged 18 and older		
Ireland	1,536	40.3
United States	1,310	34.4
Germany	599	15.7
England	160	4.2
Scotland	81	2.2
France	45	1.2
Canada	36	.9
Others (14 countries)[a]	43	1.1
Totals	3,810	100.0
Aged 17 and younger		
United States	2,601	94.4
Ireland	70	2.6
Germany	41	1.5
England	17	.6
Others (7 countries)[b]	25	.9
Totals	2,754	100.0

Note: The sampling includes residents of odd-numbered dwellings in W. Twenty-fourth Street between Seventh and Eighth avenues, in W. Twenty-sixth Street between Seventh and Ninth avenues, in odd- and even-numbered dwellings in W. Twenty-seventh, Twenty-eighth, and Twenty-ninth streets between Seventh and Eighth avenues and along Eighth Avenue from Twenty-third to Twenty-ninth Street.

[a]Cuba (1), Holland (5), Portugal (1), Poland (10), "Nassau" (2), Denmark (2), Russia (1), Switzerland (10), Wales (2), "Africa" (1), Spain (4), Turkey (1), Austria (2), Hungary (1).

[b]Canada (6), Switzerland (1), Scotland (5), Holland (3), France (5), Mexico (4), Wales (1).

he carried a concealed club and a list of "Hibernian Volunteers." At the same time, some men appeared across the street, shouting and cheering and "led by a man waving a long cane." The leader's cane fell, and a large dirk popped from its handle. Police clubbed this band into Seventh Avenue and returned to again clear Eighth Avenue from Thirtieth to Twenty-eighth Street.[5]

5. *Times* and *Tribune* ("long cane"), July 13; complaint of officer Philip Lambrecht v. Bernard McGinnis, July 13, Grand Jury Dismissals (Supreme Court, 1871), Box 10570, New York City Municipal Archives.

Then troops arrived. The first was Col. Josiah Porter's Twenty-second Regiment, carrying some 420 muskets. Hisses and jeers greeted them. Some guardsmen reportedly were spat upon. An unidentified eyewitness told the *Herald* that after the Twenty-second arrived, he saw some two hundred "Hibernians" storm up from near Twenty-third Street "carrying muskets and swords, bludgeons, and such other things as a mob bent on mischief would be likely to pick up promiscuously." The group might have been part of the Grace Church crowd; for "they were led by a man dressed in a bluish-black frock coat, black pants and straw hat, who wielded a shilleiah [sic], and every few steps he turned around to say something to his followers." Seeing the Twenty-second already in place, the band of men broke into small groups and hurried into nearby houses facing the street.[6]

The swelling crowds worried Orangemen. A man recalled seeing a Lamartine Hall sentry "at the door in the uniform of the Old Washington Continental Guards, which I had remembered as a Native American company as a boy." The guard admitted only reporters, delegates with badges, and building residents. As they entered the hall, Orange men hid their colors, but Orange women waved their ribbons and handkerchiefs, wore Orange bows tied at the throat, and seemed unruffled by the nearby angry crowds. One observer believed that the crowds at Twenty-ninth Street were "composed mostly of laboring men, a majority of whom were Irish, with a fair sprinkling of German and other nationalities." He also noticed many neighborhood women who "were evidently strong sympathizers with the Catholic element, to judge from the expressions used by many of them." The women reminded another reporter of "the Paris *petroleuse*." Yet, significantly, the *Herald*'s observer believed that just east of Eighth Avenue in Twenty-ninth Street "there were very few members of the Ancient Order of Hibernians" and that "those who composed the crowds seemed to be without any organization or purpose, for during the entire day two men in concert never made an attack at one time on the Orangemen."[7]

Inside the Twenty-ninth Street entrance to Lamartine Hall, a rick-

6. *World*, July 13; Col. Josiah Porter (Twenty-second Infantry) to Col. W. H. Chesebrough (Assistant Adjutant General, First Division, New York State National Guard) (New York, July 13), printed in *World*, July 19 (hereafter cited as Porter's *Report*); *Irish World*, July 22; *Herald*, July 13.

7. *Herald* ("Continental Guards"), *World* ("laboring men"), and *Tribune*, July 13; *Star*, July 15.

ety, darkened stairway led to a sixty-by-thirty–foot room upstairs. By half past one, some 150 men had gathered. Thirty women and girls waited in an anteroom, gingerly fanning the heat from their faces. Guarding the door to the lodge room was a man holding a sword. Gideon Lodge master and supreme grand treasurer, James D. Askin, "dressed in plain black, with an orange and blue sash across his breast," stood at one corner of the room behind a desk. Another Orangeman presided at the opposite corner. Using heavy gavels decked with purple and orange ribbons, both men occasionally called their boisterous members to order. Members of Prince of Orange, Derry Walls, Gideon, Chosen Few, No Surrender, Enniskillen, and other lodges inspected showcases of regalia and membership certificates, or sat upon dusty, purple-cushioned benches that lined the room. They wore white aprons, and orange and purple scarves, which looped around their necks and fell below their waists.[8]

Of the several visitors who gained entrance to the room, only one later remarked that "nearly all" the men "were very much intoxicated." Disappointed that so many lodge members had not heard about Hoffman's decision and had already gone to work, Orangemen nevertheless were determined to parade, so at 10:30 A.M. they had sent a delegation to invite Newark Orangemen to join the New York procession. But Gideon Lodge No. 10 of Newark's No Surrender District telegraphed Askin that Newark's Orangemen would parade at home. He explained that separate parades "will cover more ground, exert more influence, and redound with more honor to the cause." Then a debate erupted. Why not confront the crowd in Twenty-ninth Street instead of waiting to be attacked? someone proposed. The men decided they were outnumbered and poorly armed for such a fight, so they settled on a parade and sent women and children home to avoid possible danger.[9]

Other visitors came and went. Orangemen believed one was a "Hibernian" spy and threw him out. Then a Seventy-ninth Regiment captain appeared, telling Orangemen that his "Scotch" regiment had asked Shaler for permission to parade with the lodges and protect them. Shaler said he would call on them if necessary. Other encouragement came from an honorary member of Brooklyn's Thirteenth Regiment. He told the men:

8. *Sun* (quote), *Tribune*, *Herald*, and *Times*, July 13.

9. *Herald* ("intoxicated"), *Tribune* (telegram), July 13.

> I am an American Protestant. (Cheers.) I hope you will turn out full numbers, with the American banner at your head. (Cheers.) There will be no interference, Oakey Hall or anybody else to the contrary notwithstanding. (Tremendous applause.) I trust that every man will parade without fear, and show the world that having rights they dare maintain them. (Cheering.) This, brethren, is a conquest over all our enemies, and I beg of you to have no fear. Walk the streets like men, and believe me that you will have the protection of the military, if not the police. (Cheers.)[10]

Shortly before two o'clock someone offered a prayer, the women and children left the hall, and the Orangemen filed downstairs to regroup in Twenty-ninth Street. Askin later told the *Tribune* that all processionists carried pistols hidden under their coats as a precaution. Although the *Times* believed that Orangemen were not otherwise "at all ostentatiously uniformed," its reporter did regret that one member "seemed to expose himself unnecessarily by being, of all the members, the only one attired in a uniform of blue coat, yellow buckskin leggings, and cocked hat, and, to invite an attack, by the exhibition of a pistol in a large holster, conspicuously hung at his belt." The Orangemen unfurled three banners: Sons of Liberty Lodge No. 28 supplied a large silk American flag with the lodge's insignia sewn beneath it; members of Derry Walls Lodge No. 2 hoisted a tall, purple silk banner bearing a picture of Prince Glorious on horseback in the center; and a bannerette, carried by two men, urged in black letters: "American Freemen, Fall In." All were clearly visible for several blocks. Other members carried small Orange flags. Troops in the Eighty-fourth Regiment's Company B apparently were also provocative. An officer of that regiment told the *Star*, in an account confirmed by others, that when Orangemen appeared in Twenty-ninth Street, Company B members placed their caps on bayonets, held them aloft, and cheered in support. Asked to squelch his company's demonstration, a lieutenant replied, "I cannot help the cheering."[11]

Guardsmen completed final arrangements as crowds pushed against police lines. Various regiments marched up Eighth Avenue and took their positions. Hoffman arrived and inspected the alignments, pushing through the dense police cordon that almost blocked

10. *Herald*, *Tribune*, *Times*, and *Sun* (quote), July 13.
11. *Tribune*, July 14; *Times*, *Sun*, and *World*, July 13; *Star*, July 14.

Orangemen from view. "A rough crowd skirted the line established," the *Times* described, "many of whom were perched on housetops, piles of brick, high stoops and wagons, straining their necks eagerly, to get a sight of what was going on within the forbidden ground." The reporter noticed "a gang of ruffians, said to be a party from the Fourteenth Ward under the leadership of one Casey." Tradesmen and shopkeepers slammed shutters and locked their doors. Pushcarts were hurried away from the area.[12]

Then fights broke out. Standing nearby on a pile of loose bricks, a man urged those around him to attack the police. Police at once began clubbing heads and twice cleared Eighth Avenue and Twenty-ninth Street, pushing people into Seventh Avenue or onto nearby sidewalks and occasionally trampling them on horseback. East of Eighth Avenue in Twenty-ninth Street, a *Tribune* reporter "saw three or four lying on the side-walk, and in the middle of the street, who had been knocked down in this way," while a *Herald* writer saw "several fellows, who appeared to be leaders" and who urged "those behind them to 'come on, come on, now's the time,'" similarly clubbed and trampled. Irish-born milliner John Taylor, an Eighth Avenue resident, told a *Sun* reporter two days later that just before the parade began, "a shot was fired from the corner of Twenty-eighth street, or from the roof of Daniel Quinn's livery stable, at No. 338." (Quinn's address, in fact, was 353 Eighth Avenue.) Pointing to the rooftop, he recalled that "a number of men were concealed [there] during the time the parade was forming," hidden from sight by a five-foot-tall sign that spanned the width of the building.[13]

As police cleared the area one more time, Orange grand marshal John Johnston mounted his horse and galloped down the avenue to Twenty-third Street to inspect the route, saluting the police and troops along the way. Johnston returned amid a shower of bricks, shoes, and stones. Taking his place at the head of the parade, Johnston gave the order to start. Someone fired a cannon, a band played "The Star Spangled Banner," and, sometime between 2:30 and 2:45 P.M., the procession began to move.[14]

12. *Times*, July 13.

13. *Times*, July 13; *Tribune*, *Herald*, and *World*, July 13; *Sun*, July 15, 13; testimony of policeman James McGraw, coroner's inquest, in *Herald*, *World*, *Tribune*, and *Times*, July 25. Information on Taylor is from the *Ninth United States Census* (1870), *Population Schedules*, second enumeration.

14. *World*, July 13; *Irish World*, July 22; *Times* and *Herald*, July 13.

2. Police clubbing spectators on Eighth Avenue. *Frank Leslie's Illustrated Newspaper*, July 29, 1871. State Historical Society of Wisconsin.

"Slaughter on Eighth Avenue"

The Orangemen were well-protected. Resting at Twenty-eighth Street, the head of the procession was led by police on foot and on horseback and followed by five Seventh Regiment companies, another police detachment, and some reporters. Twyford's twelve-piece band and some one hundred Orangemen, who came next, were flanked on their left by police and the Eighty-fourth Regiment, on their right by police and the Twenty-second Regiment. More police and the Sixth and Ninth regiments marched behind. Ambulances and mounted and foot police brought up the rear.[15]

Other police and guard units were deployed along the avenue. Shortly before two o'clock, Inspector George Walling had told Brig. Gen. J. M. Varian, who commanded Eighth Avenue guard units, that armed men could be seen on rooftops along the east side of the avenue from Twenty-eighth to Twenty-sixth Street. Accordingly, Varian ordered Seventh Regiment commander Col. Emmons Clark to post five companies along the west side of the avenue, the left line resting at Twenty-eighth Street. "The orders of General Varian were positive and explicit that these companies should fire upon any persons who should make any hostile demonstrations from the windows and house tops on the east side of the avenue," Clark later reported, "and I personally communicated said orders to the captains of the companies." Varian also issued orders to all other guardsmen not to fire unless they were told to do so.[16]

Varian next issued orders nearly thirty minutes later, when the head of the procession had just turned east into Twenty-third Street. At this point he ordered the column to halt so that the Seventh Regiment companies on the west side of the avenue could rejoin the other Seventh companies at the front.[17] Guardsmen opened fire on people along the east side of the avenue only moments later (see Figure 1).

15. *Tribune*, *Sun*, and *World*, July 13; *Irish World*, July 22.

16. Brig. Gen. J. M. Varian to Maj. Gen. Alexander Shaler (New York, July 12), printed in *Herald* (and others), July 22 (hereafter cited as Varian's *Report*); Col. Emmons Clark (Seventh Regiment) to Lt. Col. William Seward, Jr. (Assistant Adjutant General and Chief of Staff, Third Brigade, New York State National Guard) (New York, July 12), printed in *Herald* (and others), July 21, and in Clark, *History of the Seventh Regiment of New York, 1806–1889*, 2 vols. (New York: Regiment, 1890), 2:193–97 (hereafter cited as Clark's *Report*); Porter's *Report* in *World*, July 19.

17. Varian's *Report* in *Herald*, July 22.

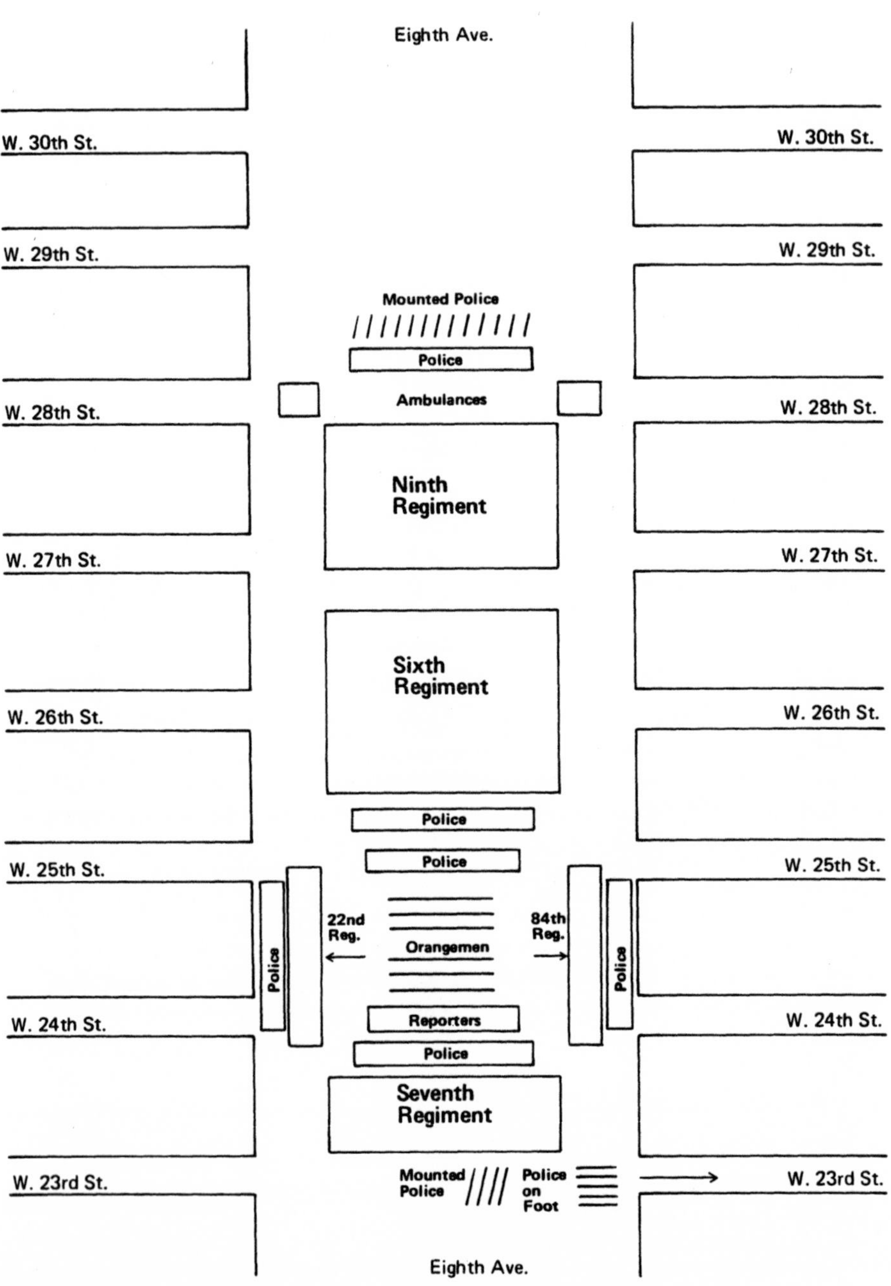

FIGURE 1. Approximate parade alignment when militia began firing. Based on diagrams in the July 13, 1871, *Tribune*, *Sun*, and *World* and the July 22, 1871, *Irish World*.

Many things sparked this attack. It would be instructive to discuss these incidents sequentially, but sources do not permit such precise treatment. Although most of the nearly four dozen accounts pinpointed the locations of violent acts, many did not locate the exact positions of parade contingents when such acts occurred, did not always indicate at whom various objects or pistol shots were directed, and often neglected to mention incidents happening at the same time elsewhere in the avenue. Yet in spite of these limitations, a careful examination of the evidence enables us to reconstruct many important details, and we can occasionally establish where and when specific acts occurred in relation to the first musket blasts.

The band's music touched off the first disturbances. Crowds in Twenty-ninth Street threw paving stones at the Orangemen and the troops. As Orangemen turned into Eighth Avenue from Twenty-ninth Street, their giant purple banner could be seen by people at Twenty-third Street. From sidewalks, windows, and rooftops came shouts of "There they come, the bloody traitors" and "Now we will give them hell, the infernal Englishmen!" There were reports that a man, "tolerably well dressed in broadcloth," hurried into the middle of the street and exclaimed, "Ain't it an outrage, boys? Oh, gorrah! to think that we should have to see it!" One writer saw "many women and children" throwing "missiles" from rooftops, and "boys" and "middle aged men" grabbing up stones, bricks, and "parts of vegetables" from the refuse spilling out from alleys. But another observer, standing at Twenty-sixth Street, claimed that as the parade began, "not a murmur from the crowd was scarcely heard, or a word of defiance uttered, save a few hisses from three or four boys."[18]

In the rush of excitement a careless guardsman accidentally discharged his musket just below Twenty-ninth Street. At the same moment someone fired a pistol and another hurled a bottle from a building at 382 Eighth Avenue. A partially finished structure stood next door on the northeast corner of Twenty-ninth Street, where many Orange taunters reportedly had hurried inside hoping to escape the police. When the first shot was fired, police rushed into the building,

18. *World*, July 13; *Irish World*, July 22; *Herald*, July 13 (crowd descriptions); W. P. (n.p., n.d.) to *Irish World*, July 22 (last quote). Locations of shops and incidents have been reconstructed from *Wilson's Business Directory of New York City* (New York, 1871); from damage claims cited in Appendix B; from the *Ninth United States Census* (1870), *Population Schedules*, second enumeration, for New York City's twentieth and sixteenth wards; and from reporters' notes and other "eyewitness" accounts.

clubbed as many people as they could reach, and quickly cleared the area. Meanwhile, another shot rang out from the southeast corner of the street, where a group of boys was perched on a wooden awning. A *Herald* informant claimed to have seen a boy throw a brick at the Orangemen and someone else toss a whiskey bottle. Both objects missed their marks. "Then some foolish man in a militia regiment stepped out of his rank," the observer went on, "and fired his musket into the awning where the rowdy boys were congregated." The shot did no damage, but it angered the witness because the guardsman "had received no order whatever, and was simply endeavoring to commit murder."[19]

It seems clear that some militia regiments not only expected trouble; they also helped to provoke it. We already have noted that members of the Eighty-fourth's Company B saluted Orangemen at Lamartine Hall. Visiting Sixth Regiment units before the parade, a Brooklyn reporter was told by apprehensive troops that they would shoot the first Irishman who fired at them. And Eighty-fourth members again caused a disturbance just after the parade began. Hoping to exonerate his own Company C, James P. Ross complained to the *Herald* and *World* that "as soon as the procession moved[,] Company D, which was in our rear, cheered for the Orangemen." His company informed Lt. Col. Cornelius B. Mitchell "in the most positive and emphatic terms that we would not march if such conduct was allowed in the regiment."[20]

Mitchell stopped the demonstration at once, but by then the commotion brought crowds of people off the sidewalks and into the streets. So the procession came to a halt after it had moved only a short distance. As police tried to clear a path, people pelted Orangemen and others with "bottles, paving stones, and other missiles." An Orangeman later claimed that he could see pistols being readied in windows and that even poisoned sandwiches had been thrown at them![21]

The parade resumed, the band this time playing "Columbia, the gem of the Ocean" (Twyford had been told to play only "American"

19. *Sun*, July 13. An account of the fight at the northeast corner of Twenty-ninth Street was given by a *Brooklyn Union* writer to the *Sun*, July 14; see "Personal Narrative" in *Herald*, July 13.

20. *Brooklyn Union* writer's account in *Sun*, July 14; James P. Ross (n.p., n.d.) to *Herald*, July 16, and to *World*, July 17.

21. *Sun*, July 13; I.F.R. Lodge, 622, E. R., Ireland (n.p., n.d.) to *Sun*, July 15.

tunes), but the Orangemen were greeted by still more hoots and jeers. At the corner of Twenty-eighth Street another group of young men watched events from a wooden awning extending far over the sidewalk. They threw several stones and fired at least two shots as the Orangemen came into view. As the boys scrambled off the awning into a nearby house and Orangemen passed the Twenty-eighth Street corner, people fired another barrage of stones from tenement house rooftops along the block from Twenty-eighth to Twenty-seventh Street. According to the *Sun*, firing erupted from "a large body of Hibernians" who were "armed with rifles" and "were firing on the Orangemen and their escorts." Seventh Regiment commander Clark omitted reference to "Hibernians" in his report, but he did confirm the *Sun*'s account that "occasional shots were fired and stones were thrown at the Orangemen and the troops acting as their immediate guard."[22]

The first militia volley seems to have occurred soon after the attacks between Twenty-eighth and Twenty-seventh streets, with the front of the procession perhaps just at or below Twenty-sixth Street. An unnamed Varian staff member told the *Herald* and *World* that just as Orangemen reached Twenty-seventh Street, they "received a shower of shots and other missiles from the windows." One *World* reporter claimed that someone standing at the southeast corner of that street fired a shot; another *World* writer heard a pistol crack and saw a small puff of smoke come from a third-story window. These incidents may have occurred at different times. But from all accounts, it appears that Seventh Regiment soldiers, stationed along the west side of the avenue from Twenty-eighth Street to at least the middle of the block between Twenty-seventh and Twenty-sixth streets, responded to sniper shots. Varian's aide reported that several Seventh men returned about six shots at the southeast Twenty-seventh Street corner windows. But a *World* reporter saw guardsmen fire at a person on the roof of the same house, and "a beardless young man" calmly raise his musket, fire one shot without orders, and reload. A *Sun* reporter said he saw something worse, although Clark

22. On Twyford's orders, see James D. Askin interview in *Tribune*, July 14. Shots and stones near Twenty-eighth Street were reported by the *Brooklyn Union* writer in *Sun*, July 14. See also *Tribune*'s account, July 13. Descriptions of incidents between Twenty-eighth and Twenty-seventh streets are found in two separate *Sun* stories, July 13; in the *World*, July 13; and in Clark's *Report* in the *Herald*, July 21, and in his *History of the Seventh Regiment*.

flatly denied this account. He claimed that after the shots from tenement houses, soldiers suddenly and without orders blasted the houses, killing at once some twenty people. Clark, however, was adamant that his troops strictly followed orders. Whenever "missiles came from the upper windows or housetops of the buildings opposite the position of the five companies of this regiment," he stated in his report, "shots were fired in return by individual members of said companies, under the immediate direction of their officers. At no period was any volley fired by any company of this regiment, and the individual shots fired were only at persons engaged in some hostile act."[23]

Assaults on Orangemen and soldiers increased as the parade neared Twenty-third Street. Seven witnesses—three of whom testified at the coroner's inquest—told of seeing a woman dash out from Adolphus Schinkel's bakery at 324 Eighth Avenue, pick up a garbage or ash barrel from the curb, and throw its contents at Orangemen and a Sixth Regiment soldier. When she repeated this act, the guardsman clubbed her head with the butt of his musket, pushed her back onto the sidewalk, and struck a bystander who came to her aid.[24]

Meanwhile, there was much activity near Twenty-sixth Street. According to Walling, "a dense crowd, including many women, had collected," and "it was with the greatest difficulty that my men could clear the way for the Orangemen, who were obliged to come to a halt." Almost at once, someone threw "a cobblestone" from the southwest corner of the street, while simultaneously shots rang out from housetops on the northeast and southeast corners, and people threw other objects at the parade. "I saw a man from a small crowd in front throw two or three stones in rapid succession at the Orangemen moving in the centre of the procession," a Dr. Van der Weyde described, "and then he and the crowd ran off, and created a temporary panic among the rest, who also ran." As police chased portions of the crowd on the east side of the avenue into Twenty-sixth Street

23. For Varian's staff member's account, see *Herald* and *World*, July 15. The two *World* versions are in the July 13 edition. See also *Sun*, July 13; and Clark's *Report* in *Herald*, July 21, and in his *History of the Seventh Regiment*.

24. See the testimony of Aaron Parker, Abraham Drake, and Charles (or Christian) Smith, coroner's inquest, in *Herald*, *World*, *Tribune*, and *Times*, July 25; the interview with Samuel Shottick in *Herald*, July 15; the account of William H. Carr in *Tribune*, July 15; a Mr. Atwater's description in *Herald*, July 13; and Col. Frank W. Sterry (Sixth Regiment) to Col. William H. Chesebrough (New York, July 13), printed in *Tribune*, July 21.

and finally into Seventh Avenue, one woman, apparently undaunted by the panic, broke through the Eighty-fourth's flank and began tearing regalia off an Orangeman. *Herald* and *Tribune* reporters who saw her attack, and one of whom described the woman as "ferocious-looking," saw her pushed back to the curb at the front of a bayonet, shrieking and raging all the way. "Almost at the same instant," the *Herald's* writer continued in a classic caricature of a crowd member, "a half-grown boy, of a slouchy, pockmarked and wretched guise, almost idiotic in expression," took from his coat "a large paving stone as big as his double fist" and threw it at the Orangemen. The stone hit no one, and the boy dashed behind Christian Smith's saloon for more ammunition. Shutters and windows slammed closed, still more bricks crashed to the pavement, and Seventh or Ninth Regiment members reportedly fired at the upper stories of houses on the east corners of Twenty-sixth Street and then fell back along the west side to reload.[25]

Rushing into a doorway at the corner of Twenty-sixth Street to escape panicked bystanders, Van der Weyde peered around the corner and heard what he thought was a shot coming from the Twenty-fifth Street corner. Another witness—this one standing on the south-east corner of Twenty-fifth Street—may have confirmed the doctor's account. John H. Banner told the coroner's jury that he saw a man, dressed in a linen suit and wearing a straw hat with a broad black band, fire a revolver into the air and then dash east to Seventh Avenue. Banner mentioned no other incidents at that corner and said he saw no assailants hiding on rooftops, but clothier Peter D. Brower's vantage point gave him a wider view of events. His account added much more. From his second-story window at 307 Eighth Avenue (on the west side of the street), Brower heard several shots fired and saw many stones thrown at the military on both sides of Eighth Avenue. He thought the military began firing six or eight minutes later, but Banner, whose hat was shot off by a musket ball, believed only thirty seconds elapsed. Since neither man identified which regiment fired, it is possible that Brower referred to the Eighty-fourth's fusillade, which occurred after the head of the parade reached Twenty-third Street, whereas Banner's hat was lost to sporadic action by

25. George W. Walling, *Recollections of a New York Chief of Police* (New York: Caxton Book Concern, 1887), 158; *Tribune*, July 13. Van der Weyde's account is in *World*, July 13. See the interview with clothier Samuel Shottick in *Herald*, July 15; Ex-Army Officer (New York, July 14) to *Herald*, July 16; *Herald*, July 13; and *Tribune*, July 14.

guardsmen attempting to return shots at nearby buildings. This version is also suggested by a report of an Eighty-fourth captain who said that his men were fired upon just below Twenty-fifth Street (perhaps near Bryant's butter store) as the company's thirty-one members briefly slowed their pace to enable Orangemen to catch up. Apparently as they were doing so, police surgeon Beach said "an old boot and tin kettle . . . [were] thrown down from some roof into the midst of the Orangemen." Police crashed into the crowd, opening head wounds with their clubs, "shots were fired," and more stones streamed down from rooftops and windows, some of them hitting policemen and soldiers. Beach claimed the militia fired soon afterward, and Van der Weyde—still back at Twenty-sixth Street—claimed to have seen members of an unidentified regiment fire a volley at the Twenty-fifth Street intersection. Just south of where the physician huddled, Ninth Regiment soldiers then aimed their muskets in his direction. Van der Weyde was pushed inside the door as people scrambled past him and into the cellar and coal hole.[26]

As the lead units neared Twenty-third Street, Orangemen were still about a block and a half behind. Most of the Eight Avenue violence committed by all parties occurred during these last two blocks. Five shopkeepers between Twenty-fifth and Twenty-fourth streets reported many assaults on Orangemen by persons in buildings or on sidewalks. Butter and cheese dealer T. W. Roche claimed he saw "many scoundrels" loading revolvers in the alleyways leading to tenement houses; he believed there was a conspiracy of "several gangs of rowdies" to wait along the avenue and shoot at Orangemen through gaps in the guard's left column. He saw "several shots" fired in this manner and said that when troops began firing, a man rushed into his shop bragging that he had unloaded three rounds at Orangemen and soldiers. Roche, tinsmith John Koehler, tea merchant Joseph Anguin, Patrick J. Meagher, a used furniture dealer, and others all agreed that "two Irish girls, dressed in white" repeatedly fired revolvers at Orangemen from the upper windows of a "dingy cream color" building at 284½ Eighth Avenue. Moreover, in confectioner Henry N. Helfst's store at 317 Eighth Avenue, "a young man" al-

26. Van der Weyde in *World*, July 13; testimonies of John H. Banner and Peter D. Brower, coroner's inquest, in *Herald*, *World*, *Tribune*, and *Times*, July 25; Eighty-fourth Regiment Capt. John G. Norman (New York, July 14) to *Sun*, July 18 (Norman is not listed as a captain in the roster of men on duty on July 12 in New York State Adjutant-General's Office, *Annual Report* [Albany, 1872], 103); *Times*, July 14 (Beach).

leged that four shots were fired from the top of Koehler's store—the same address where the girls were seen shooting. Anguin added that people fired more weapons and threw bricks and stones from rooftops two and three doors from his shop and that he saw "one man deliberately draw a Derringer" and fire it without being caught. George Walling recalled that "stones and other missiles were now thrown from the housetops" at Twenty-fifth Street. Many struck Ninth Regiment soldiers. Dodging these objects, police captain Joseph Petty and his men charged the crowds at the corner and drove them into Seventh Avenue.[27]

Eighty-fourth Regiment commander Cornelius B. Mitchell reported generally that near Twenty-fourth Street "several shots were fired from the windows and housetops injuring three members of this command," but other observers provided more detailed accounts. A Mr. Audley, a clerk in George Andrus's drugstore on the southeast corner of Twenty-fourth Street, later said that the militia's behavior was justified because troops were pelted with stones and bricks as they approached that intersection. Moreover, both Audley and Dr. C. L. Lordly, who was also at the drugstore, said that people fired shots from windows above Sullivan and Green's dry goods store at 275 Eighth Avenue and from atop other buildings between Twenty-fourth and Twenty-fifth streets. Several other witnesses saw two shots fired in front of George McMurtry's grocery. McMurtry himself heard explosions there, and furniture dealer Daniel Laughlin said he saw someone ignite a loud blast while he (Laughlin) stood on a chair in front of his store a half block away. A *Sun* reporter also saw the incidents. Police reportedly arrested the assailant. Yet other *Sun* writers said that one or two men fired a revolver from an awning over McMurtry's store and that both were either shot or chased away by the police and soldiers but not arrested.[28]

Moments later, bricks and other objects showered down on the parade from a housetop on the northeast corner of Twenty-fourth Street and from adjoining houses, while at the same time, "a man dressed in a light suit" fired a pistol from the sidewalk. Still another

27. Accounts are in *Times*, July 14; *Herald*, July 14, 15; and Walling, *Recollections*, 158.

28. Lt. Col. Cornelius B. Mitchell (Eighty-fourth Regiment) to Maj. Gen. [Alexander] Shaler (New York, July 12), printed in *Herald* (and others), July 21 (hereafter cited as Mitchell's *Report*); Audley interviewed by *Times*, July 15; Lordly's account in *Herald*, July 14. See testimonies of George McMurtry and David Laughlin in the coroner's inquest as published in *Herald*, *World*, *Tribune*, and *Times*, July 25; *Sun*, July 13–15.

person reportedly fired from an upper-story window. One of the bullets was said to have narrowly missed Orangeman John Johnston but hit instead an Eighty-fourth soldier. Police sergeant James M. Miller, who lived at that intersection, said he had to call other policemen to help him protect his family from people escaping angry guardsmen and the police.[29]

Then horror struck. In front of Andrus's drugstore across the street, Audley and Lordly watched as an unidentified man "put a pistol" to the head of a "poorly dressed" woman who was waving a white handkerchief with yellow-orange borders at Orangemen just a few feet a way. The blast blew off the top of her head. Lordly claimed to have kept the bloodied handkerchief as grizzly evidence for the coroner's inquest, but the official report mentioned no such death. The *Sun* reported that a Mrs. Linnahan had "one finger on each hand and [the] top of [her] head shot off." Yet because of the additional mutilations, it is unlikely that Linnahan was the same person Audley and Lordly saw.[30]

Scores were killed and injured within no more than the next five minutes. The parade stopped as the front ranks reached Twenty-third Street; people again fired bullets and objects at Orangemen and soldiers; and then the avenue exploded with the sound of musket fire, shattering glass, and screams. As police and soldiers just began turning into Twenty-third Street, cheering "ladies and men" waving white handkerchiefs greeted them, but so did a large paving stone thrown by a boy from the corner. Police and a few guardsmen dashed after the boy. Varian halted the column and ordered the five Seventh Regiment companies in the rear to the front.[31]

In the subsequent confusion, crowds of people rushed into Eighth Avenue from cross-street blocks between Eighth and Seventh avenues. Others dashed toward Twenty-third Street from blocks farther north. Someone on horseback (perhaps it was Orange marshal Johnston) reportedly rode up and down the entire column and was struck

29. See the "eyewitness" descriptions by an Eighth Avenue businessman in *Sun*, July 15, and by an unidentified "Gentleman," who was a former Seventh Regiment member, in *Tribune*, July 13; and also *Herald*, July 13.

30. Testimony of Dr. C. L. Lordly and Oliver Timms, coroner's inquest, as reported in *Herald*, *World*, *Tribune*, and *Times*, July 25. Lordly made the same statement to the *Brooklyn Daily Eagle*, July 13. The incident was also mentioned in the *Tribune*, July 13. On Linnahan, see *Sun*, July 14, and Appendix B.

31. *Irish World*, July 22; *Herald*, July 13; Varian's *Report* in *Herald*, July 21; the account of an unidentified member of Company B, Seventh Regiment, in *Tribune*, July 15.

on the shoulder by "an old shoe." Many men stood on the roof of a four-story building on the northeast corner of Twenty-fourth Street. Gaping men, women, and children filled the building's windows. As the men on top fired shots and threw stones, pistols crackled from the dense crowd in Twenty-fourth Street east of Eighth Avenue, from inside Bruce and McQuinton's plumbing shop, and from the east side of the avenue at Twenty-fifth Street. Neighbors reported seeing a Mrs. Arnold shoot a revolver from a middle second-floor window at 288½ Eighth Avenue. Painter John H. Schmitt of 292 Eighth Avenue told the *Sun* "that just previous to the firing by the troops, he saw a man with a red moustache" shoot from atop an awning at 290 Eighth Avenue. Frightened soldiers shouted warnings to others, and just then a rifle exploded from the second story between Twenty-sixth and Twenty-fifth streets (perhaps at Number 310), the musket ball ripping off the tassel from Ninth Regiment lieutenant colonel Charles R. Braine's shako.[32]

The final assaults that culminated in the Eighty-fourth's firing occurred at the southeast corner of Twenty-fourth Street, probably at the same moments as the above incidents. By all accounts, several people at that corner committed provocative acts. Yet the militia's undisciplined behavior was sparked not only by these attacks but also by the commands of one frightened Orangeman and one Eighty-fourth Regiment officer.

Two pistol shots rang out from above Cregan's liquor store on the northeast corner. At the same time, a woman hurled "a piece of crockery" from the roof above Dan Ryan's liquor store on the southeast corner. Someone else fired from a window in the same building. In front of Ryan's store, people threw bricks and other objects from an awning and a newsstand. An *Irish World* observer said that "a crowd of boys" fired revolvers at Orangemen and soldiers "from behind three milk wagons which were standing near the sidewalk." Shots hit two Eighty-fourth guardsmen, a brick opened a large

32. *Irish World*, July 22; *Herald*, July 13. On the Twenty-fourth and Twenty-fifth Street incidents, see *Tribune* and *Sun*, July 13, and policeman Timm's coroner's inquest testimony in *Herald*, *World*, *Tribune*, and *Times*, July 25. Baker Aaron Parker mentioned the shot from the plumber's shop in his inquest account, as reported in the same papers. The *Sun*'s item on Mrs. Arnold (July 14) was partially corroborated in the *Irish World* (July 22), which did not identify the woman but gave similar details. Schmitt's story is in *Sun*, July 14. See also *World*, July 13; and Seventh Regiment Private A. C. Evangelides (n.p., n.d.) to *Herald*, July 16.

wound in the head of Company K captain James Douglass, and Orangemen and other soldiers were hit too. As someone quickly ordered the Orangemen to lie down, police captain Joseph Petty and his men darted after the boys into a nearby alley, toward Seventh Avenue. Other police charged crowds on all eastside corners of Twenty-fourth Street. More pistols popped. Stones pelted Orangemen even as they lay on the ground. One Orangeman, himself struck on the ear by a stone, explained what happened next: "I looked up and saw Capt. Douglas's head and face streaming with blood. I shouted, 'fire a volley, and it will frighten the murderous scoundrels.' Then an order came beside me, from some one in the Eighty-fourth, and a volley was fired down that street toward the mob." While the Orangeman did not identify who gave the order to fire, others maintained it was Douglass, and still others claimed that *no* order was given. All agreed, however, that the troops acted without specific orders from Varian. One *World* reporter even suggested that all regiment and company officers reacted spontaneously: "In clear, distinct tones were heard the orders of the officers of the regiments, 'Ready——Aim——Fire!' and the Eighty-fourth Regiment was the first to pour volley upon volley into the mob of rioters."[33]

In his official report, Colonel Mitchell was vague about his Eighty-fourth's Eight Avenue behavior. He said only that "it was an utter impossibility to prevent" the firing and that he used his "utmost exertion to check the movement on the part of the troops" once it began—an action verified by Pvt. James P. Ross, who later bitterly denounced his regiment's behavior but did report seeing Mitchell try to restore order by waving his sword. Shaler later accepted Mitchell's account and said the troops fired only after they had been attacked and hurt. "It is the opinion of the most experienced officers of the police force and the military present," he said in his annual report, "that the troops did not fire any too soon; that, in a very few minutes more, it would have been difficult, if not impossible, to

33. For incidents on the northeast and southeast corners of Twenty-fourth Street, and for Douglass's injury, see *Sun*, July 14; *Brooklyn Union* reporter's account in ibid.; report by an unidentified Varian staffer in *Herald*, July 15; *Times*, July 13; Lordly's account in *Herald*, July 14; *Irish World*, July 22; Walling, *Recollections*, 158; W. P. (n.p., n.d.) to *Irish World*, July 22; Anguin's account in *Times*, July 14; and *World*, July 13. See also the Orangeman's letter, I.F.R. Lodge, 622, E. R., Ireland (n.d., n.p.) to *Sun*, July 15. Douglass's action was mentioned by Anguin and James G. Hitchcock in *Times*, July 14; by *Irish World*, July 22; by Lordly in *Herald*, July 13; and by *Times* and *World*, July 13 (another account in the *World* made the general indictment of officers' orders).

3. Ninth and Eighty-fourth regiments firing on the crowd at Eighth Avenue and Twenty-fifth Street. From a sketch by A. Berghaus. *Frank Leslie's Illustrated Newspaper*, July 29, 1871. State Historical Society of Wisconsin.

overpower the mob, and that the lives lost at Eighth Avenue and Twenty-fourth Street saved the sacrifice of a much greater number at some other point."[34]

Yet Shaler glossed over details of the carnage in Eighth Avenue. The first musketry blast was directed at the upper stories of buildings and sidewalk crowds on the northeast corner of Twenty-fourth Street. "Not a moment's warning was given," one *Irish World* reporter accused, "nor was the volley preceded by an order for the crowd to disperse." The sudden outburst trapped the police in a crossfire, as they were charging the crowd at the same corner, and sent them sprawling onto the pavement along with innocent bystanders and those who, only moments earlier, had hurled epithets or worse. Perhaps mistaking Douglass's order to his company for a general license to fire, other Eighty-fourth troops quickly shot into crowds of people dashing for cover. Heavy fire also came from portions of the Sixth, Twenty-second, Ninth, and the remnants of the Seventh, then on the way to the front between Twenty-sixth and Twenty-fifth streets. Windows shattered everywhere. Pieces of brick fell to the ground as errant minié balls crashed into buildings. These volleys, which "lasted several minutes," were described by a *Sun* writer as being "indiscriminate, reckless, pointed at no one in particular, but . . . all the more terrible for that." He found it "remarkable" that almost all of the shooting was "directed against the people and houses on the east side of the street," because some of "the first shots had come from McMurty's [sic] grocery store on the west." Still another *Sun* reporter said that "many fired wildly, shooting into the buildings, against the walls, the windows, or the air, and but few taking aim."[35]

Calling its account of the violence "Slaughter on Eighth Avenue," the *Irish World* emphasized that much of the militia fire was purposeful and not random. Believing that some troops fired "indiscriminately into the windows," the paper's reporter claimed that "others appeared to take a more deadly aim, and fired directly into the crowd of men, women and children, mowing them down in a shocking manner." According to a C. Merritt, four men fired a "small

34. Mitchell's and Clark's *Reports* in *Herald*, July 21 (it was Clark who claimed that no shots were fired by the five Seventh Regiment companies under his command at the front of the procession); Shaler's *Report*, dated December 1, 1871, 33; Pvt. James P. Ross (n.p., n.d.) to *Herald* and *World*, July 16.

35. *Irish World*, July 22; *Sun*, July 13, 14. See also *World* and *Tribune*, July 13, 14.

cannon" in front of Appel's saloon at 292 Eighth Avenue. The shot added to the panic. Merritt joined several others who leaped through a broken window into a building at the Twenty-fifth Street corner. Elsewhere, dozens of people fell wounded or were killed outright. Others frantically sought safety in nearby buildings, alleys, or basement stairways. And some just huddled on the pavement, risking more militia fire or being trampled by screaming and terrified people. "The scene was rendered all the more terrible by the mounted police," a stunned *Herald* reporter recalled later, "who at this point took advantage of the panic, and, dashing down the streets ahead of the procession, rode roughshod into every crowd they met on the corners."[36]

Trapped with the police at Twenty-fourth Street when the troops fired, Omaha physician Edward H. Clark fell to the ground, was struck in a boot by a musket ball, and was covered by two fallen wounded policeman and a dead woman. The woman—perhaps Mrs. Linnahan—had been shot through her temples, abdomen, and hands. Another woman fell across Deputy U.S. Marshal H. S. Russell as he lay on his stomach. Two policemen reportedly were shot as they and Captain Petty frantically tried to stop militia volleys.[37]

Elsewhere, a shower of rifle balls blasted the awning above 290 Eighth Avenue, where the red-moustached man had fired his revolver. Another volley, aimed at Mrs. Arnold, blew out the glass in her window and riddled the front of the building, but it apparently missed Arnold and a man on the awning. Others were not as fortunate. Seventy-two-year-old Philip J. Ackerman, a retired shoe manufacturer living with his family on the northeast corner of Twenty-fifth Street, was shot through the chest by a minié ball as he checked on the safety of a fourth-floor neighbor. Just after leaving his paper collar business in Twenty-sixth Street, James A. Clark was wounded in his right thigh and arm. Irish-born Thomas Dugdale and Patrick Slattery, who like Clark later died from their wounds, by all accounts were innocent bystanders. Dugdale had watched the parade from the

36. *Irish World*, July 22. Merritt's account is in *Sun*, July 13. General descriptions of the crowd's panic can be found in *Times*, *Tribune*, *Sun*, *Herald*, and *World*, July 13.

37. *Herald*, July 13; Clark's account in *Times*, July 13; Russell's story in *Sun*, July 13. On the police, see the interview with an unidentified Eighty-fourth Regiment officer in *Herald*, July 15, and *Sun*, July 13, and the *Brooklyn Union* staffer's account in *Sun*, July 14; "An Eye Witness" (n.p., n.d.) to *Sun*, July 18; and a policeman's remarks as reported in *Irish World*, July 22.

steps of the Utah House, where militia fire tore into his left arm and breast. A minié ball pierced Slattery's lung as he returned from a nearby job. Schoolboys Thomas McCormack and Thomas Spring were shot in the back and groin, respectively. Spring bled to death in twenty minutes, but McCormack died at once. Ship steward Richard Douce, a black man, also bled to death. Germans William Hartung, Conrad Sieger, and Frederick Hiners were killed by chest wounds. And butcher Charles H. Pettit was killed by a single ball as he and an uncle were about to enter Sarah Green's Twenty-fifth Street furniture store in search of goods for Pettit's forthcoming marriage.[38]

Soldiers killed many others that afternoon. Some were Irish immigrants. Laborers John Riley, Morris Holway, John Mullen, Patrick Monaghan, John Lavery, Michael O'Shea, Timothy Sullivan (a hod carrier), and Michael McCormack all died in the first militia blast, but their exact location when the procession halted is unknown. All but McCormack died immediately from head wounds. Immigrants Michael Kelly (a quarryman), William Tigh, John A. Whiteside, and Walter J. Scott were killed by chest or abdomen wounds. Richard McCummings and James McDougal also were shot in the chest. Fifteen-year-old Hannah Hanby was shot as she watched the parade. She died two days later. Sarah Kenney succumbed to a skull fracture, most likely caused by a musket ball. Coachman William McGrath's left arm was so badly shattered by a musket ball it had to be amputated that night at Bellevue Hospital. He died from "exhaustion" on July 14. Joseph Love lingered just long enough to reach Mount Sinai Hospital with a ball in his head. Another minié ball entered Dennis McMahon's right hip and then ripped its way through his abdomen. He too died later. But thirteen-year-old Patrick Maualean was taken directly to the morgue with pieces of his back and a musket ball lodged in a lung.[39]

As the white smoke from National Guard muskets slowly lifted into the air after the final volley, the streets were suddenly quiet—except for the groans of those who lay injured or dying on the hot pavement. Stunned and shocked, people gazed for some moments at the unforgettable sight. Then, perhaps realizing by nothing more than

38. Schmitt's account of the red-moustached man and the Arnold incident are in *Sun*, July 14. On the deaths, see Appendix B.

39. See Appendix B.

instinct that the fighting was over, they began drifting back into the avenue from side streets and buildings to help whom they could. Some shrieked in horror when they recognized relatives or friends in the carnage. Rivulets of blood began to run slowly down the gutter. Irish women and a few priests knelt beside the dead and dying. One woman reportedly collected several bonnets bedecked with green ribbons from the grieving women, flaunted them in the troops' faces, and shouted defiantly, "Down with the Orangemen!" Between Twenty-fourth and Twenty-fifth streets, at a window that had been shattered by a minié ball, a young woman appeared and hysterically waved a white handkerchief as she cried for help from those below. Fearing another round of musket fire, some of the wounded tried to drag themselves into alleyways or down stone basement steps, occasionally slipping on the blood-covered sidewalks or stumbling over bodies. A few trudged toward Seventh Avenue in Twenty-fifth and Twenty-sixth streets. Banging on neighborhood doors, they begged for help from terrified residents who had heard the shooting and were suddenly confronted by people with parts of their bodies shot off. To one *Times* reporter, the scene just after the militia volleys was, in all its gruesome details, "a panorama of blood, a vista of gore, an arena of agony."[40]

Witnesses reported seeing as many as sixteen bodies at Twenty-fourth Street. There, "a man with a fearful wound in the head, which covered his face with blood, writhed in agony for some moments, and then slowly crept to the door-step, and feebly strove to raise himself upon it, presenting, as he did so, a full view of his ghastly injuries." The same *Tribune* writer counted eleven bodies, "two or three" of which "were piled together as they had fallen." Ten bodies were taken into Andrus's drugstore. On the northeast corner, a *Times* writer found parts of a head in a pool of blood on a basement stairway leading to a restaurant. On the corner itself a *Sun* reporter saw "the bodies of seven men and one woman," whose "wounds were mostly in the head" and who "presented a sickening sight." "The street literally ran with blood," he continued, "and for fully ten minutes nothing was done for the dying ones." Other witnesses counted from one to sixteen bodies between Twenty-fourth and Twenty-fifth streets. One may have been Joseph Garity. His sister, Margaret, later found him at Twenty-fourth Street shot through the heart.

40. *World*, *Tribune*, *Herald*, and *Times*, July 13; *Irish World*, July 22.

Lying on the southeast corner of the street, his right jaw and half of his tongue ripped off by a minié ball, was William T. Latimer, a forty-nine-year-old Brooklyn resident whose stationery business had brought him to the area. A second ball had smashed Latimer's neck. Blood ran off his body onto Owen Stanton, a young Irish immigrant whose own leg wound bled badly. Two musket rounds had fractured Michael Leahy's arms. Another ball had lodged in Augustus P. Gilbert's back. All four men later died at Bellevue.[41]

"At the corner of Twenty-fifth Street," a *Sun* writer recounted, "the walk ran with blood. To pass, you had to pick your way among the corpses." C. Merritt emerged from Appel's saloon to find six bodies lying where he had been standing only shortly before. The *Sun* reporter found several dead and many wounded in side-street houses and backyards. At various places in Twenty-fifth Street he spoke with John Rourke, John Matthews, Patrick Ahern, James W. Firehock, and Thomas Hugh, all of whom suffered leg or hip wounds. He also saw Jeremiah Maloney's body. Maloney had been shot in the jaw, and other accounts suggest the young Irish laborer survived. At least fourteen musket balls smashed the front of Bryant's butter store, and many others killed four men and fatally wounded Peter McCaffrey. All of the men tumbled downstairs toward a basement barber shop. The steps "were smeared and slippery with human blood and brains," a shaken *Herald* writer vividly remembered, "while the landing beneath was covered two inches deep with clotted gore, pieces of brain and the half digested contents of a human stomach and intestines. Floating in this horrid puddle was an old, low-crowned felt hat, such as laborers wear." The "window sills, shutters and doors" of Bryant's store "were speckled with bullet marks and splashed with blood," he continued. "The sidewalk in front of the door was thickly coated with a red mud, and the clammy way in which it stuck to one's boots made living men's hearts cold and sick." Farther up the avenue, four men were killed in front of Patrick O'Shea's oyster bar at 308 Eighth Avenue, several bodies were seen at Twenty-sixth Street, and as many as six reportedly were

41. *Tribune*, *Times*, *Sun*, and *Herald*, July 13; Lordly's testimony at the coroner's inquest, as reported in *Herald*, *World*, *Tribune*, and *Times*, July 25. See also David Laughlin's testimony in the same sources; and other descriptions in the *Irish World*, July 22. The deaths are described, and the sources cited, in Appendix B.

stacked up at Twenty-seventh Street (one with six bullets in the head). Another three were found at the corner leading to Seventh Avenue.[42]

The accuracy of such accounts cannot be determined, but surely many people died. Some of those who were killed and wounded, and whose names are listed in Appendix B but not mentioned here, may have been among those seen by reporters and others between Twenty-fifth and Twenty-seventh streets. We know for certain only that Daniel Mulvey, an Irish-born laborer whose home was on East Twenty-sixth Street, was killed instantly while he watched the parade at the Twenty-sixth Street corner. Others, like Charles M. Keltenbach, Benjamin Franklin Erskine, and Peter Sherry died in following days from severe musket wounds. A Sixth Regiment volley sent three-to-five balls into Keltenbach's arms and back. Other regiment shots tore open leg wounds in Erskine and Sherry.[43]

National Guardsmen were not responsible for all of the civilian deaths and injuries. Lordly and Audley did not describe the "woman" they claimed to have seen shot from behind at Twenty-fourth Street, but it is unlikely that the person they saw was Mary York. Warned by her parents to remain inside her West Eighteenth Street house, the twelve-year-old girl was persuaded by a neighbor woman to join her for the parade. Wearing an orange scarf—a family heirloom—York and her friend escaped the Eighty-fourth's barrage at Twenty-fourth Street. But according to the woman, York was killed moments later by an unidentified but obviously incensed man, wearing a green ribbon, who shot her in the back of the head.[44]

The barrage of objects and shots fired by people along Eighth Avenue took their greatest toll among the police and guard troops. Only one Orangeman, John W. Storey, was reported wounded, and the Gideon Orange Lodge later claimed that no one by that name was a member of the order. Two policemen died from unknown causes. Henry Ford died on July 12 at the Twenty-ninth Precinct station. Patrolman John Hamil died on August 28. Of the thirty-four other police casualties, five were sunstroke victims, one was thrown from a horse and another from a coach, one somehow suffered a bayonet

42. *Sun*, July 13; *Herald*, July 13, 14. See also Appendix B for more information on the wounded and killed; and *Sun*, July 13, for Merritt's account.

43. *Herald, Sun, Tribune*, and *Times*, July 13. See also Appendix B.

44. Appendix B.

wound, and still another was struck in an elbow by a spent militia ball. Twenty other policemen were injured by stones, clubs, or rocks, and four were wounded by gunshot. The cause of one other policeman's injury could not be determined.[45]

Twenty-four guardsmen also were injured, although Shaler's official report listed just thirteen. Many of them suffered body bruises or cuts from stones and bricks. Three Ninth Regiment soldiers died from gunshot wounds. Henry Paige, the business manager of James Fisk's Grand Opera House, was fixing his musket when a bullet ripped off a portion of his head. Samuel Wyatt was shot in the abdomen. Walter R. Prior died on July 17 from complications associated with a fractured leg. Yet some military injuries, and even perhaps one death, may have occurred when troops accidentally fired into other regiments. Just after the Eighty-fourth's first volley, some Ninth members broke ranks and dashed to the west side of Eighth Avenue near Twenty-seventh Street. Crashing through the line of Seventh companies marching to the front, Ninth soldiers turned their muskets toward the east side and began firing indiscriminately, thus apparently shooting through both the Seventh companies and the remainder of their own regiment still in the street. It is not known how many of the five soldiers who were wounded by gunfire were shot by fellow guardsmen. Of the other injured soldiers, a Twenty-second sergeant was moderately bruised in a struggle with an angry Irishman over his musket. Ninth Regiment captain Bird W. Spencer was jumped and struck on the head by someone hiding in his wagon. Col. Jim Fisk also was injured. "Prince Erie," as Fisk was known, had a memorable, if inglorious, day. After stopping the Erie ferries as Hoffman had ordered, Fisk returned to his Grand Opera House, donned his sword and coat, mounted a horse, and tried to find his regiment nearby in the avenue. "The crowd came for me," he explained. "I was set upon by the mob with stones and brickbats and pitched into the gutter. When I got up my coat was torn off and [I] found I was wounded." Fisk said he then limped into a nearby house, disguised himself in "a big overcoat and hat," and leaped over a backyard fence. There he found a waiting coach (some claimed Jay Gould was in it), drove to the Hoffman House, and from there to the Pavonia ferry, where he hired a tug for Sandy Hook.[46]

45. Appendix B.

46. Injuries and deaths are cited in Appendix B. On the troop disorder, see the reports

General Varian and the police showed no concern for the scores of casualties. Leaving even his own men behind, Varian quickly ordered the Eighty-fourth to the rear and the Ninth to the front, reassembled marching columns, and led the parade into Twenty-third Street. There the brass band struck up a festive Orange tune, and Orangemen retrieved banners from the pavement and held them aloft. Some processionists apparently even smiled. Yet, despite scattered applause and cheers for the Orangemen, only two blocks later the lead militia units encountered a large crowd near Booth's theater and the new Masonic building. Police cracked open heads and made a few arrests to clear a path to Fifth Avenue. On the northwest corner of Twenty-third Street and Fifth Avenue, police beat some thirty men about the head.[47]

Police encountered more trouble along Fifth Avenue down to Fourteenth Street. Some "two or three thousand well-dressed people" assembled at the Fifth Avenue Hotel cheered the parade, but persons in Madison Square and in side streets occasionally hurled stones and other objects. Dense crowds at Fourteenth Street and Union Square led to still more skirmishes. Reports indicate that people fired shots from windows near Union Square and that a man who waved a large revolver in the square itself was clubbed and dragged away bloodied. As the procession turned into Fourth Street, someone fired a shot from a crowd at the Union Place Hotel. Hisses and

---

of Clark, Varian, Porter, and Braine, in *Herald* (and others), July 19, 21; *World* and *Herald*, July 13; Evangelides to *Herald*, July 16; the account of an unidentified Company B Seventh Regiment member in *Tribune*, July 15; *Herald*, July 15; Varian staff member in ibid.; interview with Ninth Regiment captain Henry Miller in *Sun*, July 15; and W. P. (n.p., n.d.) to *Irish World*, July 22. *Harper's Weekly* 15 (August 5, 1871): 272, immortalized Jim Fisk's exploits of July 12 in a mocking, twenty-seven-verse poem, "The Flight of Fisk," which included these lines:

> Who struck the blow that laid Fisk low
> Remains a hidden mystery;
> His name, bedad, a Mac or O,
> Will ne'er be writ in history.

Fisk's story is detailed in *Herald*, July 13; *World*, July 14; and Don C. Seitz, *The Dreadful Decade* (Indianapolis: Bobbs-Merrill, 1926), 77–79. A *Sun* reporter found Fisk at Sandy Hook two days later, in a ten-room suite at the Continental Hotel. He was being fanned by a "pretty young lady," while "a small negro [sic]" attended his other needs. Fisk "was elegantly attired in white duck pantaloons, a blue sack coat, and his admiral's cap," the reporter described. "His right foot was encased in a tiny red slipper, embroidered with gold. Above it, beneath the pantaloons, ran a white silk stocking. The ankle was swollen" (*Sun*, July 15).

47. *Sun*, *Herald*, *Times*, and *Tribune*, July 13; *Irish World*, July 22.

jeers accompanied the parade to Cooper Union, but many girls merrily waved orange ribbons as tired Orangemen marched by the American Bible Society's building. Fresh troops and police met the parade at Cooper Union. Hundreds of people reportedly crowded into adjacent streets or glared from windows or rooftops, but only one incident occurred there. Police beat and carried off six men who shouted obscenities at the Orangemen. At four o'clock, the Orangemen quietly dispersed, shed their regalia, and melted into surrounding crowds.[48]

"humanity held cheap"

As word of the riot spread, people rushed to Eighth Avenue to view the scene and check on friends and relatives. Those arriving thirty minutes after the shooting could still find many fly-covered bodies piled on street corners and in alleys. At Twenty-fifth Street a man's brains oozed out onto the pavement. Another body lay nearby, atop a soda water stand. Dazed men and women and curious children shuffled through the pools of blood that covered sidewalks. Under a blanket at the same corner lay a man whose eye had been shot out. Just east of the avenue on Twenty-seventh Street one *Sun* reporter found the bodies of "a countryman," "an Irishman," and "an old negro [sic]." Policeman Oliver Timms saw Charles Buckland's body sprawled across a butcher's cart and the bodies of soldiers Paige and Wyatt inside Abraham Drake's drugstore at Twenty-sixth Street. Just after Timms left, Pvt. Daniel Burns was stabbed by one of several men who broke into the store and attacked the soldiers. The men escaped before police arrived. Elsewhere a *Herald* reporter found Denis King nursing a head wound. King said he had admonished a policeman who fired at a crowd. The cop yelled, "What have you got to say you God damned – – – –; get out of here," and then clubbed King twice. King produced an honorable discharge from the Third Illinois Cavalry and said he was angry at "them peelers and Orangemen" who stayed home while he fought Rebel soldiers.[49]

King's wounds were not serious. But others who did need medical

48. *Tribune* (quote), *Herald*, *World*, and *Times*, July 13; *Irish World*, July 22.

49. *Sun*, *Herald*, *World*, and *Tribune*, July 13; *Irish World*, July 22. See also the coroner's inquest testimonies of Oliver Timms, Abraham Drake, Jacob Gesween, Joseph White, and Peter D. Brower, as given in *Herald*, *World*, *Tribune*, and *Times*, July 25; and Appendix B.

care were taken to hospitals or police stations in bakers' and grocers' wagons and even in pushcarts. The dead and wounded often traveled together. It was an awful sight. One observer said that "in many years of residence in this city never has this reporter seen humanity held so cheap as it was in this quarter of town" that afternoon. The last victim was not cleared off the street until five o'clock. Other remnants of the day's disaster remained long after. People's "blood, brains, or intestines" lay strewn about into the night.[50]

Scores of persons followed the makeshift ambulances to the Sixteenth Precinct station on West Twentieth Street. There they saw Mary York lying on a slab floor next to Mrs. Linnahan, who was dressed "in a plain calico suit, with black gaiters," her brains oozing from one side of her head. Nearby lay an unknown laborer, "dressed in black pantaloons, dark vest, linen coat, plaid undershirt, and calf boots," who had been shot in the back. Many other similarly dressed unknown men were stretched out for inspection. They had variously been shot in the neck, bowels, face, back, and heart. Frantic people besieged officials at Bellevue and Mount Sinai for information about missing relatives. One elderly woman's inquiry was answered, and she found herself at Bellevue next to a pine coffin that held her son. A kindling-wood vendor, the unidentified man had been shot in the breast by a stray musket ball while pulling his wagon near Twenty-seventh Street. From his bed, Christopher Longworth told a *Sun* reporter that he had been shot in the groin at Twenty-eighth Street while watching the parade. Cuban Gaspar Silva said he was shot in the leg as he walked with his wife and a friend toward Ninth Avenue along Twenty-fifth Street. Patrick Hughes, Edward G. Hussey, Henry Langstaff, and others recounted similar stories. Many were confined to hospitals for days, some with serious wounds. Ellen Carey, Patrick Harvey, and John O'Brien left much later, each with only one leg.[51]

Who were these people? The *Times* summarized a prevailing opinion about the identities of the civilian casualties: "Nearly all of the killed and wounded belong to the laboring class. Some were mechanics, and a few others in trades of some kind. If it is to judge from the outward appearances, many of them were engaged in the fray at the time they were shot down. Nearly all were young, hale and

50. *Times* and *Tribune* ("humanity"), July 13; *Irish World*, July 22 ("intestines").

51. *Times* (quotes), *Tribune*, and *Sun*, July 13. See also wounded accounts in Appendix B.

hearty men, very commonly clothed, and apparently in poor circumstances. The innocent were in the minority, and evidently were rushing away to a place of safety when overtaken by their sudden and untimely doom." By contrast, the *Irish-American* claimed that "not a single member of the Irish societies, from whom it was alleged an attack was to be made, was found near the spot." Numerous Irish organizations had announced they would not interfere with the Orangemen. "The victims, therefore, were persons whom chance or business had brought to the spot, or who were attracted by a momentary curiosity to see the turn-out."[52]

Table 2. 1871 riot: Civilian casualties by source of death or injury

			Killed		Wounded	
	Number	%	Number	%	Number	%
All casualties						
Militia	115	86.5	55	98.2	60	77.9
Pistol	3	2.2	1	1.8	2	2.6
Club	12	9.1	0	0.0	12	15.6
Beaten	3	2.2	0	0.0	3	3.9
Total	133	100.0	56	100.0	77	100.0
Unknown	29		6		23	
All casualties	162		62		100	
Irish						
Militia	53	39.8	27	48.2	26	33.8
Pistol	1	.7	0	0.0	1	1.3
Club	6	4.5	0	0.0	6	7.8
Beaten	0	0.0	0	0.0	0	0.0
Total	60	45.0	27	48.2	33	42.9
Unknown	10		1		9	
All Irish	70		28		42	
Others and unidentified						
Militia	62	46.8	28	50.0	34	44.1
Pistol	2	1.5	1	1.8	1	1.3
Club	6	4.5	0	0.0	6	7.8
Beaten	3	2.2	0	0.0	3	3.9
Total	73	55.0	29	51.8	44	57.1
Unknown	19		5		14	
All others	92		34		58	

52. *Times*, July 13; *Irish-American*, July 22.

An analysis of the available evidence about the identities of civilian casualties reveals that both the *Times* and the *Irish-American* were only partially correct. Despite many unknowns, Tables 2 and 3 demonstrate that troop fire accounted for the great majority of all civilian casualties, that Irish-born residents suffered the greatest number of deaths and injuries, but that at least forty-two of the dead were born in the United States or in foreign countries other than Ireland. But one's place of birth does not alone indicate sympathy with or hostility toward the Orangemen. We cannot be certain that all people called "Irish" were Catholic, except where funeral accounts mentioned burial in Catholic cemeteries. A person described as "Irish" *usually* meant an Irish-born Catholic. But "Irish Catholic" is a social statistic; it does not describe social behavior. Nor can we be certain how many of the American-born dead had Irish-born parents.

We can, however, combine statistical and other evidence and draw reasonable conclusions about who the people were who gathered in Eighth Avenue that July afternoon and why they were there. Given the random nature of the military's fire, those who died can be considered as fairly representative of the entire crowd. It is likely that Irishmen Thomas McCleary, Brian Burke, Michael McCormack, John Mullen, Daniel Mulvey, John Riley, and Peter Sherry intentionally went to Eighth Avenue to watch the activities. John Ward, a Scot, and Mary York, did too. Thomas McCormack and Thomas

Table 3. 1871 riot: Civilian casualties by place of birth

			Killed		Wounded	
	Number	%	Number	%	Number	%
United States	20	17.8	12	25.0	8	12.5
Ireland	70	62.5	28	58.3	42	65.6
Germany	8	7.2	4	8.3	4	6.3
England	9	8.0	1	2.1	8	12.5
Scotland	1	.9	1	2.1	0	0.0
Canada	1	.9	1	2.1	0	0.0
Australia	1	.9	1	2.1	0	0.0
Cuba	2	1.8	0	0.0	2	3.1
Totals	112	100.0	48	100.0	64	100.0
Unknown	50		14		36	
All casualties	162		62		100	

Spring were returning from school. Others who accidentally were caught in the militia's fire were Richard Douce, Benjamin Franklin Erskine, Frederick Hiners, Charles Pettit, Conrad Sieger, and Patrick Slattery. James Clark, Alfred Harrington, Charles Keltenbach, and William Latimer were in the area on business. Philip Ackerman was the local resident shot looking after a neighbor in his building. By all accounts, Thomas Dugdale, Hannah Conor Hanby, Augustus P. Gilbert, and William Hartung were "innocent bystanders" who came to see the parade but were not otherwise involved.

These names account for twenty-six of the sixty-two civilian deaths. Information is lacking for another sixteen persons who died, and we can only infer that most of the other twenty Irish who died were hostile to Orangemen. Two of them—Sarah Kenney and Walter Scott—traveled from Brooklyn. Many of the others were laborers who lived or worked nearby. They included Morris Holway, Michael Kelly, Thomas Kerrigan, John Lavery, Michael Leahy, Peter McCaffrey, and William McGrath. Dennis McMahon, James McMahon, R. Madden, Patrick Maualean, Patrick Monaghan, Michael O'Shea, Owen Stanton, Timothy Sullivan, William Tigh, and John Whiteside also likely were Irish Catholics.

The data in Tables 4 and 5 tell us more about the composite identities of the civilian casualties. Most victims were young to early middle-aged unskilled workers. Of the 104 persons whose ages are known, 71 (or 68.3 percent) were between the ages of eleven and thirty, and 26 were not over twenty years of age. Patrick Maualean, Thomas Spring, and Mary York (all killed) and James Dillon and Robert Warren (injured) were younger than seventeen years old. At least 10 of those who were not yet twenty-one years old had been born in Ireland, while 16 more of similar ages were born in identifiable or unknown countries. Few Irish-born victims were forty or older. They included Timothy Hanlon, Peter McCaffrey, Michael McCormack, John Benton, W. P. Coleman, Patrick Harvey, and Elizabeth Lutenberger. Of these, McCormack was the only apparent recent immigrant, and except for Lutenberger, all lived at some distance from Eighth Avenue.

The occupations of only 51 of the riot casualties could be determined. Yet 35 held unskilled jobs, and 25 of them were Irish. Among the unskilled Irish, there were 14 laborers, a quarryman, 2 hod carriers, 2 clerks, a coachman, an expressman, a cartman, a bartender, a domestic servant, and a streetcar conductor. The skilled Irishman

Table 4. 1871 riot: Civilian casualties by age

	Number	%	Killed Number	Killed %	Wounded Number	Wounded %
All casualties						
10–20	26	25.0	13	24.1	13	26.0
21–30	45	43.3	23	42.6	22	44.0
31–40	20	19.2	9	16.7	11	22.0
41–50	5	4.8	3	5.5	2	4.0
Over 50	8	7.7	6	11.1	2	4.0
Total	104	100.0	54	100.0	50	100.0
Unknown	58		8		50	
All casualties	162		62		100	
Irish						
10–20	10	9.6	6	11.1	4	8.0
21–30	27	26.0	15	27.8	12	24.0
31–40	11	10.6	4	7.4	7	14.0
41–50	1	1.0	0	0.0	1	2.0
Over 50	2	1.9	2	3.7	0	0.0
Total	51	49.1	27	50.0	24	48.0
Unknown	19		1		18	
All Irish	70		28		42	
Others and unidentified						
10–20	16	15.4	7	13.0	9	18.0
21–30	18	17.3	8	14.8	10	20.0
31–40	9	8.6	5	9.3	4	8.0
41–50	4	3.8	3	5.5	1	2.0
Over 50	6	5.8	4	7.4	2	4.0
Total	53	50.9	27	50.0	26	52.0
Unknown	39		7		32	
All others	92		34		58	

was James McMahon, a blacksmith. Thomas McCleary owned a Brooklyn saloon. Ages are known for 23 of these 27 working people. Except for Thomas Dugdale, Michael McCormack, Patrick Harvey, Terence Maloy, and John Mitchell, the rest were not more than thirty years old.

Most of the Irish Catholic riot victims lived in predominantly Irish working-class neighborhoods where the Orange parade had been discussed for days. Those who lived close to the Eighth Avenue parade route likely were outraged by the prospect of an Orange invasion of

Table 5. 1871 riot: Civilian casualties by occupation

	Number	%	Killed Number	Killed %	Wounded Number	Wounded %
All casualties						
Unskilled	35	68.6	18	62.1	17	77.3
Skilled	7	13.7	4	13.8	3	13.6
Business/professional	9	17.7	7	24.1	2	9.1
Total	51	100.0	29	100.0	22	100.0
Unknown/children	111		33		78	
All casualties	162		62		100	
Irish						
Unskilled	25	49.0	12	41.4	13	59.1
Skilled	1	2.0	1	3.4	0	0.0
Business/professional	1	2.0	1	3.4	0	0.0
Total	27	53.0	14	48.2	13	59.1
Unknown/children	43		14		29	
All Irish	70		28		42	
Others and unidentified						
Unskilled	10	19.6	6	20.7	4	18.2
Skilled	6	11.7	3	10.4	3	13.6
Business/professional	8	15.7	6	20.7	2	9.1
Total	24	47.0	15	51.8	9	40.9
Unknown/children	68		19		49	
All others	92		34		58	

their neighborhood. Nearby apartment buildings were crowded with Irish working-class families. For example, according to the 1870 census schedules, John Whiteside's building at 207 West Twenty-sixth Street housed 41 people. Among people who were over eighteen years old, 18 were born in Ireland, 9 in the United States, and 2 in Scotland. All 12 younger people had been born in the United States. Before he was killed, Whiteside shared an apartment with his Irish-born parents, an older sister, and a younger brother. Besides Whiteside and his father, who were laborers, the other residents of the building included two other laborers, a coachman, a gardener, a carman, a hackman, and a stonecutter. Another victim, Peter Sherry, had lived with his younger sister and their aging, widowed mother at 144 West Nineteenth Street. All three had come from Ireland, as did eighteen of the other twenty adult residents. Four, including Sherry, were laborers. There also was a grocer, a seaman, a carpenter, a tailor, and a maker of chair bottoms.

John Mitchell, Terence Maloy, John Kierney, John Feeney, James Dillon, and Patrick Harvey, all of whom were injured, came from similar Eighth Avenue area neighborhoods. Mitchell, Dillon, and Harvey had large families. Maloy supported his mother. Kierney and Feeney, who lived in the same building, moved in after the 1870 census was taken, but they lived among many large Irish families that had begun in Ireland and grown in New York. Census takers recorded 360 people in the five buildings where these people lived in 1870. Of the 182 who were over seventeen years old, 136 (or 74.7 percent) were Irish. But 167 of the 178 children (93.8 percent) were born in the United States. In his apartment building between Seventh and Eighth avenues, Terence Maloy probably talked often with his Irish-born neighbors, Michael and Margaret Lavy. Lavy, a liveryman, and his wife were each twenty-five years old and had an infant son. The young Irish families of hotel waiter Barney McKenna and shoemaker James O'Conor may also have been Maloy's friends. Elsewhere in the building lived Teresa Laxe, a German-born laundress and widow who struggled to support her three young sons. Barber James Whitter and his wife Sarah, both Irish, lived there with their three American-born children. Up the street toward Eighth Avenue in Mitchell's building, one found marble polisher Daniel McGowan and his wife Catherine, both forty and Irish. They had five children ranging in age from eighteen to four. Mitchell most likely knew the laborer James Murphy, his wife, Catherine, and their six children. Such persons with varied occupations could be found in all five buildings. There were peddlers, beer and pie wagon drivers, wheelwrights, numerous laborers, a dyer, a marble polisher, a wood turner, a mason, a cooper, a door maker, a butcher, a grocer, seamstresses, a chair caner, night watchmen, a wine maker, and many others.[53]

Most of the Irish Catholic victims probably came from such neighborhoods. It merits repeating that not all casualties were Irish, that many—including some Irish people—were drawn to Eighth Avenue by curiosity or by accident, and that the militia was responsible for at least 115 of the 162 known casualties. Troop fire presumably caused

53. Information is from the *Ninth United States Census* (1870), *Population Schedules*, second enumeration, and from sources cited in Appendix B.

many other casualties that went unreported. For example, Edward Clark, the Omaha physician who witnessed the riot, believed "that a great many were shot slightly, and went at once to their homes, and the newspaper list of the wounded does not begin to cover the entire number." Concerned citizens like John C. Hannan, Jeremiah Murphy, and Thomas Cremmen formed a committee to raise funds for riot victims. They uncovered evidence supporting Clark's suspicions. Murphy reported to a July 21 meeting that he had "found that there are many sufferers of whom the public knows nothing. I found a man yesterday who had been shot through the lung. He was at home in his little hut, with four children around him, and there was not a dollar in the house." Murphy was convinced that "he is an honest laboring man" who, like "nearly all the injured persons," was only a spectator and had "no intention to molest any one." Still more evidence emerged from a bundle of clothing discovered in an ash barrel on July 14 by a policeman. The clothes included "a black sack-coat with a bullet hole in the back, a pair of black pantaloons, a white overshirt, an undershirt, and a pair of drawers. All these articles, which were of very common quality, were saturated with blood."[54]

Many accounts indicate that many of the known victims wore the long, dark linen coats; black vests and pants; and white shirts that were common working-class clothes. In spite of the heat, even street laborers and quarrymen were said to have worn such items. So while not all of those who viewed the Orange parade were Irish Catholics, many surely were Irish laborers who left work after they learned of Hoffman's proclamation.

Their numbers were not as large as suggested by those who had reason to exaggerate Irish working-class provocation, however. Most reports of roving bands of laborers on the morning of July 12 proved to be rumors. Worried police commissioner Benjamin F. Manierre said he personally had asked many Boulevard foremen and contractors on July 12 to fire laborers who missed work without a good excuse. In 1863, Manierre had confronted angry workers as a captain and provost marshal, and he now urged the public to support his demand that rioting laborers be fired. "Teach these men," he insisted, "that they must submit to the laws if they expect to gain a living by receiving employment. Starve them into submission." Yet a Croton Water Works engineer and supervisor rebutted Manierre's

54. *Times*, July 14 (Clark); *World*, July 15 (clothes), and 22 (Murphy).

claims. The man had warned "over 600 laborers" that they would be fired if they quit work on July 12. He admitted that "a few" had been "frightened off" by "gangs of men" but claimed that "at roll call . . . we still had 600 left. I investigated the case of every man who left work, and am satisfied that none went down town or joined in the disturbances in any way," he said. "None have been dismissed." Rumors that arguments among Boulevard laborers on July 13 resulted in widespread fights, and that laborers attacked Orangemen and Orange houses, also proved false.[55]

Many laborers undoubtedly did go to Eighth Avenue. But, as an *Irish World* reporter observed, "If any came with the purpose of provoking a riot they certainly, as the course of events showed, came without organization, leaders, or [a] premeditated plan of attack." The various AOH meetings and movements of laborers did not result in organized plans to stop the Orangemen. The names of leaders of scattered mobs did emerge in newspaper and police reports, but their identities usually remained anonymous. There were some exceptions. Police captain Henry Hedden arrested Patrick Hogan just outside the First Precinct station for carrying "a large fragment of brick" up his sleeve and rallying a crowd, which demanded the release of suspected rioters. There were also, as noted earlier, three separate accounts of a man with a drawn sword who rallied others on the morning of July 12; another person seen at Grace Church waving a sword cane; and still another opposite Lamartine Hall just before the parade began. Yet once Orangemen began to parade, it became clear that those who hurled paving stones or shot pistols from rooftops acted spontaneously or made no attempt to preserve their anonymity. Papers like the hostile *Sun* acknowledged that "there was apparently no organization on the part of the mob," but they still insisted that Irish bigots were responsible for the riot. The mob "seemed to have no leaders," the paper admitted, "but every Ribbonman went into the business of assassination on his own hook." In a classic caricature of a riot leader, one *World* reporter more accurately described a class mentality than his intended Irish subject. In other words, he reported what his consciousness "saw":

55. Manierre quoted in *Tribune*, July 14; Tracey (waterworks) quoted in *Times*, July 18; *Sun* and *Herald*, July 14. On Manierre's draft riot activities, see Adrian Cook, *The Armies of the Streets: The New York City Draft Riots of 1863* (Lexington: University Press of Kentucky, 1974), 70, 71, 73, 119, 185.

> The writer of this had seen in the early part of the day, near Hibernian Hall, in Prince street, a more than mortal man; his frame was herculean; his face not unlike that which Mirabeau describes as his own—that of a tiger who had the small-pox. He seemed filled with suppressed ferocity not pleasing to see. He was the centre of no group, yet no bystander, interested or not in what was to be the order of the day, could help looking at him as the type of a bad and dangerous class. He stuck out his jaws, twisted his hands about nervously, and evidently was bursting for a row. The better sort of man about Hibernian Hall did not seem to like him, but a wiser sort afterward followed him into Broadway, up which they went. Later in the day the writer saw the same man near the St. Denis Hotel [on Broadway near West Eleventh Street], when the Orangemen were marching up to their rendezvous. Again he saw the same ominous actions, and, looking for result, saw one when on the heads of his comrades, for good cause, descended the policemen's clubs, and where they fought they fell, but not the hero, whose thoughts were then bent on safety. Still later the same man was seen urging a crowd up Twenty-Sixth street to do deeds of valor at Eighth Avenue. He pressed his way to the first ranks, there was a volley fired, and the reporter had the pleasure of looking at the dead face of the bully, shot right in the mouth and lying in the gutter.[56]

This reporter only inferred that his subject had committed violence. Nothing is learned from his account about either the man's attempts to incite to riot or his actual identity.

These solitary crowd "leaders" were never given names. But other lone figures lost their anonymity for a brief period after they were arrested for various acts on July 12. Police statistics suggest that many persons wanted to attack the Orangemen but that few actually did. Detectives searched more than three hundred people along the parade route. They reportedly confiscated seventy-eight weapons, including many pistols, knives, and paving stones. One account said 169 were arrested, but available court records and newspapers named only 105 taken into custody. At least 34 of them were charged with two offenses, such as disorderly conduct and carrying a pistol

56. *Irish World*, July 22; complaint of Capt. Henry Heddin v. Patrick Hogan, July 13, Grand Jury Dismissals (Supreme Court 1871), Box 10570, New York City Municipal Archives. Hogan was released on $1,000 bail. The grand jury later dismissed the case. See also *Sun*, July 14; and *World*, July 13.

(see Appendix B). Some 32 people were charged with carrying pistols (26 of them also with rioting or disorderly conduct); 13 were charged with carrying knives, clubs, or other weapons; and 2 were arrested for intoxication.

Most of those arrested for whom charges are known were accused of "rioting" or "disorderly conduct" (the terms seemed to have been used interchangeably). Some of the 54 persons arrested for "disorderly conduct" seem to have been arrested for appearances alone. For example, William Dalton was found running in the street with a bloodied head, and John Montgomery was arrested for "running away from the crowd at Hibernian Hall." Details are lacking about charges filed against 14 of the 105 known arrested persons.[57]

The only known person arrested for firing a pistol on Eighth Avenue was Edward Croak, who was charged only with disorderly conduct. Two policemen claimed to have seen him shoot at Orangemen on Twenty-third Street. Officer Phillip Farley did not see Martin Follett fire his revolver but nevertheless arrested him in Mott Street when he learned that two chambers in Follett's gun were empty. The three others who were accused of firing weapons—John Gallagher, Barney Martin, and Patrick Radigan—apparently aimed their pistols into the air on the night of July 12. Thirty-one people were charged with carrying pistols (again, some faced other charges too).[58]

57. *Tribune*, July 14; *World*, July 13. Sources for arrests are cited in Appendix B. The 21 men who were arrested for "rioting" were Thomas Coleman, John Connor, John Darian, Hugh Deery, John Dewey, John Falon, Daniel Flynn, Thomas Gilmartin, Patrick Green, Edward Kelly, Patrick Kelly, Gustavus Kershner, Michael Lanihan, Thomas Leen, John McCabe, Frank McDermott, James McDonald, Thomas O'Neill, Patrick Powers, George Riester, and Thomas Wallace. The others arrested for "disorderly conduct" were Sherwood Bellington, William Blair, Andrew Bowney, John W. Clark, John Connell, Patrick Connolly, Michael Cox, Edward Croak, John Curtain, William Devine, John Dorman, Edward Dwyer, William E. Dwyer, Thomas Fitzharris, Martin Follett, Michael Frantoni, John Gallagher, Henry F. Gibney, John Hayes, John Henricks, Patrick Hogan, Francis Keelt, John Kelly, Peter J. Kelly, John Kennedy, Thomas Kilmartin, Edward Lamb, James Lynch (two men by this name were charged with disorderly conduct), Thomas Lynch, John McCabe, John McCarty, Arthur McClinchey, Thomas McDonald, Patrick McGowan, Barney Martin, Patrick Merrigan, Michael Norton, William O'Guire, Patrick O'Mahony, Joseph Plunkett, Patrick Radigan, Thomas Regan, Gustavus Reicher, Michael Riordan, Frank Russell, Thomas Ryan, Washington Serres, Michael Shaw, William Tobin, William Tucker, and James Walsh. Details are lacking on Patrick Bowers, Frank Connolly, Michael Enwright, Michael Finley, James Fleury, James Henry, Michael Kellaher, Michael Kelly, John McCarthy, F. McDonald, Michael Maloney, Frederick Orst, Patrick Shaw, and James Ward.

58. They were Bellington, Bowney, Connor, Curtain, John Deery, Devine, E. Dwyer,

Of the others who were arrested, police charged that William Blair, John Flayes, Thomas Gilmartin, John Hayes, John Henricks, and John McCarty carried knives. Thomas Lynch and Thomas Ryan were arrested on Twenty-third Street and on Fifth Avenue for concealing weapons. Daniel H. Flynn was arrested for waving a razor in a crowd, and Cornelius Mahony for carrying an unidentified weapon. Three others—*Star* reporter Bernard McGinnis, Thomas Coleman, and Samuel Sapulen—were accused of wielding clubs. James Lahey and Michael Ward were intoxicated. Edward O'Neill apparently was bent on serious violence; he was arrested for carrying a shotgun.

Little more is known about those who were arrested. Published accounts and court records seldom included more than names and charges. Although only twenty-four arrest locations were given, it appears that police were busy throughout the day, especially along the parade route. Three were arrested on Eighth Avenue, and five at or near Hibernian Hall. Patrick Hogan was arrested at the Fifteenth Precinct station in Mercer Street, between Prince and West Houston. Fifteen others were arrested at various points on Sixth, Fifth, and Fourth avenues, on Broadway at Lafayette Place, at Cooper Union, and in Bleecker, Bowery, South, and Fourth streets.

"you have saved this fair city from ruin and disgrace"

Anxious and grieving families maintained vigils outside hospital gates throughout the night. Civil and military officials kept vigils of another kind. Fearing that the day's events might spark a night of disorder, Kelso stationed already weary policemen at Hibernian Hall, at Fenian headquarters, in Eighth Avenue, and elsewhere throughout the city. Seventh Regiment soldiers returned to their armory and found a bitter proclamation posted prominently: "Highly Important," it began. "Prince William of Orange is dead (drunk). Von Abram O'Hall will be reelected Mayor of New-Cork. The Orange market quiet; Fenian market rampant. Pat, don't tread on the tail of

---

Falon, Follett, Gallagher, Gibney, Green, Keelt, E. Kelly, P. Kelly, Lanihan, Leen, one of the John McCabes, McDermott, both John McHughs, Michael Malvin, Martin, Norton, O'Mahony, Thomas O'Neill, Plunkett, Powers, Radigan, T. Ryan, and Martin Toylet.

my coat." Elsewhere in the building "was an effigy of a 'flannel mouthed' Irishman looking dubiously at a grinning Orangeman."[59]

Fears of nighttime violence did not materialize. Given the day's events, the city was surprisingly quiet. People enjoyed the evening breeze outside their houses but did not go beyond their immediate neighborhoods. Even after dark, those living near the riot scene roamed up and down Eighth Avenue inspecting bullet holes and the many blood-stained articles of clothing left behind from the afternoon. There were no disturbances.[60]

Less than twenty-four hours earlier, Hoffman had guaranteed the Orangemen's right to parade. His promise had proved costly. At ten o'clock that Wednesday night, three city officials tried to assess some of that cost as they addressed some five hundred policemen from the Colored Methodist Church steps near police headquarters. John R. Fellows, the assistant district attorney, expressed gratefulness "from my heart that you have saved this fair city from ruin and disgrace." He commended the police for "rushing boldly into the face of deadly opposition" and "sweeping the savage bands of armed riot[ers] before you as waves blown by the wind." They had saved "the people from sorrow and suffering." Then Kelso announced that the Police Board had voted to dismiss all but a few complaints against policemen in gratitude for a job well done. Cheers greeted his statement. A last speaker, police commissioner Isaac Bell, said that "as treasurer of the [1863] Riot Relief Fund, I am happy to be able to say that if any of you shall die in the discharge of your duty [your] families will be well provided for." There were more cheers.[61]

None of the men, however, offered consolation to the grieving families who did business with the many coffin shops and pharmacies that remained open throughout the night. Dozens of people waited outside Bellevue Hospital's high brick wall and iron-gate entrance in Twenty-third Street near the East River. While hospital personnel cared for the wounded, other workers carted bodies down the few steps leading to a small, unobtrusive building at one end of the out-patient dispensary for the poor. The low shed with a darkened ceil-

59. *Tribune*, July 13 (quote), 15; Shaler's *Report*, in *Herald*, July 22.

60. *World*, *Herald*, *Times*, and *Tribune*, July 13.

61. *World*, July 13. The city also paid for the funerals of the three guardsmen and for troop rations, damages, and other riot expenses. Total cost: $13,732.52. See *Irish-American*, January 13, 1872. For damage costs, see Appendix B.

ing contained five marble slabs and more than thirty crude red coffins. Letters etched on a dingy lamp above the entrance identified the building as "The Morgue." Erected in 1866 over the objections of area residents who believed that curses would accompany a death house, the morgue had since become a place of interest to neighborhood children, who often stared through the large plate-glass window separating them and others from the bodies inside. Thoughts of curses and much else—but certainly not youthful curiosity—undoubtedly accompanied those who rushed through the gates when the grounds opened at six o'clock Thursday morning. Among those who waited all night was Timothy Sullivan's wife. She quickly found her husband's body, obtained a burial permit, and went home.[62]

Not all Thursday morgue visitors sought missing friends or relatives. Bellevue warden Thomas S. Brennan did not explain to a coroner's jury what brought over twenty thousand people to the death house that day. But surely the presence of so many Irish was due to more than just curiosity. Although not all the dead were Irish, those who braved the stench and stifling heat expressed a common Irish grief for all who died in a confrontation that was historically important to Irish Catholics. Eschewing such scenes, fashionable men and women rode in comfortable carriages along Eighth Avenue, pointing out particular street corners or buildings as they read morning newspaper accounts. "Each separate pool of blood, each broken window or shattered door had its individual story," a writer observed, "and in the course of half an hour four different localities were pointed out, each as the spot on which the little girl, Mary York, was killed." Such details were irrelevant to York's parents, as they claimed her body at the morgue that morning. Yet on Thursday and Friday, Coroner Nelson W. Young came to understand that each body had its own story. Young even occasionally displayed compassion for grieving relatives. When a cousin identified John Mullen's body on July 14, Young suggested that Mullen's ring be removed and sent to his parents in Ireland as a remembrance of their dead son.[63]

62. *Irish World*, July 22; *World* and *Tribune*, July 14; William H. Rideing, "Hospital Life in New York," *Harper's New Monthly Magazine* 57 (July 1878): 179.

63. Testimony of Thomas S. Brennan, coroner's inquest, in *Herald*, *World*, *Tribune*, and *Times*, July 25; *Times* and *Tribune* (quote), July 14; *Sun*, July 15.

5 / Judgment

In the weeks after the riot, a broad segment of New Yorkers bitterly debated the violence and its meaning for America. We can learn much from their views about the class and ethnic barriers that separated them. What is especially interesting is how contemporaries and historians of the riots have distorted both events by referring to them as the "Orange and Ribbon Riots." The 1870 and 1871 riots had only three things in common: they stemmed from historically antagonistic experiences and beliefs; they involved Irish Catholics and Protestants and the police; and they resulted in many deaths, injuries, and arrests. But the confrontations differed considerably. In 1870, Orange provocations sparked a general melee in which both sides exchanged blows and pistol shots. Police and city officials seemed unprepared. The spontaneity characterizing the Elm Park violence was not evident in 1871. Plans for an Orange celebration were announced weeks before July 12. Rumors that Irish Catholics and the Ancient Order of Hibernians planned to attack Orangemen appeared almost daily in city newspapers. Both sides denounced each other, as Tammany officials tried to resolve the crisis. Although the Catholic clergy, Irish-American nationalist spokesmen, and even the Orange grand master all helped Hall's efforts, the mayor eventually decided

Note: Unless otherwise indicated, all dates in the footnotes are from the year 1871.

to ban the parade and not risk a riot. That way, he could disrupt Irish Protestant and Catholic plans, shift political responsibility from City-Hall to Albany, and hope to emerge only somewhat tainted by then cooperating with Hoffman's order to protect the Orangemen. If violence occurred, Hall could claim vindication for his original plan and argue that his cooperation with Hoffman showed that he had not "surrendered to the mob," as critics charged before Hoffman's intervention. Indeed, after July 12, Hall continued to insist that his plan was not a ruse and that Kelso's order "was intended to be executed." He took credit from former critics for cooperating with Hoffman, but he also tried to distance himself from Hoffman in a play to his Irish constituents, claiming, "If the Governor of the State wants to take care of a principle [the right to parade] at sacrifice of life and property he has the right to do so."[1] Such sticky political considerations were not present in 1870.

The 1871 violence differed in two other important ways. In the events leading to July 12, 1871, there was an element of public theater that transcended party considerations and made the Boyne Day confrontation inevitable. All participants seemed to have understood their roles well. Surely Hall and others knew that some Orangemen would defy Kelso's ban, that Irish Catholics would oppose them, and that city authorities would try to squelch disruptions. City and state officials also understood that Hoffman's proclamation signaled a day of violence, as evidenced by their deployment of massive forces throughout the city. Police and militia units also must have expected violence, as one tragic incident suggests. Fearing he might have to fire on fellow Irishmen, Ninth Regiment soldier Edward Gaffney remained home on July 12. He could hear the gunfire from his Twenty-fifth Street house and saw victims later that day. Distraught over the slaughter and from charges of cowardice, the twenty-nine-year-old drugstore clerk became depressed. On July 16, he slit his throat with a razor.[2] Orangemen were no less naïve about the possibility of violence than their protectors and Gaffney. And those who went to Eighth Avenue for whatever reason similarly understood that provocative acts would not go unchallenged.

Yet none could have foreseen the extent of death and injury caused by militia muskets. Four days of rioting in July 1863 had re-

1. See interviews with Hall in *Leader* and *Star*, July 15.

2. *Herald*, *World*, *Times*, and *Sun*, July 17.

sulted in 105 confirmed deaths, 23 of which were militia victims.[3] Neither troops nor police were responsible for deaths in 1870. But guardsmen required only a few seconds to kill outright or fatally wound 55 of the 62 people who died in 1871.

The militia presence was the greatest difference between the 1870 and 1871 riots, and not only because of the troops' capacity to inflict injury and death. Like Orangemen, they were surrogates for nativists, Republicans, and propertied interests who sought either to capitalize on Tammany's predicament, to crush the perceived designs of Irish Catholics, or to suppress working-class disorder in general. Because many Orange supporters embodied all of these motives, the 1871 violence may be best understood as a militia riot perpetrated by political reformers and men of property whose views reflected ethnic and class interests more than they did party affiliations. There is no question that deep and bitter religious hatred helped to provoke this riot and the one in 1870. Many Irish Catholics clearly hated Irish Protestants merely because they were Irish Protestants. But, as I have argued earlier, for most other Irish workers, this hatred stemmed more fundamentally from their experiences in Ireland and from their class position in America; and it fueled one side of the contending debate that led to violence. The class interests of Orangemen and their supporters fueled the other side and contributed more weight than did the Irish workers in bringing the city to its moment of crisis in 1871.

It is not only these different class interests, but even more, the way civil and military authorities dismissed criticism and fact immediately after July 12 in order to conceal their own complicity in the deaths and injuries of many innocent people, which requires examination. Ignoring the riot victims' identities and the circumstances that brought people to Eighth Avenue, officials argued that mere presence at the riot scene constituted guilt. Demands for investigations were brushed aside. Police and militia dissidents were punished. Most of those arrested were set free, probably to avoid embarrassing evidence that might have emerged in court. Officials perpetuated the view that the public order had been breached. They made substantial monetary awards to even slightly injured policemen

3. The number may have reached 119. See Adrian Cook, *The Armies of the Streets: The New York City Draft Riots of 1863* (Lexington: University Press of Kentucky, 1974), 194, 213–18.

and lavishly praised the troops. For various reasons, this judgment was supported widely, even among the Tweed Ring's critics. Yet government officials revealed, in their justifications and actions, that they had much more in common with reformers than with their supposedly staunch Irish Catholic supporters.

"The guardianship of . . . honor"

Civil authorities began constructing an official version of the riot immediately after July 12. While Hoffman and Kelso left for vacations at Newport and Cold Spring Harbor on July 13, Hall eagerly appeared at City Hall to defend his actions. Asked why no one had read a riot act before troops fired or why soldiers had not warned spectators by firing a blank round, the mayor replied that no riot act existed and that some persons evidently believed rioters *deserved* no warning. More important, he insisted that his actions had saved the city from a pitched battle between as many as five thousand Orangemen and twenty thousand opponents. Imagine the havoc! he implored. "Then the very Wall Street gamblers and butter merchants who in public meeting denounced the authorities would have been the first" to criticize him.[4]

That same morning, sixty-five prisoners marched from police headquarters to the Tombs police court. Accompanied by squads of detectives and police, the men reportedly were "all dressed in the coarse garb of the laboring classes, and many were stained with the dried blood which had oozed from the wounds inflicted by the detectives when they were beaten down in the streets the previous day." Justice Hogan lectured them briefly. "Where are your leaders now?" he asked. Although some were released immediately, Hogan accused them all of having been deceived by the "scoundrelly demagogues" who were their leaders.[5]

Hogan and Edward J. Shandley, who handled most of the arrests, were Irish Catholics who owed their positions to Tammany. Indeed, Shandley had been honored at a meeting in Tweed Plaza the previous September. While there is no conclusive evidence that Tammany pressured judges and prosecutors to be lenient, there also is no

4. *Leader*, July 15; *Herald*, July 14, 16; *Sun*, July 14 (quote).
5. *Times* (clothing), *World* (Hogan), *Herald*, and *Sun*, July 14.

evidence that any of the 105 arrested men were brought to trial. The disposition of ninety-one cases is known. The judges dismissed thirty-eight cases when no arresting officer appeared in court to press charges, or because they believed cases did not merit prosecution. Most of those set free in this manner had been charged with disorderly conduct or rioting. Twenty-six more were released with the court's instruction to keep the peace six months to a year or forfeit bail, which usually amounted to five hundred or a thousand dollars and was posted for them by friends or bondsmen (see Appendix B). Many of the twenty-one other persons discharged on bail probably were given the same orders. Three remained in jail for several days because they were unable to post bail. John Curtain was finally released on his own recognizance on July 19. Hogan reasoned that Curtain must not have been a rioter because no Hibernian society member had yet appeared to obtain his release! The seven cases known to have reached the grand jury were all dismissed.[6]

In conducting their inquests, city coroners followed the judges' examples. There are no coroner's reports to be found in city archives, but newspapers did report some proceedings. At least five inquiries were held on July 13. A coroner's jury composed solely of Ninth Regiment soldiers heard Lt. Col. Charles R. Braine describe briefly how Henry Paige died and then returned its verdict of death by skull fracture. Similar proceedings took place in houses and hospitals as doctors and relatives told how Philip J. Ackerman, Charles H. Pettit, John Ward, and Benjamin F. Erskine died, but no efforts were made to determine culpability. The jury's verdict in Ward's death was typical: "Death by gunshot wound of bladder received during the riot in Eighth Avenue, July 12, 1871."[7]

Coroner Nelson W. Young convened a more formal inquest on July 24 to consider the deaths of thirty-six others. Jurors included a

6. On patronage in courts, see Alexander B. Callow, *The Tweed Ring* (New York: Oxford University Press, 1965), 134–35. On Shandley, see the *Irish-American*, September 17, 1870, and details about another Tammany dinner in his honor in ibid., November 26, 1870. Between August and December, the grand jury refused to indict Thomas Coleman, John Hayes, John Henricks, Patrick Hogan, Bernard McGinnis, Thomas O'Neill, and Samuel Sapulen. *Sun*, July 20; Grand Jury Dismissals (Supreme Court, 1871), Boxes 9580 and 10570, New York City Municipal Archives. See also Appendix B. Official police reports indicated that seventy-one people had been arrested for rioting in 1871; see *Second Annual Report of the Police Department of the City of New York: For the Year Ending April 5th, 1872* (New York: Pease and Jones, 1873), 22.

7. *World*, July 14.

galvanizer, Eighth Avenue undertaker Frederick P. Wood, butcher Henry Comstock, William H. Roome (an agent), a billiard parlor operator, and three men whose occupations are unknown. Young told these men that most deaths appeared to have been caused by gunshot wounds and instructed them to determine "who, if any one, was guilty of causing such death[s]." Sixteen witnesses testified. Eleven were Eighth Avenue shopkeepers; three were policemen; one (Lordly), a physician; and one, John Banner, claimed to have been a passerby. None were able to identify anyone who fired a pistol. Stephen J. Meany asked to cross-examine the witnesses in defense of the Irish people. His appeal was denied. Only Patrick O'Shea, who kept an oyster saloon, claimed that troops fired without provocation. The other witnesses provided the general accounts already described. Three minutes after they retired, the jurors returned with their verdict "that the deceased persons came to their death from gunshot wounds received at the hands of some parties to us unknown, on the 12th day of July, 1871."[8]

The *Irish World* and *Irish-American* were incensed. Both argued that authorities tried to conceal evidence that would exonerate the city's Irish Catholics. The *Irish-American* called the proceedings a "Mock Investigation," which nevertheless had performed a public service:

> The care exhibited to prevent any attempt to sift the matter and show whether there was any justification for the firing by the military, was, in itself, an evidence that a thorough inquiry would have elicited the true facts of the case—that the efforts of the police were entirely sufficient to have put down any riotous demonstration that was likely to take place; that there was no real necessity for the interference of the military under the circumstances; and that their using their arms, without proper orders, was the effect of their own undisciplined condition, of groundless and disgraceful panic, and of a brutal desire to inflict injury on the crowd before them, without seeking to discriminate whether they were friends or foes, rioters or innocent spectators. In fact the worst and only mob in New York that day were [sic] the mob of undisciplined militiamen.[9]

8. *Times*, *Tribune*, *World*, *Herald* (Young, verdict), and *Sun*, July 25.
9. *Irish World*, August 12; *Irish-American*, August 5.

Others shared this view. Few better understood how official civil and military evidence might be misused than an anonymous correspondent to the *World*:

> The newspapers, which make history, will carry down to posterity the narrative of the heroism, the gallantry, and the superhuman bravery displayed by the militia of this city on the 12th of July, 1871. The dastardly outrage in massacring our innocent fellow-citizens will be entirely overlooked[;] it will not be told that a body of raw and inexperienced soldiery, with little or no provocation, maliciously fired upon a mass of innocent spectators whom curiosity or accident had drawn to the spot.

The writer criticized troops "for firing indiscriminately into a mass of respectable men, women, and children" and argued that "the very small number of Orangemen or their protectors who were injured is evidence that the shots and missiles fired by the mob could not have been very numerous, else the damage to the ranks would have been much more severe than it was."[10]

That writer overlooked the deaths of soldiers Paige, Wyatt, and Prior and of policemen Henry Ford and John Hamil and the treatment for injuries (excluding sunstrokes) of twenty-four guardsmen and twenty-nine policemen. Moreover, there *had* been provocations. But there is little doubt that troops fired indiscriminately. Civilian victims represented almost a random sampling of Eighth Avenue sidewalk crowds. Causes of deaths and injuries could be determined for 133 of the 162 known civilian casualties (see Table 2). Troop fire accounted for 115 (or 86.5 percent); pistol shots, policemen's clubs, and fistfights inflicted almost all of the other casualties for which causes could be determined. Moreover, soldiers were responsible for at least 55 of the 62 deaths and for at least 60 of the 100 injuries. Having killed 27 of the 28 persons whom sources identified as being born in Ireland, troops also wounded at least 26 Irish natives and took an equally heavy toll on those born in other foreign countries or in the United States. Although the Irish clearly suffered more casualties than any group of people whose birthplaces are known, Tables 2 and 3 also demonstrate that the Irish alone were not singled out by troops and police, even though they appear to have made up most of the Eighth Avenue citizen crowd. Casualties also included immi-

10. L.M.W. (n.p., n.d.) to *World*, July 19.

grants from Germany, England, Scotland, Canada, Australia, and Cuba as well as native-born Americans.[11]

Because of such evidence, even those who called themselves "non-partisan" found the numbers appalling. One believed that if "Kelso's proclamation had been enforced fifty innocent persons and double that number of rioters would not have been slain and mutilated by a 'panic-stricken military.'" Another, who was "neither a Catholic nor an Orangeman, but an American actuated by justice, and with the feeling that the guilty should be punished, but the innocent spared," criticized that "no effort [was] made to lessen the sacrifice of human life" and that "the troops were ready and eager for the opportunity to fire." Their irresponsibility resulted in "an un-called for and wanton massacre." Reports that "several gentlemen" heard "a drunken sergeant or lieutenant" give the initial order to fire were partly supported by one of Shaler's aides, who charged that Capt. Peter MacDonald was drunk when he left police headquarters with his Eighty-fourth Regiment. MacDonald later claimed that he had been temperate for three years, and the matter was dropped. Another source berated soldiers because they "gave no warning whatever when they fired" but acted "solely on the impulse of the moment." Still another alleged that some members of the Eighty-fourth's Company C belonged to the APA and that the company enrolled Orangemen and gave them uniforms on the morning of July 12—a charge that cannot be substantiated and which the regimental commander denied. Some demanded an investigation of troop behavior. The *Times* dismissed such demands but suggested that the troops needed better training, and a *World* editor believed that such an untrained and disorderly militia "is no better than an armed mob."[12]

Not all officers and enlisted men condoned the military's behavior. One unidentified officer of the infamous Eighty-fourth considered "this slaughter one of the most wanton outrages ever perpetrated." Another found it inconceivable "that when the regiment returned to

11. Figures derived from Appendix B.

12. B. (New York, July 13) to *World*, July 16 ("'panic-stricken military'"); "American" (New York, July 13) to *World*, July 14 ("neither catholic"); *Sun*, July 14 (reports); *Tribune*, July 13; Capt. Peter MacDonald (New York, July 13) to *Tribune*, July 18; "A Personal Narrative" in *Herald*, July 13 ("no warning"); "One Who Was Present" (New York, July 13) to *World*, July 14. The allegation about Company C membership is in the *New York Freeman's Journal and Catholic Register*, July 22. For editorials, see *Times* and *World*, July 18. No records can be found for the Eighty-fourth Regiment or the APA.

[its] armory, not a single musket was examined to discover which men had fired and which [had] not." The regiment's Board of Officers did not consider such complaints at its July 15 meeting, but it adopted resolutions praising police and city authorities for their bravery and then expelled Lt. John Macklin "for cowardice and conduct unbecoming an officer." Macklin replied to the board's decision in a letter to the *Herald* and *Star*. Macklin, who was not even told of the hearing until almost an hour after it began, called the proceedings a "mock trial." Claiming that other members of the Eighty-fourth "had murder in their hearts," he had a different understanding of proper military conduct:

> How the charge of cowardice can be sustained by the butchers of Eighth Avenue I cannot conceive, unless it consists in my failing to shoot down a defenceless [sic] and inoffensive mob, like the others of my regiment, without orders. In any case, I esteem the separation from such a body called for by the dictates of honor, as I could not continue my connection with the regiment without incurring a share of the responsibility for what the people will always regard [as] an indefensible massacre.[13]

Other Company C soldiers also protested. James P. Ross believed "the record of the Eighty-fourth regiment is no longer a respectable one" and suggested that the entire unit should resign. He explained: "We cannot shoulder the crime nor accept the disgrace. The regiment marched out to uphold the law, to protect the people and to add to its reputation for courage and discipline. It returned with the stains of the most unjustifiable murders on its colors. I will never again shoulder a musket in the Eighty-fourth regiment." Ross and seventeen other Company C members signed a July 16 resolution supporting Macklin, announced their resignations, and condemned "the disgraceful conduct" of soldiers who "committed a most foul and deliberate outrage by firing on a comparatively defenseless mass of men, women, and children." The act was "in violation of all military discipline" because "no order to fire . . . [was] given by the commanding officer of the regiment." Calling himself "an impartial Irishman," Company C secretary David Nugent similarly resigned. He

13. Officers quoted in *Star*, July 13, rpt. *Irish World*, July 22 (the *Star*'s July 13 issue is missing from the microfilm copy), *Star*, July 14; *Herald* and *World*, July 16 ("cowardice" charge); John Macklin (n.p., n.d.) to *Star*, July 15, and *Herald*, July 17.

had "no desire to associate in the future with . . . cowardly assassins." At least two Seventh Regiment members—Charles Williamson and E. G. Haight—resigned their commissions, and the regiment continued to lose members in the following months.[14]

Several policemen who also objected publicly were sternly punished for doing so. Thomas O'Grady and Michael Harrison had been fired by Kelso on July 12 for refusing to obey orders and for criticizing the police raid on Hibernian Hall. Officials disciplined at least four others, one of them a prominent police captain. Calling the Eighty-fourth Regiment "a Protestant brigade," Joseph H. Petty censured that unit for endangering police lives at Twenty-fourth Street. Petty and other Thirteenth Precinct policemen who saw duty on July 12 adopted resolutions the next day charging that the Eighty-fourth's barrage "was unnecessary, ill-timed and an outrage." They demanded an investigation. Only Petty, Sgt. William Quinn, and John W. Polk signed the document. On July 14 Kelso's acting chief clerk charged all three with "unofficer-like conduct." Petty later recanted, claiming he had been distraught after seeing one of his men (John O'Connor) shot by troops and had failed to consider the consequences of signing the resolution. Referring to his good record, Petty begged for forgiveness. Polk did too. The commissioners dismissed complaints against both men but fined Petty ten days' wages.[15]

Two days later the Police Board dealt more severely with Patrick Logan. Accused of "improper conduct and insubordination" for refusing to help disperse a crowd at Eleventh Street and Broadway, the ten-year police veteran was not repentant and called witnesses to support his claim that the police and militia used unnecessary violence. Commissioners acted quickly when Logan concluded his de-

14. James P. Ross (n.p., n.d.) to *World* and *Herald*, July 16; *Herald*, July 17; David Nugent (New York, July 16) to *World*, July 17. Those resigning from Company C were Joseph G. Weldrick, William Ahearn, William Shea, George Allen, James Eardley, Gilbert O'Grady, William Anderson, Daniel Mulvey, Phillip Mallin, William Costello, James Nolan, John P. Hamilton, James P. Ross, Peter B. Mulvey, John J. Bergen, Charles Carey, Peter Meagher, and F. Fogarty. See also Company C Sgt. William Ahearn (n.p., n.d.) and "Shields" (New York, July 13) to *Star*, July 15, both of whom also called for investigations of troop conduct. On the Seventh, see Seventh Regiment, Company G, New York State National Guard, *Minutes*, July 8, October 13, November 10; and the circular sent by Col. Emmons Clark to all companies about absenteeism since July 12 in the regiment's *Letter Book*, November 23. Both items are in the New-York Historical Society.

15. *Tribune*, July 13, 20; *Herald*, July 14 (Petty and precinct quotes); *World*, July 16 (charge against Petty), 20; *Times*, July 20.

fense by arguing that he could not get a fair hearing because commissioner Henry Smith disliked Catholics. Logan was fired but had the last word, throwing his badge at his judges and shouting, "There's the shield; I don't want it."[16]

Such protests had no apparent effect. Officials and civilians alike defended the Eighth Avenue police actions. As for charges that the Eighty-fourth Regiment was anti-Catholic, Company C captain William H. O'Neal said his men were partial to no "sectarian organization" but would "always be ready at short notice to rush to the rescue of civil, political and religious liberty." He asserted that those who resigned his unit were not committed to preserving law and order. His troops faced "sorties, brickbats, garbage and missiles of every description" and "a motley crowd, most of whom were hooting, howling and uttering the most horrid and fearful oaths that any being ever was witness to." He believed his men had helped to preserve law and order.[17]

O'Neal implied that troops had undertaken a political and religious mission. Presbyterian minister David Gregg made that view explicit in his July 16 sermon. "The balls which carried death to so many were sent upon the errand of protection to liberty," he said. "Had you been where you are to-day you would have heard the rifles of American patriots ringing out their salutes to religious freedom, and proclaiming death to religious tyranny and prejudice." Ninth Regiment chaplain Edward O. Flagg expressed a similar view during funeral services for soldiers Wyatt and Paige at the packed Calvary Episcopal Church. He chose his sermon text from Micah: "The Lord's voice crieth unto the city." He implored mourners to heed God's imperative and purify New York of "avarice," "theft," "murder," "disrespect," and "debauchery." Wyatt and Paige had died fighting "a growing evil" in city government and city life. Flagg used his text to make four points. First, "mob violence and Christianity are just as widely at variance as are heathenism and Christianity." Mobs required the state to inflict death "where it would not otherwise have been meted out, the innocent suffering with the guilty."[18]

Flagg made clear who were heathens and Christians in moving to a second point. He asserted that "no foreigner has any business to

16. *Herald*, *World* (quotes), and *Irish-American*, July 22.

17. William O'Neal (New York, July 16) to *Herald*, July 17, and *Sun*, July 18.

18. *Tribune* (Gregg), *World* (Flagg), *Sun*, *Times*, and *Irish-American*, July 17.

4. Bravo! Bravo! Thomas Nast cartoon. *Harper's Weekly*, July 29, 1871.

wrest from us those rights for which our forefathers fought and bled" and that "a foreigner should least of all, by word or deed, dare to impugn the institutions which gave him the home and opportunities afforded by our own free, beloved country." The divine imperative also required that America remain free from sectarian animosity, and, finally, "the Lord's voice on the present occasion requires us never to surrender our religious liberties." The minister found a lesson in recent events. "You have learnt how easily your liberties may be wrested from you," he thundered. "While you respect the good men of every creed, stand ready to assert your rights at the ballot-box and wherever duty may call you. Let your vote be like your sacred honor."[19]

Other military defenders focused just on the militia's actions. They argued that troops could not distinguish between actual rioters and innocent spectators and that even the innocent and the curious unwittingly may have concealed assailants. The "innocent" therefore were "guilty." If troops fired in panic and without orders, their indiscretion nevertheless saved the city from "frightful butchery and pillage" later that night when darkness, time, and whiskey would have transformed the mob into a ferocious beast. If soldiers were disorderly, they should be better trained. But no one should expect soldiers to coddle an angry mob. *Harper's Weekly* concluded: "There is nothing more conclusively proved than that in repressing a mob the promptest and sternest measures are the most humane and the most efficient. There must be no threatening, no blank cartridges, but point-blank broadsides." Col. John S. Loomis agreed. The North Pacific Railroad's land commissioner, Loomis demonstrated his appreciation for the military's action by awarding a quarter-section of land to the families of Wyatt and Paige.[20]

Such support enabled military officials to ignore the serious charges of troop misconduct, except when "misconduct" meant "cowardice." The dismissal of Macklin and Company C sergeant William Ahearn reflected an official military judgment that disobeying orders was a more serious offense than succumbing to panic. No troops were chastised in the regimental commander's final reports. Varian and Shaler exonerated the Eighty-fourth. Varian told Lt. Col. Cor-

19. *World*, July 17.

20. *Tribune*, July 13 ("butchery")–15; F. (New York, July 17) to *Times*, July 18; "Innocent Persons," *Harper's Weekly* 15 (July 29): 691.

5. The lesson of the twelfth. *Frank Leslie's Illustrated Newspaper*, July 29, 1871.

nelius B. Mitchell that he had ordered his Eighty-fourth to the rear merely to reorganize the unit after assaults broke company skirmish lines. His order was not meant to imply dissatisfaction with troop performance; for he also said "most emphatically that the attack made upon you, as has been represented, required prompt and immediate repulsions and had I been present in person would have given orders to fire without hesitation."[21]

Shaler closed the issue of troop misconduct in his lengthy final report to Hoffman. The general said that he felt compelled to comment publicly on military matters because "so much has been said by certain classes, and so much has been written calculated to bring into disrepute at least a portion of that organization, which alone can protect and defend law-abiding citizens in their rights of person and property in times of riot and anarchy." Shaler therefore believed he would "be pardoned for assuming the guardianship of the honor and reputation" of his soldiers, declaring that misconduct charges had "a partisan origin and an unmanly aim." A review of the evidence disclosed that soldiers "acted with coolness and discretion." His commanders' reports, numerous letters of praise, and the opinions of Eighth Avenue area residents had convinced him that "while New York possesses so brave and self-sacrificing a body of protectors, she has little to fear from internal dissensions."[22]

"Traitors to law and Me arise, and to the reward
stand; It is not fit that they should rule who
fear a mob's command."

Thus did *Harper's Weekly* poetically express a view, through its portrait of "Columbia," which others also shared.[23] Many agreed with Shaler that state troops should control working-class violence, but for them the problem was even more serious. Irish Roman Catholics

21. Reports are in *Times*, *World*, and *Herald*, July 21. See J. M. Varian (New York, July 15) to Lt. Col. C. B. Mitchell, printed in *Times* and *Herald*, July 16.

22. Maj. Gen. Alexander Shaler (New York, July 19) to "Sir" [Hoffman], printed in *Herald* (and others), July 22, and in Shaler, *Report*, 33. Twenty years later, Seventh Regiment Colonel Emmons Clark recalled that while some members of the Seventh and Eighty-fourth "fired without proper orders, the conduct of both regiments was generally approved by the public, and was never censured by the military authorities" (Clark, *History of the Seventh Regiment of New York, 1806–1889* [New York: Regiment, 1890), 2:195.

23. *Harper's Weekly* 15 (July 29): 696.

formed a "dangerous class" that threatened American Protestant society. Critics argued that the Tweed Ring should be ousted even before the fall elections because official city action revealed that Tammany embodied Irish Catholic subversive designs.

Nativists were convinced that the Irish rioted on July 12 to further Rome's objectives. "We do not accuse the Pope of Rome, nor Archbishop McCloskey, nor the Roman Catholic priests in this city, of getting up this riot," the Presbyterian *New York Observer* editorialized. "But we do say that it was in the interest of Romanism, and that Roman Catholic hatred of Protestants inspired those who meditated and made the assault upon a Protestant procession." Claiming that America belonged to "American Protestants," one writer wondered if Irish attacks on Orangemen were not just "a cover and a blind" for "the intense hatred and bitterness directed against the 30,000,000 American Protestants as well?"[24]

To many others, attacks on American Protestantism were inseparable from Irish assaults on American republicanism. The Reverend Mr. Gregg, a Presbyterian, thought that the riot "delivered a practical sermon on the spirit of Roman Catholicism"; for "whenever it has the opportunity it is sapping the very foundation of our freedom." To the Republican *Boston Advertiser*, "the riot was the outbreak of *a dangerous spirit*, and not the sudden outburst of resentment against some grievous wrong. It was a deliberate assault on one of the most precious privileges of the American people." Such concerns prompted one New Yorker to "question whether Roman Catholicism is consistent at all with the duties and obligations of republican citizenship." The question was easily answered. He found, in the riot, evidence that "whoever submits his mind to the Church of Rome cannot raise it to the conception of that citizenship which gave to history a WASHINGTON, an ADAMS, or a JEFFERSON, or a LINCOLN." Lamenting that "if such things can occur, you can't call the United States a free country any more," Jay Cooke promised that "if Catholics overstep their rights, they will have trouble." And the *Herald* viewed the riot outcome as "A Glorious Victory" and as "a battle of having been fought and won for equal rights, the constitution, liberty and law."[25]

24. *New York Observer*, n.d., rpt. *Tribune*, July 21; "A Native American Protestant" (n.p., n.d.) to *Herald*, July 16.

25. *Tribune*, July 17 (Gregg); *Boston Advertiser*, July 13 (emphasis mine), rpt. *Herald*,

Nativism and racism often combined in assessments of Irish character. The Irish were intolerant, demonic, savage, and morally inferior. By turns "cowardly" and "brutal," George Templeton Strong believed "their bestiality was of the type peculiar to France, Erin, and carnivora." He was gratified "that the Irish roughs have had a rough lesson." These implications of Celtic inferiority were expanded into a full-scale racist attack in a *Times* editorial: Louis Jennings contended that the French and Irish shared

> the same passionate impetuosity, the same tendency to harbor feelings of revenge. Fondness for glare, glitter and noise, for somewhat puerile forms of excitement, and for fighting considered as a pastime, are equally distinctive of the Celt of remote history and the nearest approach we have to his lineal descendants. Celtic worship has always inclined to the sensuous type, and the social organization of the race has inevitably tended to the slavish subjection inherent in the clan, rather than to the personal independence that has come to us from the forests of Germania. The Celt, in his very struggles to be free, moves in masses wherein all individual opinions are silenced, and where, consequently, the natural tendency is to excess.

Other papers said the Eighth Avenue Irish crowd included "evil-looking wretches, lowering browed, hallow-cheeked, shabbily dressed, and evidently the lowest of the low," whose "instincts . . . were hideously brutal." It was "natural" for Irish Celts on July 12 to try to steal the bodies of Wyatt and Paige "for purposes of mutilation"; for they were nothing less than "barbarous assailants."[26]

For many, Catholicism and its priests only strengthened the inherent barbarity of Celtic people. *Scribner's Monthly* acknowledged that priests publicly denounced attempts to interfere with Orangemen but maintained "the fact is that the influence of their teaching through all the centuries has been to foster these brutal exhibitions

---

July 14; E.S.B. (New York, July 14) to *Times*, July 18 (New Yorker); *Sun*, July 13 (Cooke); *Herald*, July 14. For a related view, see "Processions," *Harper's Weekly* 15 (July 29): 690–91.

26. George Templeton Strong, *The Diary of George Templeton Strong*, vol. 4, *The Post-War Years, 1865–1875*, ed. Allan Nevins and Milton H. Thomas (New York: Macmillan, 1952), 371, 372; *Times*, July 16; *World*, July 13 ("wretches"); *Sun*, July 14 ("assailants"). For similar views, see E. W. Hitchcock's sermon in *Times*, July 17; and *Methodist*, n.d., rpt. *Tribune*, July 21.

of intolerance." *Scribner's* told priests it was now their responsibility to transform Irish character. "Give them some culture," the editors demanded, "so that they shall be reflective and rational. The great masses engaged in the late riot were as ignorant as horses. They did not know enough to know that the Orangemen were intellectually and morally their superiors." With that knowledge, the Irish would learn tolerance and the "charitable spirit of Christianity." Without it, Catholics would become "public enemies."[27]

Others agreed that the Irish threatened "American" values. "The Irish of this city . . . are not satisfied with things as they are," E. L. Godkin wrote just after the riot. "They want more money, and less work, and fewer Protestants, and cheaper whiskey." Class, and not just nativist, concerns informed Godkin's critique. A similar view was expressed by the banker Rufus Hatch, who grumbled that "if this city is to be given over to a set of drunken Irish rioters it's about time to stop it." The riot "beats the worst religious outrage of the Commune." W. A. Wheelock, vice-president of the New York Stock Exchange, considered the Irish so serious a threat to America that if Hoffman had not intervened, "it would have been time to take the law into our own hands" by organizing "a vigilance committee."[28]

Like Godkin, Hatch, Wheelock, and many others, the *Times* editor Jennings believed it was the duty of "the intelligent, the wealthy and the patriotic" to "reform" Irish character and thereby prevent future attacks on property. In his sweeping nativist and class judgment of "'The Dangerous Classes,'" the Englishman Jennings expressed the concerns of many early Gilded Age reformers who viewed the riot as final proof that Irish thought and behavior undermined American society. The riot should remind "the comfortable classes" that they rested atop a "volcano." New York harbored young boys, "roughs," "ruffians," street gangs, criminals, and a vast laboring class, "who [caring] nothing for our liberty or civilization," were jealous of their employers and the rich, and had no hope of improving their lives. They burrowed "at the roots of society, and only [came] forth in the darkness and in times of disturbance, to plunder and prey on the good things which surround them." "This class of working men in our City are mainly Irish Catholics," Jennings con-

27. "The Riot of Romanism," *Scribner's Monthly* 2 (September 1871): 546.

28. "The Irish and the Riots," *Nation* 13 (July 20): 36. See the editorial "Holiday Violence," in *Times*, for that paper's view on how Old World drinking habits increase violence during and after holidays. Hatch and Wheelock were quoted in *Sun*, July 13.

tinued. "They are densely ignorant, and easily aroused by prejudice or passion. Let them once break forth, and their passion and violence would soon take its direction toward the property of the rich and well-to-do." The police and militia had performed a great service to all propertied interests by crushing the Eighth Avenue Irish rioters.[29]

So disorderly Irish Catholics needed periodic lessons. Police commissioner Henry Smith was especially pleased with the militia's performance, but he regretted to a *Tribune* reporter "that there was not a larger number killed." A bank president and Republican, Smith believed "that in any large city such a lesson was needed every few years. Had one thousand of the rioters been killed, it would have had the effect of completely cowing the remainder, nor would any threatening demonstration have been made again for years." A veteran guardsman arrived at a similar conclusion after fighting "traitors" in the draft riots and again in 1871. Arguing that mobs never were persuaded by reason, he maintained that to crush a riot "somebody has got to be killed, and it is better to kill the few than the many." The *Springfield Republican* cautioned New York's "worthy citizens" that their city might become another Paris, and it hoped Orange assailants would be severely punished. The Massachusetts paper assumed that many 1871 rioters had been involved in the draft riots as well: "They and their fellow scoundrels got off a great deal too easily then; we hope that if there is any mistake now it will be on the side of severity. The dangerous classes need a lesson that will last them for a decade at least."[30]

Others believed that the Orangemen, like guardsmen, were surrogates in the crucial confrontation between opposing sets of values

29. *Times*, July 16.

30. Smith's remarks paraphrased in *Tribune*, July 14; "Veteran" (New York, July 22) to *Times*, July 23; *Springfield Republican*, July 13, rpt. *World*, July 14. For similar views, see also "American Metropolis" (New York, July 12) to *Times*, July 14; R.M.C. (New York, July 14) to *Tribune*, July 18; the comments of an unidentified former judge in *World*, July 14; and *New York Evangelist*, July 20, which demanded stern retribution for "conspirators" against Orangemen, who "have not been ambitious to attract attention." On Henry Smith, see Callow, *Tweed Ring*, 146–47. Views similar to Smith's were expressed in 1857 by Col. Abram Duryee. As a police commissioner in 1874, Duryee praised his men's handling of the Tompkins Square riot as "the most glorious sight I ever saw"; see Cook, *Armies of the Streets*, 44–45; and Herbert G. Gutman, "The Tompkins Square 'Riot' in New York City on January 13, 1874," *Labor History* 6 (Winter 1965): 56. Pleas for more such "lessons" emerged after the 1877 strikes and the Haymarket Square violence in 1886; see Robert V. Bruce, *1877: Year of Violence* (Chicago: Quadrangle, 1959), 313; and Henry David, *The History of the Haymarket Affair* (1936; rpt. New York: Collier, 1963), 186–88.

and class interests. Ministers Henry Aston, Henry Ward Beecher, and Samuel Burchard worried that American Protestants did not appreciate the battle that Orangemen had waged on their behalf. In his Sunday sermon at the Second Street Methodist Chapel, Aston said "the Catholic mob declared [its] intention to murder Orangemen, and as Protestants and Americans, we may justly compare ourselves with these Orangemen." Romanism subverted American laws, which came from "our primitive fathers," who forged the Constitution according to godly principles. That some people believed Orangemen had no right to parade revealed the importance of Protestant unity. To Beecher, Orangemen were transformed into "the representatives of a principle which lies at the foundation of modern civilization." A question of right was now "a sacred duty." "It is high time Protestants were awake to this subject," Burchard appealed. In 1882, Burchard would become famous for his slanderous remark that the Democrats were a party of "Rum, Romanism, and Rebellion." That sentiment emerged from his pulpit just after the 1871 riot. "We must suffer no foreign sect to come in and monopolize the public funds," the Presbyterian minister said, "occupy all the high places of public trust, and then say who shall parade in our public streets."[31]

Burchard's views about Democrats caused a sensation in 1882, but they were common stuff just after the 1871 riot. One "Native American" reminded "a class of the better portion of the Democrats" that it aided and abetted "the baser portion of our own people, who have proved their utter disregard of principle by mixing in with such a horde of foreign vagabonds for the sake of power." Others condemned Democratic officials for condescending "to a threatening papist rabble," for helping to transform America into another "priest-ridden Ireland," and for representing in official government "a lawless and bloodthirsty mob." The *Times* believed that "for the first time since 1863," Tammany officials realized "the risks they run by suffering the Irish to usurp all power in this City." The *Sun* rested its case merely by reminding readers that Hall's initials were "A.O.H."[32]

Some demanded that Hall and Kelso resign; others broadened the

31. Aston, paraphrased, in *Times*, July 17, and *Christian Union*, July 19, rpt. *Herald*, July 21; *Herald*, July 21 (Beecher); Burchard paraphrased in *Herald*, July 17.

32. "A Native American" (New York, July 17) to *Times*, July 18; "American Metropolis" (New York, July 12) to *Times*, July 14; *Nation* 13 (July 13): 17–18; *Times*'s editorial of July 13; *Sun*, July 18. See also the Republican *Troy Whig*, July 13, and *Hartford Courant*, July 13, excerpts rpt. *Herald*, July 14.

6. Religious processions. Thomas Nast cartoon. *Harper's Weekly*, July 29, 1871.

appeal by insisting that native-born Protestants replace the Irish working-class domination of the city. "Alas! for the Republic," a Jersey City resident cried, "if we do not soon force a change and place true Americans to rule us, instead of a foreign mob." The *Tribune* concluded its July 13 editorial "The Tammany Riot" by declaring, "These frightful scenes will not cease until that corrupt party which depends for its existence upon the votes of the ignorant and vicious loses its tyrannical control of our public life." "So long as the City is governed by men to whom the Irish vote is a vital necessity," the *Times* maintained, "so long will their dupes be shamefully corrupted and their worst passions fed." The Reverend Mr. Gregg and the Baptist *Examiner and Chronicle* urged that the Tweed Ring be voted out in the fall elections by "free-born" citizens and a "law-and-order party." "If we afford ignorant Irish Catholics an asylum and protection," said one nativist Democrat, "intelligent Irish Protestants must equally find protection. It may be time to revive the old cry, 'Put none but Americans on guard.'" "We are to-day governed too much by foreign influence," said another. "This should not be. Let Americans govern America. Let the offices be held by American-born citizens."[33]

Some formed nativist groups. On July 14, a group of young men organized a Washington Post branch and vowed "not to allow any foreign mob to rule this City." There also was a report that more than sixty divisions of the Patriotic Order of Sons of America had been formed in New York City within the previous year and that the riot also had increased membership in the Organization of Americans United.[34]

Nativists worried about the ethnic and religious threats Tammany embodied because they believed Tammany embodied an evil, foreign, anti-Protestant spirit. Business and financial leaders urged well-to-do citizens to join in opposing the equally dangerous threat posed by Tammany's *working-class* constituency. Even the Congregational

33. Demands for resignations: *Tribune*, July 14, 15; *Times*, July 13, 15; *Christian Leader*, n.d., rpt. *Tribune*, July 21; "Justitia" (New York, July 14) to *Tribune*, July 18; B. H. (n.p., n.d.) to *Times*, July 14. Quotations: K. (Jersey City, July 12), to *Tribune*, July 13; editorial in ibid.; story in ibid., July 17; *Times*, July 16; *Examiner and Chronicle*, n.d., rpt. *Tribune*, July 21; "An Ex-Democrat" (n.p., n.d.) and "An Old Style Democrat" (n.p., n.d.) to *Herald*, July 16.

34. *Times*, July 15, 16; "Native" (n.p., n.d.) to *Sun*, July 21.

minister Merrill Richardson made such an appeal from the pulpit of his fashionable Madison Avenue church on July 17:

> If the educated, the Christian, and the law-respecting citizens of New-York will only throw off their political objectivity and take, as they can, the government of this city into their own hands, no more such bloody and disgraceful scenes as took place last week will again occur. If, however, the higher classes will *not* govern, the lower classes *will*; and what kind of government it will give, you have sadly experienced. The pulpit and the press must work together to impress upon the consciences of our best classes the duty of wresting our city government from the hands it is now in.

New York Stock Exchange president Thomas E. Clerke and two anonymous writers to the *Times* and *World* all expressed alarm and disgust that businessmen were not more active politically. Describing himself as a recent Republican convert, Clerke said the violence and misrule "looks like the precursor of civil war." Another convert feared the establishment of Irish class rule in America or "a religious war." The third claimed that "every sound-minded business native American" would agree that no political candidates should be elected who favored continuing the kind of Old World street parades that fostered ethnic and class unrest. On July 13, the Union League Club incorporated such views in a lengthy resolution condemning Tammany and urging the immediate removal of "this infamous clique." Members reasoned that city officials, in not punishing the Elm Park rioters, had given the Irish license to commit more serious crimes in 1871. Tammany was "a gang of aiders, abettors, and supporters of ruffianism and disorder," which brought shame to the city and state. The Seventeenth Assembly District Republican Association adopted similar resolutions on July 17.[35]

"pious Orange Massacres"

Irish Catholics paid little public attention to nativist attacks. Many blamed the militia and Hoffman for the "slaughter" and promised to

35. Richardson paraphrased in *Tribune*, July 17; Clerke quoted in *Sun*, July 13; "A New Republican" (n.p., n.d.) to *Times*, July 13; "An Old School Democrat" (n.p., n.d.) to *World*, July 14; *Tribune*, July 14; *Times*, July 18.

vote their outrage in November's elections. While few defended the ring, many praised Kelso and Hall for attempting to prevent Orange affronts and troop violence. Some even believed Republicans provoked the riot to discredit Irish Catholics and Democrats. Others promised vengeance. But the overriding Irish Catholic concern was about the implications of state support for Orange parades and principles, because such support would harden class lines and pauperize the city's Irish workers, just as Orangeism had helped pauperize Irish peasants. These concerns are discussed below, but they were aptly summarized in an *Irish World* poem called "The Great Orange Massacre." The anonymous poet claimed that Orange parades were as insulting to Irish Catholics as Gen. Benjamin Butler celebrations would be to the South:

Come let us sing in joyous songs
What late befell in New York City,
How heroes shot at helpless throngs,
And butchered scores with mocking pity,
    In a glorious Orange Massacre.

These Orangemen, like loyal fellows,
In Ireland fight for "Church and King;"
And to improve our laws, they tell us,
Their royal maxims here they bring,
    With pious Orange Massacres.

Our Orangemen in secret swear
No Democrats should office hold,
For freedom these too freely share,
And spread o'er countries new and old,
    Without great Orange massacres.

Show us an Orange Democrat!
For sight so rare, we safely promise,
With golden coins we'll fill your hat,
And vote for Mayor some Orange rat
    To lead in Orange Massacres.

To keep men out, and keep men down,
Are plainly Orange rule and creed;
Then citizens should freedom crown
By spreading wide this Orange breed,
    And bloody Orange Massacres.

The North shall dim this Orange glory
By marches through the Rebel cities;
And yearly make their streets all gory,
For Butler flags and loyal ditties,
With pious Northern Massacre.[36]

Other anonymous protests occurred. Two effigies emerged in Brooklyn's Irish neighborhoods to express anger at Hoffman and sympathy for a riot victim. On July 17, a group of Irish workers paraded down Hamilton Avenue bearing the governor's straw symbol. The men hung the effigy from a police telegraph pole and affixed a placard reading: "John T. Hoffman, Governor of New-York, died July 12, 1871." Police captured the effigy but made no arrests that day—or two days later when friends of White House saloon owner Thomas McCleary, who died on July 19, hung another likeness of Hoffman near the Washington Avenue Bridge.[37]

More widespread public displays of community sentiment accompanied the funerals of other Irish Catholic riot victims. Long corteges followed Hannah Conor Hanby and Michael McCormack to Calvary Cemetery on July 14. That same afternoon, John Riley's wife and two children watched from the steps of their East Sixteenth Street apartment as friends carried a mahogany casket to a waiting hearse. Riley's casket was sealed with silver nails and was identified by a silver cross inscribed "John Reilly, aged twenty-six years." Eighty men and twenty-eight carriages accompanied the body to Brooklyn for burial. An aging, grief-stricken Irish woman who remained at the house told a reporter she hoped that "the curse of Cromwell wud rest on the head of the black-harted basthard that killed poor Johnny Reilly." All afternoon, Thirty-fourth Street was crowded with black carriages and hearses on their way to the Greenpoint ferry and thence to Brooklyn's Calvary cemetery. One hearse carried the body of Daniel Mulvey, while nearly one hundred of Mulvey's fellow members of the Society of Immaculate Conception walked beside.[38]

Similar scenes were repeated at the July 16 funerals of Michael O'Shea, James Monaghan, and Patrick Slattery. As many as fourteen hundred members of St. Patrick's Mutual Alliance accompanied Michael Kelly's body from his parents' home on East Thirty-seventh

36. *Irish World*, August 19.

37. *Tribune*, *Star*, and *Times*, July 18; *Sun* and *Herald*, July 20.

38. *Times*, *World*, *Herald* (curse), and *Tribune*, July 15. "Riley" is the coroner's spelling.

Street. Elsewhere in the city, one hundred Ancient Order of Hibernians wore white mourning scarves as they led Timothy Sullivan's funeral procession. (Sullivan was the only known AOH riot casualty.) They were followed by an open hearse, as many as eighty carriages, and two hundred Tweed Benevolent Association members. Bedecked with white sashes, black rosettes, and a badge reading "We mourn our loss," association men selected eight from their numbers as pallbearers and paid for most of the funeral expenses.[39]

No violence occurred at these events, but frustration and anger led to a July 15 fight, at Doyle's saloon on Roosevelt Street, between an English sailor and brothers John and Patrick O'Brien. The sailor tried to break up a fistfight between the O'Briens and a saloon patron by boasting he could lick the brothers better than Irish Catholics had been beaten on July 12. The ensuing brawl spilled into the street, where one O'Brien mistakenly stabbed a close friend, who died shortly afterward. The following day, several Irish men attacked Seventy-first Regiment soldiers Charles N. Swift and Emile Cardozo as they returned from the funerals of Wyatt and Paige. The group's leader reportedly was John Mahony. A blacksmith and Sixty-ninth Regiment member, Mahony tried and failed to stab Swift and Cardozo with a sword cane. He was arrested. And on July 17, Jersey City Orangeman Timothy O'Leary lost an ear in a scuffle over the riot with two men.[40]

How much other violence stemmed from the riot is unknown, but much Irish bitterness and resentment was channeled through Irish-American nationalist groups and local political organizations. Members of such bodies criticized the militia, Orangemen, and especially Hoffman. On July 14, for example, Irish Democratic Club No. 11 members heard a Mr. Lawrence denounce Hoffman for allowing Orangemen to revive an old feud. Lawrence urged Hoffman's defeat in the next election. That night at a Fenian council meeting, John O'Mahony, William G. Halpine, Stephen J. Meany, and George Cahill drafted a resolution that bitterly criticized Hoffman and the Orangemen. The council supported constitutional guarantees of peaceful assembly but said Orangemen were "aliens . . . sworn to uphold monarchical institutions . . . inimical to the government and laws of

39. *Times*, *World*, *Herald*, *Tribune*, July 17.

40. *World* and *Sun*, July 16; *Herald*, *Tribune*, and *Times*, July 17; *Sun* and *Times*, July 18.

the United States." Moreover, the council found that Hoffman was "morally guilty of the wanton and unprovoked massacre of a large number of our fellow citizens, and of the wounding and maiming of many more, by his uncalled-for usurpation of the powers that properly belong to the Mayor and Municipality of New York." It also demanded that "all parties in these wanton outrages [be] arrested and punished according to the law for the unprovoked murders committed by them on the 12th day of July, 1871." Irish Confederation members adopted a similar resolution promising that if "the laws fail to punish the guilty, it will then become the *duty* of the sovereign people of this state to administer justice as should be through the medium of the ballot box, at the next and subsequent elections."[41]

Irish residents of the Fifth, Eighth, Fourteenth, and Nineteenth wards also took action. Meeting on Canal Street July 17, Fifth Ward citizens blamed the riot on "fanatical bigots, who desire to create a hatred towards Irish Catholics and renew the spirit of Know-Nothingism." They held Hoffman responsible for the July 12 carnage and promised to oppose him in future elections. Here, nativist charges did not go unanswered. Meeting participants repudiated "the stigma by which prejudice and bigotry is sought to be attached to the character of Irish Catholics, viz.: that they are not law-abiding citizens and are the promoters of riot and disorder." The following night, Fourteenth Ward Irish residents met on Mott Street and adopted almost identical statements. At their July 19 meeting, Eighth Warders added only a demand for a thorough investigation.[42]

Perhaps the largest Irish meeting that night took place at Brevoort Hall at Fifty-fourth Street near Third Avenue. Fully two thousand people cheered when Stephen J. Meany promised that neither Orangemen nor Know-Nothings would ever "rule this country." Meany said that he and D. P. Conyngham witnessed the Eighth Avenue slaughter. "I saw armed and clubbed ruffians shooting innocent men, for the crime of looking at Orangemen," he said. As he "stood in Irish blood my own blood curdled, and I prayed that I might see the day when my countrymen's blood might be avenged." Yet Meany counseled that "immediate vengeance may do harm." Instead, he urged all Irish to vote against Hoffman on election day. The group's resolu-

41. *Times* and *Herald*, July 15; *Tribune*, July 19; *Herald*, July 16; *Tribune* and *Times* July 17 (Fenians); *Irish-American*, July 29 (Irish Confederation).

42. *World* and *Herald*, July 18 (quotes); *Star*, July 19; *Tribune*, July 18–20; *Times*, July 20.

tions also protested against "the willful and malicious accusations made against our race" and affirmed that the Irish were "liberty loving and loving people" who resented "the charge that we are a sectarian people."[43]

Divisions within the Irish community prevented a unified Irish political response to the riot. Fearing that all Irish-Americans would be maligned because of the actions of a minority and that Irish-American nationalist efforts would suffer, prominent nationalists, though they condemned Hoffman and the militia, also condemned Irish working-class opposition to the Orangemen. These divisions became more clear in following years when economic depression and labor unrest combined with Irish Land League demands in the 1880s to provide a radical thrust to Irish working-class politics. Time and circumstances widened the psychological and political breach between the increasingly successful, status-conscious Irish businessmen and professionals and the Irish-American workers.[44]

That gap—so important to understanding varied Irish-American nationalist movements—was reflected in the responses of two "Irish nationalists" who spoke to a *Herald* reporter in Union Square on July 12. The "gentlemen" belittled "longshoremen" for being insensitive to the nationalist cause. Fearing that Americans would think longshoremen represented all Irish sentiments, they vowed that longshoremen would "have to succumb to the spirit of toleration and the power and talent of education." Claiming there were "at least three thousand Fenians" who would not allow riotous behavior to deter nationalist efforts, Thomas Costello pledged to call a mass meeting within a few days to denounce "mob rule in New York." The discredited Fenian leader, John Savage, echoed Costello's concerns.[45]

Members of the honored Irish Brigade Association were equally concerned about the Irish image. In spite of the riot, these Civil War officers decided to hold their long-scheduled annual picnic on July 13. Cruising leisurely up the Hudson to Dudley's Grove, they discussed the previous day's events with a *World* reporter. The reporter claimed that these men reflected Irish "middle class" opinion. Some blamed Hall for "advertising" the riot; others criticized Hoffman for "inducing" it. One officer thought the mishandling by civil authori-

43. *Tribune*, *Sun*, *Times*, and *Star*, July 20.
44. These themes are discussed in Chapter 6.
45. *Herald*, July 13, 14.

7. The unconditional surrender. Thomas Nast cartoon. *Harper's Weekly*, July 29, 1871.

ties "was only equalled by the 'horrible incapacity and insanity of the military mob.'" Many others complained "of the 'dastardly slaughter' of innocent people."[46]

On July 15, Brigade Association member Gen. Martin T. McMahon and a number of others called for a mass meeting. Their Astor House Brigade conference produced a carefully worded resolution:

> *Resolved*, That as an organization representing in a great measure the Irish soldiery of New York, who fought to maintain the government of the United States, and thereby gave substantial evidence of respect for law and love of liberty, we deeply deplore the calamitous events of Wednesday, the 12th inst., and denounce as slanderous and unjust the imputation made in many quarters, and supposed to be implied in certain official acts of public officers, that the great body of the Irish citizens of New York are in any manner responsible for those occurrences. That we fail to perceive in the published reports of those events the evidence of any riotous combination too great or widespread for the civil powers to subdue, and we, therefore, believe that the employment of the militia and the firing upon the people demand a searching and thorough investigation.

After hearing the resolution at a reconvened July 19 meeting, Col. James Magee moved to disband McMahon's committee and dismiss plans for a mass meeting. Magee explained that the Brigade Association was a social and benevolent organization, not a political one, and should not be involved in such controversial matters. Honorary member Stephen J. Meany replied that it *was* the association's business because the good name of the Irish people everywhere had to be protected. Magee's motion failed, and the resolution itself was tabled. Meagher's Irish Brigade joined the effort, putting up one thousand dollars for a legal fund "to prosecute to conviction" anyone who "fired upon the people without proper orders and due warrant of law."[47]

No mass protest meetings or investigations occurred. Brigade members presumably agreed that prolonged public protests would only hurt Irish-American nationalism. They also may have been influenced by city priests and a final rebuke from a recent Irish arrival.

46. *World*, July 14.
47. *World* and *Tribune*, July 17 (resolution); *Times* (Meagher) and *Tribune*, July 20.

Less than two years after his escape to Boston from a British penal colony in Australia, John Boyle O'Reilly addressed a *Boston Pilot* column to the American Irish, "who are made to bare the blame and the shame of the disgraceful proceedings that have marked the 12th of July in New York for the past two years." O'Reilly asked and answered a simple question that only helped perpetuate nativist fears and a historical myth: "Do we or do we not defend the New York rioters? As Irish-American Catholic citizens, we answer, we condemn the rioters, and ignore them both as Irishmen and Catholics." The New York *Freeman's Journal*'s James McMaster agreed. Saying that Orangemen really were members of the APA, which "is made up of the scum of the most degraded class of Irish servants of the British crown," McMaster tried to disassociate himself and the Catholic Church from Irish rioters by claiming that there were other Irishmen in the United States who were "baptized Catholics, but not in the communion of the Catholic Church. They are bound to the 'Ribbon-men's' oath" and not to Rome.[48]

Such views did not deter other Irishmen and their supporters from criticizing Orangemen and city officials. They argued, first, that Orangemen sought to establish a "Church and King" society and ruin America. "It is an incontrovertible historical fact," wrote John H. Greene, "that the main, if not the sole, object of this organization, at its very incipiency in the county of Armagh . . . was the extermination of its Catholic landholders for the purpose of *seizing their farms*." Here, they could make workers dependent too. Greene and others believed that because Orange principles were inimical to American institutions, Orangemen did not deserve public protection. They "are hostile to our American republic" and claim "the right to

48. *Boston Pilot*, July 29, quoted in James Jeffrey Roche, *Life of John Boyle O'Reilly* (Philadelphia: John J. McVey, 1891), 118–19. Twelve years later, O'Reilly repeated his contempt for the 1871 rioters in a speech to the Massachusetts State Convention of the Irish National League of America. The convention was purposely called for July 12, 1883, to symbolize Irish Catholic and Protestant unity. O'Reilly said he recognized "in this meeting a symbolic and a unique purpose. Twelve years ago this day, in a great American city, . . . the militia regiments were called out to protect the peace, because the lives and property of the great city were in danger from an imported Irish abomination and nuisance" (quoted in ibid., 232). In his memoirs, the Fenian John Devoy recalled that "there was no real riot," claimed that the crowd fired only one errant shot, and dismissed the incident as a somewhat amusing event; see Devoy, *Recollections of an Irish Rebel* (1929; rpt. Shannon: Irish University Press, 1969), 339. See also the *Freeman's Journal and Catholic Register*, July 22.

set apart one day each year on which to rake up every memory of past contest, re-inflame each subsided passion, and by all manner of appeal to the eye and the ear and the recollection to stimulate hate and evoke violence." After all, asked "An English Dissenter," "what has 'religious liberty' to do with an order established for the avowed purpose of putting down all dissent—Protestant and Catholic alike—from a church established by law?" To claims that the Orange parade marchers actually were all "respectable" APA members and not Orangemen, "Amicus Veritas" asked why did "they carr[y] the Orange flag, if they were not Orangemen?" Moreover, Irish Confederation president Thomas Kerrigan and port warden Edward Carey claimed that AOH members had *stayed away* from Eighth Avenue and Hibernian Hall on July 12. So the Orangemen, not Irish Catholics, were to blame for the riot. And to *Irish World* editor Patrick Ford, the Orangemen sought to convey a message in their parade. "They say: Slave-born Papists, our fathers met and defeated your fathers in 1690, and we, their sons, are ready to meet *you* now! Down, Croppies, and know your place! This is the meaning of the Orange parade." To New York's *Catholic World*, charges that Irish Catholics sparked the riot and hoped to weaken republicanism were nonsense: "Not a few of us have fled from the tyranny and oppression of Protestant governments; expatriated ourselves for the sake of liberty; and do you believe us such fools as to destroy it the moment we have found it?"[49]

A second and related argument focused on Hoffman and the militia and took its cue from the thrust of O'Neill Fitzgerald's poetic blast:

> Sublime spectacle, says the *Times*,
> Three thousand armed men
> Pour volleys and volleys into legs and groins;
> Ground arms and load again.
> Forward the lead, pull the dead,
> Cover the sidewalks with slaughter.

49. See John H. Greene (Washington, D.C., July 17) to *Irish-American*, July 29; "An English Dissenter" (New York, July 15) to *World*, July 18; "Amicus Veritas" (n.p., n.d.) to *Sun*, July 21; Kerrigan and Carey in *Tribune*, July 24; *Irish World*, July 22; and *Catholic World*, n.d., rpt. *Irish-American*, September 30. See also editorial in *World*, July 13; R. K., A.P.A. (n.d., n.p.) to *Sun*, July 17; "Justice" (New York, July 16) to *World*, July 18; "Anonymous" (n.p., n.d.) to *World*, July 14; J.S.G. (Philadelphia, August 12) to *Irish-American*, August 19; W.C.D. (n.p., n.d.) to *Herald*, July 30; Michael J. Callihan (New York, July 15) to *Irish-American*, July 22; and *Irish-American*'s July 15 editorial.

Several wondered if Hoffman did not believe that it was more important to preserve public order and citizens' lives than to satisfy the "malignant vanity" of Orangemen. If a parade did occur, the police had proved they were capable of maintaining order. "There seems to have been on the part of some of the authorities a nervous readiness to employ the troops," an anonymous writer lamented, "and on the part of some of the militia a murderous promptitude in the use of their guns." "If a party of Ku-Kluxers came to New York in order to celebrate the anniversary of some horrible murder perpetrated in the South," asked James O'Donnell, "would Governor Hoffman, in open defiance of the greater position of the citizens of New York say that they should parade and call out the militia to protect them[?]" Others, like William Anderson, "An Exile from Dublin," agreed. "I hope my countrymen will never again be used as tools in helping to put into power the renegade who is the cause of all this bloodshed," he wrote. Many of New York's Irish did not use words to express their outrage at Hoffman. The governor's portrait was torn from walls and trampled in saloons throughout the city.[50]

Hoffman's role was tied to troop misconduct. Repeating their demands for investigations, the *Irish World* and *Irish-American* offered rewards to anyone identifying the real July 12 "murderers" and announced the formation of a "Citizens' Defence [sic] Fund" to pay legal fees. The *Irish World* argued that it was important "to show whether the Irish people of New York are *chronic rioters*, as the daily papers would represent them," or whether it was the military which "made the only riot and committed the only murders that were perpetrated in our city on that day." *Irish-American* editors believed that the fundamental question was whether "Governor Hoffman or President Grant [could] send into our streets a mob of armed ruffians, who, at their own pleasure, may shoot into our own windows, and murder our wives, friends, and children."[51]

A final argument focused on politics. Irish-American and Democratic newspapers accused both regular and Radical Republicans with conspiring to foment the riot. Since Grant's victory in 1868, they

50. O'Neill Fitzgerald (n.p., n.d.) to *Star*, July 17; "Anonymous" (n.p., n.d.) to *World*, July 14; James O'Donnell (New York, July 14) to *Star*, July 15; and William Anderson (New York, July 13) to *Star*, July 16. See also opinions of the Democratic *Philadelphia Age*, *Buffalo Courier*, *Rochester Union*, and *Boston Post*, all rpt. *World*, July 18; *World*, July 13 and 18 ("vanity"); *Irish World*, July 22; and *Sun*, July 15.

51. *Irish World*, August 26; *Irish-American*, July 29.

argued, Radicals had sought ways to convert crucial city and state Democratic votes to the Radicals and thereby help to oust the president in 1872. Republicans of all persuasions had courted Fenians. In 1870, they had convinced Grant himself to send federal troops to protect ballot boxes in city and state elections. This maneuver might not endear them to Tammany's Irish, but it would ensure that Republican votes were not "lost."[52]

These Irish saw Radicals and regular Republicans as class opponents. They argued that desperate Radicals decided to exploit Irish Catholic and Protestant animosity and to marshall nativist sentiment because they were frustrated by their waning power and their inability to weaken Tammany's hold on the Irish. Radicals demanded that city officials protect Orangemen, fully expecting that many Irish Catholics would be killed and that thousands more would desert the Democrats. Orangemen were hapless and unwitting tools: "The Radicals intended to use the Orangemen as a cat's-paw to pull their chestnuts out of the fire." Moreover, Irish defenders argued that the *Tribune* and *Times* purposely exaggerated accounts of Hibernian plans to attack Orangemen in order to force cancellation of the parade and thereby create indignation against Tammany for not protecting Protestant rights. When Kelso's order was published, Hibernian military drills for July 12 were postponed. "The plot was so worked up that the 'Hibernians' should *not* be on the ground," the *Irish World* maintained; "but it was also contrived that the whole Irish element should bear the odium." One New Yorker believed the odium belonged elsewhere. Describing himself as "an American citizen," and "a property-holder," "Civis" agreed that city authorities had "surrendered to a mob." But he claimed that the mob "was made up of Wall Street brokers, of produce-merchants, of bankers, and I am sorry to say of lawyers. I have heard rioters loudly talking treason to the local government of New York at my club within the last six hours." He believed that "on Wall Street and the Exchange be the blood of that day."[53]

The Irish and Democratic press found a flaw in Radical and Republican schemes. Hall had satisfied the city's Irish Democrats by banning the parade; Hoffman sought to appease rural nativist Demo-

52. *Irish-American*, July 15, 22; *Irish World*, August 26. See also New York *Leader*, July 15.

53. *Irish-American* and *Irish World*, July 15 and 22; *World*, July 17 ("cat's-paw"); "Civis" (New York, July 17) to *World*, July 18.

crats. Both Irish papers, while they unequivocally attributed the massacre to Hoffman, clearly understood and condemned the Radical involvement. The *Irish-American* noted perceptively that "the origin of this Orange nuisance is purely political in Ireland; in this country it is doubly so; for it depends upon [sic] its existence, first, on the English influence, . . . and next it leans on the Radical element here, who hope, out of this *embroglio*, to derive a certain advantage."[54]

All elements of the conspiratorial drama were brilliantly captured in an *Irish World* cartoon. An explanatory key accompanied drawings of the Boyne Day celebrants. Shown first was a press band. The *Herald*'s James Gordon Bennett played Scottish bagpipes, Horace Greeley strummed a banjo, *Times* editor Louis Jennings tinkled on a triangle; the *Sun*'s Charles A. Dana tooted a flageolet, and one of the Harpers blared on his horn. The band played an English tune, "Thunderer." Riding on "a spirited Animal of the O.U.A.-sses (Order United American) Genus," standard-bearer John T. Hoffman "(Our Orange Viceroy)" held aloft an emblem of the English crown inscribed "O-U-Asses." Next came the "Orang(e)-Outangs" and the "A.P.A.-pes." The latter carried a banner describing them as "Darwin's Connecting Link" between the O.U.A.-sses and the Orange-Outangs. Supporting all these next in line was a large segment with a simple placard reading "Fanatical Happy Family." This was "A Riotous and disorderly Mob, with bludgeons and rifles in their hands, which they carried to kill any one who would laugh at the Procession." The paper concluded that "the pageant was worthy of the occasion. The weather was a little stormy, but the processionists wavered not an iota. The Viceroy looked splendid. The band played 'Croppies lie down' vociferously. The troops fought nobly. On the whole, it was a grand day for England—Old and New."[55]

"A fierce, vindictive and passionate class"

Charges that Radicals or Republicans conspired to provoke a riot to gain support from disaffected Irish Democrats cannot be substantiated, but surely there were those who sought to capitalize on Tammany's predicament by supporting the Orangemen. Still, the varied

54. *Irish-American*, July 15; *Irish World*, July 22. See also *World*, July 17; *Leader*, July 12; and "Counselor-at-Law" (n.p., n.d.) to *World*, July 19.

55. *Irish World*, August 24, 1871.

8. Grand turnout of the "Apes" and "Orang-outangs." *Irish World* cartoon, August 12, 1871.

pieces of the riot puzzle form many separate pictures that are not linked by a web of conspiracy. They form instead a mural of contending visions that sparked the initial confrontation over Orange pretensions. A second confrontation occurred after Kelso prohibited the parade and embroiled party politics in the controversy. A third took place on July 12 in New York streets. A final fight erupted in the days after the violence as all participants evaluated riot events and interpreted the consequences for themselves and the nation. The riot intensified, without changing the focus of, those visions, which did often include conspiracy theories. Although nativists and other Tammany foes did not conspire to provoke a riot, they did perpetrate it. Frightened and rattled soldiers, the police, and Orangemen were not unwitting parties to a conspiracy; instead they were surrogates for class interests and for worried Democratic officials. Neither did Irish Catholics conspire to attack Orangemen or APA members. If AOH members developed plans for such attacks in their military drills before July 12, the pattern of violence does not reveal they tried to carry them out. Moreover, quarrymen, longshoremen, and Irish workers do not appear to have harbored schemes for subverting republican institutions, as their detractors charged. Rather, their opposition to Orangemen seems rooted in their belief that Orangemen threatened republicanism's potential for creating equality.

Conspiracy theories became part of the event itself. They helped to reinforce the myth of "the wild Irish" and to reveal much about their advocates' mentalities. We have seen how military and civil authorities dismissed accusations that troops fired indiscriminately, punished dissident officers, and suppressed inquests. They were supported by many persons who blamed the riot on Irish Catholics, who claimed that civilian victims were actual riot participants, and who believed that the rabble had been taught a proper lesson. Generous rewards to policemen further strengthened that myth. Genuine gratitude was combined with efforts to convince the public that the police had saved the city from plunder. While Hoffman publicly saluted the men for their "disciplined, intelligent, dutiful, and fearless" service, the Police Board lauded the force for its honor and courage and for "alacrity, zeal, and efficiency with which you performed every duty imposed upon you during the riotous disturbances." The board granted three days' leave with pay to all patrolmen on duty on Boyne Day and pardoned all policemen (except Quinn and Logan) who had been charged with violating regulations before July 16. A more permanent expression of gratitude was suggested by Henry S. Olcott, an official of the National Insurance Convention headquartered in New York. Olcott sought donations for a series of flags for police to carry in their official parades. Flag inscriptions would acknowledge New Yorkers' gratitude to the police for their "Gallant behavior—July, 1863, And July, 1871."[56]

Injured or ill policemen also received substantial gifts from the 1863 Riot Relief Committee. Nearly $10,000 was awarded to twenty-eight of the thirty-four police casualties. Even sunstroke victims received as much as $400 each. Only two policemen apparently were seriously injured. Henry Hedden was cut above the nose and left eye during a scuffle; John O'Connor suffered a gunshot wound in the side. But Hedden was a captain, so he received $800. Patrolman O'Connor's injury was worth just $225. Henry W. Farbush and Thomas C. Joyce were hurt when they were thrown from their horses. They received $500 and $450 respectively. Patrolman Edward Gilger fell off a stagecoach, bruised his back and arms, and was awarded $350. Most of those who received money had been struck by bricks, stones, or clubs. The *Times* urged its readers to contribute more money to the fund. "If people of means and property only knew how much they owe to the Police at all times," the paper editorialized in announcing the awards, "they would especially seize every opportunity of encouraging the force to act cordially on the side of law and order." The police protected such citizens from "a fierce, vindictive and passionate class, stimulated by the fires of fanaticism and by the incendiary appeals of reckless demagogues."[57]

The *Times*'s opinion was only one of many judgments rendered by contending segments of New York's population before and after the riot. City and state officials successfully sealed avenues for further investigations, but they could not eradicate the perceptions and attitudes that those involved brought to the debate. Fundamental Irish political concerns had become embroiled in American political party considerations.

Governor Hoffman might have pondered that and more as he recuperated from his ordeal at Newport and Albany. A battle fought

56. John T. Hoffman (Albany, July 14) to James J. Kelso, printed in *World*, July 17; Henry Smith (New York, July 15) "to the Officers and Men of the Police Force," printed in *Times*, July 17; *World*, July 18, 19; *Tribune* and *Times*, July 19; Henry S. Olcott (New York, July 19) to *World* and *Tribune*, July 20.

57. Amounts and sources are cited in Appendix B. See also *Times*, July 21.

181 years before along the banks of an Irish river now threatened his political career. Less than two weeks after the riot, Peter B. Sweeney informed him that New York's "Irish element are permanently disaffected toward you." And while a year later his friend George J. Magie claimed that Stephen J. Meany had offered to help reconcile the city's Irish to support Hoffman for reelection that fall, Magie said to Hoffman, "I think he is mistaken as regards some of them. Here, at Elmira and Corning, they are very bitter, and swear they will never support Governor Hoffman." Irish disaffection did force Hoffman to step aside in 1872. If he foresaw this possibility as he vacationed in July 1871, perhaps he found comfort in other things. His militia's muskets had stilled a dangerous mob. Now, Orange muskets in Phoenix, New York, tendered him a one-hundred-gun salute. Irish Catholics blamed him for the "massacre." But friends rushed to tell him "that when I read [his proclamation] aloud to my family, we instantly gave shout and joyful cheer for the man who . . . saved the honor of the city & the state." They also congratulated him for actions that were "both right and expedient and such as all good citizens are bound to sustain" and were "for the cause of liberty." Members of Gideon Loyal Orange Lodge No. 10 tendered him their thanks, publicly acknowledging that "as citizens, all rejoice that the laws have been carried out impartially, and that it has been fully demonstrated that in this 'free country' all are equally free, and every class is entitled to the fullest protection." Effigies lasted but moments. Buildings could endure decades. And Hoffman learned that the Toronto Loyal Orange District Lodge planned to erect a new Orange building called "Hoffman Commemoration Hall." The governor's role was indelibly stamped in Irish-American history in a much less auspicious but more telling manner by an unknown historian who recorded it for Calvary Cemetery visitors: "Timothy Sullivan, aged 27. Died July 12, 1871."[58]

58. Peter B. Sweeney (New York, July 21), George J. Magie (Watkins Glen, N.Y., August 13, 1872), David A. Ogden ("right and expedient") (Pen Yan, N.Y., July 15), and Smith M. Weed ("liberty") (Plattsburgh, N.Y., August 4)—all to John T. Hoffman, in Hoffman Papers, Personal (Misc.), New York Public Library; Anson D. F. Randolph ("joyful cheer") (New York, July 17) to Hoffman, in John T. Hoffman Folder, New-York Historical Society; and *Tribune*, July 20 (Orange thanks). See also *Times*, July 20; *Tribune* and *Herald*, July 21; *World*, July 17; and Jerome Mushkat, *The Reconstruction of the New York Democracy, 1861–1874* (Rutherford, N.J.: Fairleigh Dickinson University Press, 1981), 206 (on the Irish influence on Hoffman's decisions not to run for reelection).

6 / Aftermath

The Orange riots had important consequences for city politics and the Irish working class. First, they stoked the nativist reform crusade that toppled Tweed's ring from power. Led by wealthy merchants and lawyers, most of whom were Protestants, reformers sought to restore "respectability" by lessening the Irish Catholic influence in government and city life. To achieve their goals, they fought for a new city charter, supported upper-class candidates for public office, opposed public aid to parochial schools, and tried to unite with other Protestants to curb papal power in America. Many of the reformers were active in the Committee of Seventy, the New York City Council of Political Reform, and the Union League Club. Some also were figureheads of Democratic reform organizations that governed city politics into the 1880s and then merged with Tammany Hall to support Abram Hewitt against Henry George's surging working-class campaign for mayor in 1886.[1]

A second important consequence of the riots was that they led reform Democrats in Tammany to seek respectability for the organi-

1. See David C. Hammack, *Power and Society: Greater New York at the Turn of the Century* (New York: Columbia University Press, 1982), chaps. 4–6. For the connection between pre– and post–Civil War nativism, see Douglas V. Shaw, *The Making of an Immigrant Community: Ethnic and Cultural Conflict in Jersey City* (New York: Arno, 1976).

zation by restructuring it. By 1875, its powers and patronage rested more with centralized middle-class Irish leadership under John Kelly than with Tammany's traditional Irish working-class constituents and ward heelers. Irish workers now worried that the continuing reactions to the Tweed Ring scandals and the 1871 riot would further exclude them from American society. These concerns, the American depression of the 1870s, and the recurrence of famine and evictions in Ireland by 1879 led many Irish Catholics to believe that Ireland and America were beset by similar problems that stemmed from the monopolization of wealth by Anglo-Saxons.

Their search for political solutions to these problems was guided throughout the decade by Patrick Ford's analysis of events in Ireland and America in his newspaper, the *Irish World.* Their own interests led them to participate in the massive eight-hour strikes of 1872 and other labor revolts of the 1870s, but Ford also urged them to consider Greenbackism and land reform and to insist with him on Jeffersonian equality. By the early 1880s the Irish were ready to embrace the radical demands for land reform in Ireland and America that were urged by the Irish National Land League and city labor organizations, and by 1886 they flocked into Henry George's mayoral campaign.[2] Although the events of the 1880s are beyond the scope of this book, it is possible to explore the immediate consequences of the riots for what they reveal about the motives of the reformers and the experiences that helped to prepare the Irish to join radical labor and Irish-American nationalist activities.

Patrick Ford did not speak for all Irish-Americans, but he did help them to channel the collective Irish memory of Anglo-Saxon oppression into an analysis of class rule in America and to formulate a vision

2. On the 1870s, see Thomas N. Brown, *Irish-American Nationalism, 1870–1890* (Philadelphia: Lippincott, 1966), chap. 3; Iver Bernstein, *The New York City Draft Riots: Their Significance for American Society and Politics in the Age of the Civil War* (New York: Oxford University Press, 1990), chap. 7; and James P. Rodechko, "Patrick Ford and His Search for America: A Case Study of Irish-American Journalism, 1870–1913" (Ph.D. diss., University of Connecticut, 1968). On the 1880s, see Eric Foner, "Class, Ethnicity, and Radicalism in the Gilded Age: The Land League and Irish-America," *Marxist Perspectives* 1 (Summer 1978): 6–55; David Scobey, "Boycotting The Politics Factory: Labor Radicalism and the New York City Mayoral Election of 1884" [sic: 1886], *Radical History Review*, nos. 28–30 [combined issue] (September 1984): 280–325; and Michael A. Gordon, "Studies in Irish and Irish-American Thought and Behavior in Gilded Age New York City" (Ph.D. diss., University of Rochester, 1977), pt. II, and "The Labor Boycott in New York City, 1880–1886," *Labor History* 16 (Spring 1975): 184–229.

of the nation commensurate with their dreams of equality, much as Frederick Douglass sought to do for freed blacks. Born in Galway in 1835, Ford emigrated with his parents to Boston amid the famine in 1845. Taken with abolitionism, he began working on William Lloyd Garrison's *Liberator* at age fifteen, edited a short-lived Boston antislavery paper himself, and fought in the Union army. After the war, he edited two South Carolina newspapers before moving to Brooklyn and launching the *Irish World* in 1870.[3]

Throughout his years as editor, Ford worried about class distinctions, chided upper-class pretensions, and championed Irish republicanism. In April 1871, Ford wrote, "We are rapidly drifting away from democracy and becoming aristocratical, if not monarchical." Believing that "as it was the destiny of the Irish to create that anti-English feeling which led to the Independence of the United States," he thought "it will also be to them alone that we can look, in the future, for the preservation of democratic principles in our government." Arguing in another editorial in March 1872 that "Anglo-Americans" had no exclusive claims on rights as Americans, Ford also insisted that "Yankees" should not bludgeon immigrants into ignoring their culture in order to become "Americans," because Old World cultures would strengthen democracy, not weaken it. "Each element has a perfect right to its own traditions, its own social usages, customs, religion, modes of living, amusements," he wrote, "and no other element has any right . . . to interfere or dictate in the matter." In another editorial that month, he noted that "a titled nobility and a flimsy gentry—lords, earls, squireens, and half-sirs—have been the ruin of Ireland, and untitled oligarchy will, if not suppressed in time, be the ruin of this country." Asserting in other editorials that "the vital issue of all our political struggles" involved a clash between a "genuine democracy" and "a republican-oligarchy, which gives over the power of the country to corrupt 'rings,' monopolists, and 'nativist' cliques," Ford assailed those "liberalists" who would grant the Irish limited rights in return for "civil" conduct. Ford said they had no right "to supervise our behavior or fix our status." As "the least wealthy element in the country," Irish Catholics had a greater stake in republicanism than any other group. It was the "aristocratic class" of "Anglo-Americans and Protestants"—the descendants of Revolutionary-era Tories—"who hate our race and creed," who "would draw

3. Rodechko, "Patrick Ford," 28–34.

a line of demarcation in society between the 'upper' class and the 'lower' class," and who, by showing "their contempt for republican simplicity by dressing their lackeys in gilded liveries" tied Americans to "England's money kings" and made them "tributaries to England's great manufacturing lords."[4]

The objects of Ford's attack were the same men who had supported Orangemen and denounced Irish Catholics in July 1871. These were the "best men" reformers and nativists who destroyed Tweed and sought to restore responsibility and financial integrity to city government under the aegis of the Executive Committee of Citizens and Taxpayers for the Financial Reform of the City of New York. In its early stages, this "Committee of Seventy," as it was best known, gained support and members from the well-to-do Republican Union League Club, the Democratic Manhattan Club, the New York City Council of Political Reform, the Bar Association, the Chamber of Commerce, numerous "young men's" political clubs, and Protestant organizations and churches. Its backing came also from associations devoted to eliminating juvenile crime and vagabondage, prostitution, tenement-house overcrowding, "immorality," and even cruelty to animals (Henry Berg, the anti–animal cruelty activist, was a prominent city political reformer after 1875).[5]

The Committee of Seventy was launched at a frenzied September 4, 1871, meeting at Cooper Union arranged by former mayor and prominent businessman William F. Havemeyer and others. Speaker after speaker pledged to help drive those from power who had brought the city to financial and moral ruin. This "accusers meeting," as the *World* called it, quickly turned to action and elicited members and money from other citizens disgruntled with the Tweed Ring and its constituency.[6]

The committee was representative of New York's most prominent, influential, and successful men. Its ranks included the financiers Samuel D. Babcock, Eugene Ballin, James M. Brown, Henry Clews, Adrian Iselin, Robert Lenox Kennedy, Howard Potter, Henry G. Stebbins, John A. Stewart, E. Townsend, and William R. Vermilye. Commercial interests, represented by merchants and importers, in-

4. *Irish World*, April 22, 1871; March 2 ("each element"), 9 ("titled nobility"), April 6 ("vital issue"), and June 8, 1872 ("least wealthy"); and January 22, 1876 ("money kings").

5. See Alexander B. Callow, *The Tweed Ring* (New York: Oxford University Press, 1965), 261–67.

6. For coverage of the meeting, see *World*, *Times*, and *Tribune*, September 5, 1871.

cluded Isaac H. Bailey, John C. Green, D. Willis James, Servern D. Moulton, William H. Neilson, Joseph J. O'Donohue, Royal Phelps, William Radde, Robert B. Roosevelt, Jackson S. Schultz, Henry F. Spaulding, Jonathan Sturges, and J. B. Varnum. Among the well-known lawyers and judges were Francis C. Barlow, George C. Barrett, Joseph Hodges Choat, John A. Dix (New York governor, 1873–75), Dorman B. Eaton, James Emott, William M. Evarts, Thomas A. Ledwith, Henry Nicoll, Edwards Pierrepont, Samuel B. Ruggles, Edward Salomon (a former Wisconsin governor), Simon Sterne, and Samuel J. Tilden. There were also the manufacturers John Foley, William F. Havemeyer (a New York mayor in the 1840s and again in 1873–74), Robert Hoe, Benjamin B. Sherman, and Theodore Steinway. Also members were the publisher Jonas M. Bundy, the engineer and architect Christian E. Detmold, the physician Ernest Krackowitzer, the shipper Paul A. Spofford, and George W. Varian, who was independently wealthy.[7]

These powerful men shared similar interests and political agendas. Many belonged to the same social clubs, where they met each other daily over business or dinner, and were involved in common philanthropies. Nearly all of them were involved in commerce and finance. Sturges and Ruggles were founders, and Green was a director, of the Bank of Commerce. Havemeyer was a former president of the Bank of North America and the Rose Hill Savings Bank, and a director of the Merchants' Exchange Bank. Brown was a trustee of the Bank for Savings; Sherman, a trustee of the Bleecker Street Savings Bank, a former official of the Merchants' National Bank, and later president of the Mechanics' Bank of New York. Spaulding was a director of the Mechanics' Bank, the Central Trust Company, and the Continental Trust Company. Roosevelt was president of the Holland Trust Company; Schultz was a director of the National Park Bank; Bailey was an original trustee of the Union Square Savings Bank; Babcock was a president of the U.S. Mortgage Company; and Stewart was a founder of the U.S. Trust Company. Moreover, Roosevelt, Sherman, Vermilye, and Brown were variously affiliated with the Jefferson, Mutual, New York, and Royal life insurance companies. Clews, Brown,

7. The complete list of seventy members, with additions and deletions, can be found in *Herald*, September 5, 24, and November 29, 1871; *Tribune*, September 5, 25, 1871; *World*, September 8, 1871; and *Times*, September 5, 25, 1871.

and Potter were members of the famous Brown Brothers banking house.[8]

Many men had railroad interests. Dix had been president of both the Chicago and Rock Island and the Mississippi and Missouri lines in the 1850s, while in those same years, Sturges's congressional influence helped to get the Illinois Central Railroad (of which he was a director) on sound financial footing. Havemeyer had been the vice-president of the Long Island Railroad; Green, a financial backer of the Michigan Central; and Babcock, the president of the New York, Providence, and Boston line. Ruggles had interests in the New York and Erie Railroad. And Henry G. Stebbins, who was president of the Committee of Seventy, the New York Stock Exchange, the Atlantic and Great Western Railroad, and a vice-president of the Texas Pacific Railroad, was also the director and real estate agent of the New York, Erie, and Western Railroad until his death in 1881.[9]

These "best men" were not just concerned with business affairs. Many belonged to various social and political clubs. Joseph J. O'Donohue alone reportedly had memberships in over sixty New York and Brooklyn clubs. In 1864, Sterne was an organizer of the American Free Trade League, of which Phelps was also a founder. In 1843, Brown was a founder of the Association for Improving the Condition of the Poor, and became its president in 1869. Eaton, Emott, Evarts, and Pierrepont helped found the reform-minded Bar Association that same year. Eaton was also active in civil service reform. In 1873, Grant appointed him to the first national commission and, after Eaton helped draft the Pendleton Act, Chester A. Arthur named him as a commissioner in 1883. Radde was a founder and trustee of the Homeopathic Hospital (he had manufactured and sold the first homeopathic treatment in America), and Schultz was long a governor of New York Hospital. Brown was a founder of Presbyterian Hospital and a trustee of the city's Orthopedic Dispensary and Hospital. These men were active in the affairs of the Metropolitan Museum of Art, the Metropolitan Opera, the Astor Library, the Natural History Museum, the Society for the Prevention of Cruelty to Animals, and

8. George Templeton Strong, *The Diary of George Templeton Strong*, vol. 4, *The Post-War Years, 1865–1875*, ed. Allan Nevins and Milton H. Thomas (New York: Macmillan, 1952), 50–51 passim. For sources on many Committee of Seventy members, see Appendix C.

9. See Appendix C.

the Academy of Music. They were involved in home mission and other lay church affairs, the Mercantile Library Association, rapid transit development, the Emigration Commission, and various colleges and seminaries. Ruggles, for example, was a trustee of Columbia University from 1836 to 1881. Many had held public office. There were park, health, and education board members, aldermen, legislators, and congressmen.[10]

Committee of Seventy members represented a broad segment of upper-class experiences, interests, and activities. Many were old friends and former college classmates. Some, like Evarts, Havemeyer, Hoe, Iselin, James, Moulton, Roosevelt, and Ruggles, came from old mercantile families. Though they and other committee members often disagreed on politics and political economy, they were united on the need to drive Tammany and the Irish from power.[11]

The committee's crusade against the Tweed Ring and its constituents was conducted on several fronts. First, the committee sought to reassure worried banks and European holders of New York City bonds that an end to corruption had begun. On September 7 and 14, committee member and pen manufacturer John Foley, and the East Side Citizens Association, extracted temporary injunctions from Judge George G. Barnard (until then a Tweed loyalist) which prohibited the city from raising revenue or spending money (although it could make interest payments). This remedy bought time to begin restoring the city's fiscal integrity, but it also precipitated a crisis. With a depleted treasury and no ability to raise funds, the city could not pay thousands of laborers, who threatened a riot if they did not receive weeks of back wages. Ironically, Tweed may have helped prevent such disorder by giving fifty thousand dollars of "his own" money to loyal workers and their families.[12]

With this emergency averted, in late September and early October, committee members next appointed subcommittees on law and elections to prosecute the ring in the courts and at the polls. The city's elites were desperate to prove they could restore order and

10. See Appendix C.

11. For more on these men and their differences, see Gordon, "Irish and Irish-American Thought and Behavior," 396–404.

12. Callow, *Tweed Ring*, 272; Leo Hershkowitz, *Tweed's New York: Another Look* (New York: Doubleday, Anchor, 1977), 183–89; Seymour J. Mandelbaum, *Boss Tweed's New York* (New York: Wiley, 1965), 83.

sound government. "If we fail to punish them," Henry G. Stebbins noted, referring to ring members just before the fall election, "will not the capitalists and merchants of Europe logically conclude that our institutions are a failure, that the strength of American credit is gone and that it is unsafe to lend and to sell to a people whose rulers are thieves and whose legislators are robbers and rascals?" Attorney George C. Barrett and his law committee took ring members to court on behalf of an angry public fed up with fraud. Their efforts put Tweed and other ring leaders in jail. (Indeed, Tweed died in the Ludlow Street jail in 1878.)[13]

On a third front, the elections subcommittee urged citizens "to rid themselves of the thieves and plunderers . . . and to fill their places at the next election by intelligent, honest, incorruptible men." Scores of one-hundred-dollar donations supported these efforts. By late October, the committee had raised nearly fifty-three thousand dollars for its legal and election expenses. Aided by the Council on Political Reform, the Union League Club, and the Young Men's Municipal Association, which all shared overlapping memberships, the Committee of Seventy issued statements that detailed graft, condemned civil immorality, and urged complacent citizens to join its crusade. In their stunning victory in November, reform candidates captured all fifteen aldermanic, and thirteen of twenty-one assistant aldermanic, seats. They also won fourteen of the city's twenty assembly seats and four of five senate seats. Yet reformers lost the race they perhaps most wanted to win. In the Seventh Senate District, Tweed won reelection by ten thousand votes. His opponent, the Fenian martyr O'Donovan Rossa, could not lure Tweed's loyal Irish supporters away from the man who had given them jobs.[14]

13. *Times*, November 3, 1871 (Stebbins); on the fate of Tweed and the ring, see Callow, *Tweed Ring*, chaps. 17, 18; Jerome Mushkat, *The Reconstruction of the New York Democracy, 1861–1874* (Rutherford, N.J.: Fairleigh Dickinson University Press, 1981), chaps. 6–8; Hammack, *Power and Society*, 132–33.

14. See minutes of Committee of Seventy meetings for September 23, and October 2 (quote), 6, 9, 17, 24, 27, 28, 1871, in the bound volume *New York City Committee for Financial Reform: Minutes, 1871–1873*, New York Public Library; and *Subscription Book of the Executive Committee of Citizens and Taxpayers for the Financial Reform of the City and County of New York, 1871–1872* (Committee of Seventy), New-York Historical Society. On the campaign, see Callow, *Tweed Ring*, 277; Denis Tilden Lynch, *The Wild Seventies* (New York: Appleton-Century, 1941), 135–39; Howard B. Furer, *William Frederick Havemeyer: A Political Biography* (New York: American Press), 126–40. For coverage highlights, see *Tribune*, September 5, 25, October 16, and November 3, 6, 8–10, 18,

This one loss did not dim the reformers' euphoria. "We contended for the dearest and holiest principles of republicanism," the reform supporter and physician Adolph Kessler later noted. An "unholy regime" had been destroyed. Elected coroner on the reform ticket in 1872, Kessler viewed the political cooperation of "the Anglo-Saxon and German elements" as "the harbinger of a new era in our political life" because "as branches of the same Germanic family, they are not only kindred in blood and lineage, but also kindred in their love of liberty, truth and honesty, in their earnestness, intelligence and patriotism."[15]

Reformers interpreted their election victories as a mandate for a new city charter, through which they hoped to eliminate Irish influence and political machines. Anticipating the legislative remedy, a *Times* writer, who called himself "Non-Partisan," argued in late January 1872 that "the earnest, hard-worked professional men and men of business in New York City, who had devoted so much thought, time and money to putting down the great joint stock conspiracy of scoundrelism, Jacobitism, Jesuitism and venality, do not mean to leave these elements the same dangerous facility of absolute rule which they possessed before."[16]

During the next sixteen months the committee worked for a new charter to replace the one that Tweed had paid nearly one million dollars in bribes to secure in 1870. Tweed's "home rule" charter had replaced state-controlled city commissions with departments whose heads were appointed by the mayor and could act independently of the Common Council. The charter had brought some independence from Albany, but it also gave the Tweed Ring the keys to city funds. As head of Public Works, for example, Tweed himself had control of hefty budgets for streets and developments. He also had a seat on the powerful new Board of Audit, which had sole authority to pay claims against the city.[17]

Although Tweed's charter had been hailed at the time for restoring

---

1871; *World*, September 8, 19, 23, 24, 28, October 25, and November 3, 8–10, 1871; *Times*, September 18, and November 3, 6, 8–10, 14, 1871; *Herald*, October 3, 7, and November 24, 1871.

15. Adolph Kessler (New York, November 12, 1871) to *Times*, November 17, 1871. On Kessler's election, see *Herald*, January 3, 1873.

16. Non-Partisan, "Chapters on Reform," *Times*, January 27, 1872.

17. Mushkat, *Reconstruction*, 159–61; Mandelbaum, *Boss Tweed's New York*, 71–72; Lynch, *Wild Seventies*, 34–35; Callow, *Tweed Ring*, 78–80, 225–33.

local control, by 1871, reformers believed that it had only opened the city's coffers to rampant greed. The new charter they fought for featured both minority representation on the Common Council through cumulative voting and aldermanic checks on mayoral appointments of department heads. One version passed the assembly in April 1872, but Hoffman vetoed it, claiming it would only resurrect the old commission system and suppress majority rule. A final bill was not signed into law until April 30, 1873, but by then, Committee of Seventy member John A. Dix had replaced Hoffman as governor.[18]

The seventy-five-year-old Dix was elected governor in 1872. Irish Catholics and nativism were prominent issues in that tumultuous election. Many New York reformers quarreled over the presidential nominees—regular Republican and incumbent Grant and the Liberal Reform and Democratic nominee Horace Greeley. Because Greeley had local Democratic support, he was accused by his detractors of catering to Tammany's Irish and "papists" in exchange for their votes. But efforts were made to lure away Irish votes by charging that Greeley had cooperated with Know-Nothings in the 1850s. Scoffing at the idea, the *Irish World* and Greeley's *Tribune* alleged that Grant's running mate, Henry Wilson, was a former Massachusetts Know-Nothing, a charge Wilson admitted with qualifications. The *Irish World* was not as concerned with the "incompetent," "ignorant," "corrupt and selfish" Grant as with "the English Party, who have him in charge—that Party of whom *Harper's Weekly* is the organ—that Party that would use Grant as the unconscious instrument of their black designs for the degradation of our race, for the destruction of our creed, for the propagation of Anglicized ideas, for the provincializing of this nation and the humiliation of the nation's flag." The party sought to establish nothing less than "a purse-proud

18. For coverage highlights of the first new-charter campaign, see *Tribune*, January 20, February 12, 14, 21, March 25, April 19, and May 1, 6, 29, 1872; *Herald*, January 1, February 12, 15, 28, March 24, 27–30, April 2, 3, 12, 21, and May 1, 1872; and "A New Charter for the City of New York," *Harper's Weekly* 16 (January 1, 1872): 26–27. For background, see Mushkat, *Reconstruction*, chap. 7, esp. 200; and John A. Dougherty, *Constitutional History of the State of New York*, 2d ed. (New York: Neale, 1915), chap. 13. For coverage highlights and editorials on the final bill, see *Times*, January 22, February 20, 26, March 23, and May 1, 1873; *Tribune*, January 8, 22, February 4–8, 11, 14, 22, 24, 26, 28, March 5, 7, 8, 15, 21, 26, April 11, 17, 18, 21, and May 1, 1873; and *Herald*, January 1, 10, February 7, 21, March 5–7, 26, 27, 31, April 1, 2, 16, 23, 25, 29, and May 1, 1873.

British-American oligarchy" in America. Tracing current intolerance to colonial Anglo-Saxon practices, the paper also argued that nativist reformers had much in common with the Federalist "English Party" that had enacted the Alien and Sedition Laws to thwart Irish and Jeffersonian republicanism.[19]

Greeley's chances in New York were dampened further when Democrats nominated the Catholic Francis Kernan for governor. "He is a Copperhead and Romanist," Strong sizzled. Signing his name "No Church and State," a *Times* reader expressed the view shared by others that Kernan had been nominated "to save the Catholic vote for Greeley." "The Protestant sentiment of the community is not dead yet," the *Times* itself editorialized, "as those who are rather imprudently challenging it may find out to their cost." A September 29 *Times* article claimed that Kernan distributed campaign literature engraved with a cross, but the *Irish World* insisted that Wilson's supporters had hatched such an idea to agitate Protestants and that the *Times* and *Harper's* spread the story to appeal to Know-Nothings. Greeley and Kernan were defeated. With Republican backing, the reformer William F. Havemeyer was elected mayor over the Tammany Democrat Abraham Lawrence and Apollo Hall's reform Democrat James O'Brien, the county sheriff. In different ways, both the *Times* and the *Irish World* understood how fears of Irish Catholic domination affected the election's results. The former proclaimed

> that the rule of one class, and . . . the most ignorant class of the community, is over. The ignorant, unthinking, bigoted hordes which Tammany brought up to its support year after year are hopelessly scattered. Americans—truly so-called—are now deter-

19. On Greeley and the campaign, see *Times*, July 5, 16, 31, August 13, 14, 19, 21, and October 1, 1872; Eugene Lawrence, "The Party of Reaction," *Harper's Weekly* 16 (July 20, 1872): 651–52, and "Grant and Education," ibid. (August 3, 1872): 593–94; and "The Democratic Party and Candidate," ibid. (July 27, 1872): 578. See also Strong, *Diary* 4:424, 427, 433–34; Joseph Logsdon, *Horace White: Nineteenth Century Liberal* (Westport, Conn.: Greenwod, 1971), chaps. 10–12; Matthew T. Downey, "The Rebirth of Reform: A Study of Liberal Reform Movements, 1865–1872" (Ph.D. diss., Princeton University, 1963), chaps. 10–12; Glyndon Van Deusen, *Horace Greeley: Nineteenth-Century Crusader* (1953; rpt. New York: Hill and Wang, 1964), chap. 25; and Edward K. Spawn, *Ideals and Politics: New York Intellectuals and Liberal Democracy, 1820–1880* (Albany: State University of New York Press, 1972), 201–9. On Wilson, see *Irish World*, July 13, August 10, and October 5, 12, 1872; and *Tribune*, August 1, 21, September 6, 7, 9, 25, and October 26, 31, 1872. For quotes, see *Irish World*, July 13 and October 19, 1872.

mined to have some share in the Government of this City, and will no longer leave it to be tyrannized over by our esteemed friends from the Emerald Isle. This is going to be an American City once more—not simply a larger kind of Dublin. The iron rod of our "oppressed" friend is broken.

Patrick Ford's editorial analysis was more succinct: "*Greeley was beaten because he was supposed to be identified with the Democracy, and the Democracy was beaten because it was supposed to be identified with Catholicity*! There you have the history of the Presidential campaign of 1872."[20]

With the election behind them, committee members renewed their efforts to obtain a new charter. The version Dix approved in April 1873 provided the framework for city government until 1897. It curbed the mayor's powers in some areas but expanded them in others. Aldermen were picked through a mixture of at-large and district voting designed to curb Tammany's power through proportional representation. The forty-five-member Common Council had power to ratify mayoral appointments, although it could not raise taxes or incur debt. The mayor, who could remove department heads only with the governor's approval, became a member of three powerful boards that controlled the city's finances, street openings, and development.[21]

The elections of 1871 and 1872 and the new charter gave reformers the chance they had longed for. Havemeyer's appointments in May excluded the Irish from government, although a few Irish were elected aldermen. Committee of Seventy members and other reformers held prominent posts. John Wheeler, a new Committee of Seventy member; George H. Andrews; and Severn D. Moulton were appointed tax and assessment commissioners. Henry Smith remained as Police Board president. He was joined by the Democrat Oliver Charlick (a railroad president and merchant), the Radical Republican

20. Strong, *Diary* 4:435; "No Church and State," Albany, October 30, 1872, to *Times*, November 1, 1872; *Times*, October 27 and September 29, 1872; *Irish World*, October 12, 1872. For campaign highlights, see *Herald*, September 18, October 2, 4, 5, 10, 12, 13, 15, 19, 20, 23, and November 1–7, 1872; *Tribune*, September 18, 20, 27, 28, October 3, 11, 12, 23, and November 1–7, 1872; and *Times*, October 2, 10, 15, 20, 31, and November 2–7, 1872. *Times*, November 7, 1872 (quote); *Irish World*, November 16, 1872 (quote). Apollo Hall was the headquarters of reform Democrats.

21. Mandelbaum, *Boss Tweed's New York*, 105–7; Furer, *Havemeyer*, 162–63; Mushkat, *Reconstruction*, 215–16.

Hugh Gardner (a merchant dyer), Gen. Abram Duryee (who had seen action in the Astor Place and draft riots), and the Republican dry goods merchant John R. Russell. Fire Department commissioners included the Republican and former alderman Joseph L. Perley, Roswell D. Hatch, and the leather manufacturer Cornelius Van Cott. Havemeyer also appointed William Laimbeer as a charities and correction commissioner, and Joseph B. Varnum as the commissioner of jurors. Henry G. Stebbins remained as Park Board president; and the new Board of Education was William H. Neilson, Robert Hoe, Albert Klamroth, James M. Halsted, and Joseph Seligman—all Committee members.[22]

Havemeyer's appointments angered Irish Catholics and Democrats. Sensing reform's intent just before the 1872 election, Patrick Ford blasted the "Reform Party" for disguising "no other features than those of the old, familiar demon—Know Nothingism!" Concerns about a nativist revival spearheaded by Havemeyer increased during the months after the election. By spring, one *Irish World* reader charged that Havemeyer was "either a bigot or a weakling. His action in excluding Irishmen or Catholics from office almost entirely must be the result of either bitter prejudices against them as classes, or else his actions are dictated by a clique who combine this spirit with one of cupidity." Apollo Hall Democrats made similar allegations. Havemeyer denied the charges, but he was not sympathetic to Irish concerns. "I don't wonder that some of the Irish feel uneasy at the present outlook of things," he said. "They have been accustomed to fill nearly all the offices of the city, to draw large pay and do very little work. Now they are asked to do more work and have less pay and they don't like it."[23]

Despite the election and charter victories, Havemeyer's administration accomplished little. Beset by differences with the Common Council and his Republican and Tammany supporters over everything from charter provisions, the appointment of Democrat Andrew H. Green as city comptroller, and the replacement of Democratic police justices with Republicans, Havemeyer became the belea-

22. For biographical information and the complete city roster, see *Tribune*, May 6, 10, 13, 16, 20, and June 20, 1873; and *Herald*, May 6, 9, 10, 16, 17, 20, 25, and June 6, 20, 1873.

23. *Irish World*, October 19, 1872; "Independent" (New York, May 22, 1873), to ibid., June 7, 1873; *Herald*, June 14, 15 (quote), 1873.

guered doorkeeper of city government instead of a crusading reformer. He sparked a cleanup of city markets, a slight tax reduction for downtown merchants, more efficient garbage collection, a cut in outdoor relief, street improvement, increased gas lighting, and even stray dog collection. But these were hardly burning reform issues. Moreover, workers and others attacked Havemeyer and Green for cutting the wages of city employees early in the depression. German Republicans complained that the mayor had not awarded them enough patronage. Reformers generally became disgruntled by his ineffectiveness as a lobbyist for the city in Albany and by the slow pace of reform. Satisfied that it had at least driven Tweed and the low Irish from power and secured a new charter, the Committee of Seventy disbanded in October 1873. Havemeyer died in office in November 1874 after refusing renomination, and the diamond merchant and former committee member William H. Wickham, a Democrat, became mayor in January.[24]

Nothing is known about how much the elections and the charter actually diminished Irish working-class power in city affairs during Havemeyer's administration and throughout the rest of the decade. It may be, as Jerome Mushkat has argued, that the 1873 charter "unwittingly served the machine's interests" because, by delegating shared responsibility among the mayor, the aldermen, and the boards, the charter diffused municipal power and made it possible for Tammany to become a broker for unrepresented local interests.[25]

Mushkat's assertion remains to be substantiated, but it is clear that the ring scandals did force Tammany to join the reform movement and at least appear to disassociate itself from its former Irish working-class constituents. The process began on August 30, 1871, when Tammany replaced the disgraced Tweed as grand sachem with the banker-reformer Augustus Schell. Schell was the candidate of the "Swallowtail" Democrats, who largely controlled mayoral elections in New York down to 1886. Swallowtails were upper-class men like the attorneys Samuel J. Tilden, Horatio Seymour, and Charles O'Conor and the manufacturers Edward Cooper and Abram S. Hewitt who, as David C. Hammack writes, "entered politics after a successful business or professional career, or with the sponsorship of wealthy busi-

24. Mandelbaum, *Boss Tweed's New York*, 97–109; Furer, *Havemeyer*, 155–65, 174.
25. Mushkat, *Reconstruction*, 217.

ness and professional men in politics." Like many other reformers, they sought an end to corruption and legislation both federal and local which would encourage commercial development.[26]

To obtain efficient city government and municipal improvements, Swallowtails first had to capture city government. Most of them had sought that end by supporting Tammany or other Democratic reform candidates. In 1872 they divided their allegiance among Tammany's candidate, Lawrence; Apollo Hall's O'Brien; and Havemeyer, the Committee of Seventy–Republican nominee. But Swallowtails joined forces to control the elections of Tammany's Wickham in 1874 and the Tammany–Apollo Hall candidate Smith Ely (a leather merchant) in 1876. Swallowtails left Tammany for the Irving Hall Democratic faction after Tilden's failed presidential bid that year and successfully backed Edward Cooper for mayor against Tammany's Schell. With no viable candidate of their own in 1880, they supported Tammany's William R. Grace, even though many worried about Grace's Catholic affinities. The Swallowtails remained powerful in city politics for more than thirty years. Indeed, Hammack has shown that between 1870 and 1903, nearly all mayoral candidates, regardless of party affiliation, were Swallowtails.[27]

The Swallowtails helped to reform Tammany in important ways, first briefly under Schell, and then under his long-reigning successor, "Honest" John Kelly. A former alderman, congressman, and county sheriff, Kelly brought important credentials to his post. He had broken with Tweed in the 1860s and was not tainted by scandal. More important, as a devout Irish Catholic, Kelly helped to attract the "respectable" Irish middle class to Tammany, and, as Seymour Mandelbaum writes, he "was far removed from both the working class and the low wardheelers with whom his critics tended to lump him." By the spring of 1872, Schell and Kelly had reorganized and greatly enlarged Tammany's Central Committee to diminish the power of Tweed's remaining allies. They also replaced many of Tweed's former ward bosses.[28]

Despite his affinity for reform and his quest for respectability, Kelly was not completely estranged from the working-class Irish. He

26. Hammack, *Power and Society*, 121–23 (quote).

27. Ibid., 131–33; Callow, *Tweed Ring*, 287; Lynch, *Wild Seventies*, 249; Mushkat, *Reconstruction*, 34–35, 59, 237. Like Apollo Hall, Irving Hall was the home of an anti-Tammany faction of Democrats.

28. Mandelbaum, *Boss Tweed's New York*, 93; Lynch, *Wild Seventies*, 250.

was too astute politically to neglect such constituents entirely, and too Irish Catholic to shun his history and his people. Yet occasionally he had to be pressured to respond to their needs. On January 13, 1874, police crushed a demonstration of thousands of workers who had gathered in Tompkins Square to demand that Havemeyer create public works to help ease effects of the bitter depression. Kelly's immediate reaction to the event is not known, but when local party leaders soon complained that he put party reorganization above jobs for their constituents, Kelly blasted the insensitive frugality of Havemeyer and city comptroller Green and broke with them in the city register's race by endorsing James Hayes, a former Tweed man and friend of John Morrissey, the Irish-born pugilist, saloonkeeper, and congressman who had deep roots in the Irish working class. In May 1875, Kelly joined laborers, aldermen, and others in a fruitless protest against Mayor Wickham's plans to trim the city's debt by cutting the wages of city laborers. Kelly also occasionally squabbled with business leaders, and he argued bitterly with Tilden in 1875 over retaining Green as city comptroller—a spat that alienated some reformers. Yet Kelly also angered Irish workers and Tammany loyalists by getting the party to expel the popular Morrissey in July 1875 for rallying disaffected ward bosses against Kelly's centralizing tendencies. The purge removed a noisy thorn but resulted in a stunning and unexpected defeat that fall of many Tammany candidates for the state legislature and city judgeships.[29]

Kelly never fully patched up differences with Swallowtail Democrats or Irish workers. Still uneasy about Kelly's ethnicity, and suspicious about his commitment to reform, in 1881 many Swallowtails bolted Tammany and formed a rival organization, the New York County Democracy. Irish workers smarted at Morrissey's expulsion and Tammany's changed structure throughout the rest of the 1870s. Tammany had gone far under Irish middle-class leadership and Swallowtail influence to create distance between itself and the targets of reformers in 1871. Many Irish workers lamented that change, and at least one did so in song. In "The Hodman's Lament," Dennis Morgan, the song's fictitious Irish-born narrator, mourned Tweed's demise and criticized the new alliance between capitalists and government:

29. See Herbert G. Gutman, "The Tompkins Square 'Riot' in New York City on January 13, 1874," *Labor History* 6 (Winter 1965): 44–70; and Mandelbaum, *Boss Tweed's New York*, 111–12, 126–27, and chap. 12. On Morrissey, see Callow, *Tweed Ring*, 223, 234, 239; and Hershkowitz, *Tweed's New York*, 51–52, 151–52.

Long life and health to you, Bill Tweed, what'er your nation or
your creed,
For you always helped the poor in need when you were Senator,
No soup-house paupers then did lurk, and less poor men were
out of work,
For you fought the wolf just like a Turk when hunger did occur.
But if e'er you should come back again you'll meet the help of
honest workingmen.
For no matter who may you condemn, you were poverty's best
screen.
But now your loss we do deplore and none will say much less,
I'm sure,
Tho' you robbed the rich you fed the poor, and never acted
mean.
I could recall many facts here in my rhymes, but God be with
them good old times,
When in New York we had less crimes, and labor got its pay;
But we daily see before our sight that capital still backs up might,
And still do strive to cheat the right up to the present day.[30]

The Irish Catholic working class had more to lament than just the loss of Bill Tweed. The nativist reform movement that brought changes to city government and Tammany Hall—even under Kelly's reign—was part of a broader nativist revival that sought to root out alleged papal influence from other republican institutions and compounded Irish concerns about the nation's future and their place in it.

The Union League Club and other Protestant groups were especially concerned about the spread of Catholic parochial schools and the use of public funds to support them. Catholic efforts to get state aid for their schools had touched off nativist opposition since the 1840s.[31] The draft and Orange riots and recurring fears of papal designs rekindled attacks on Catholic schools and fueled Gilded Age reform.

Francis Lieber first aroused Union League Club interest in the

30. Hammack, *Power and Society*, 134–39; "The Hodman's Lament," in *Delaney's Irish Song Book No. 4*, 10, in box 271, Starr Music Collection, Lilly Library, Indiana University.

31. See Diane Ravitch, *The Great School Wars: New York City, 1805–1973* (New York: Basic Books, 1974), chaps. 1–6; and A. Emerson Palmer, *The New York Public School: Being a History of Free Education in the City of New York* (New York: Macmillan, 1905), chaps. 12, 15. See also the important details in William O. Bourne, *History of the Public School Society of the City of New York* (New York: William Wood, 1870).

school question at a November 24, 1869 meeting. The German-born, Columbia College political scientist accused city government of irresponsibility and claimed that there was an ecclesiastical conspiracy to undermine public education in New York. Lieber did not mention it, but he most likely found evidence for his concerns in a provision Tweed had pushed through the legislature that year as a rider on a budget bill. The measure allowed New York City and County to give public funds to nonpublic schools providing education for more than two hundred students. Lieber's alarm prompted the club to appoint a committee to investigate misappropriations of public school money for sectarian purposes. In his January report, committee chair Dexter A. Hawkins (a lawyer) stated that over $400,000 had been paid to Catholic schools from 1869 tax revenues and that another $120,000 had gone to at least seven other denominational institutions. Outraged club members endorsed the committee's recommendation that the legislature repeal the law that had authorized such allocations.[32]

In the following months, the Union League Club distributed twenty-three thousand copies of Hawkins's report, gathered support for its appeal to the legislature, and arranged a March 30, 1870, Cooper Union protest meeting. William Cullen Bryant's *Evening Post* editorial helped to set the dissenter's tone: "A moral force exists in the community in opposition to the introduction of priestcraft into politics and education; a force which will show itself irresistible if properly and directly organized." In the meeting's principal addresses, Peter Cooper, Henry Ward Beecher, William E. Dodge, Rev. Noah Hunt Schenk, and Hiram Ketchum all condemned public support of church schools, argued for the strict separation of church and state, and denounced those Catholic journals which led their readers to believe such aid was obligatory. Dodge especially was piqued. He claimed that Catholics used their schools both to shield their children from the Americanizing influence of public education and as a political base to spread papal authority. "The heart of the American people is true," he concluded, "and when once public attention is aroused to the true issue and danger, there will be such an uprising as will convince the Romish Church the world over, of the folly of their [sic] vain boast that within fifty years they will have the control of this country."[33]

32. Ravitch, *Great School Wars*, 93; *World*, November 28 and May 14, 1870.

33. *World*, May 13, 1870. On support, see, e.g., *Evening Post*, January 1, 8, 12, 29,

The Union League Club's efforts that year led to a repeal of Tweed's bill, although Catholic schools remained eligible to receive state funds for another two years. Despite this success, the club continued to hammer at parochial education. Hawkins presented another report in February 1872, which reaffirmed his belief that public schools provided the best education for democracy:

> But a single sect is taught by its head, a foreign and despotic ecclesiastical prince, that the civil authorities in a republic have not the right to control and direct the course of study and the choice and appointment of teachers in the schools open alike to the youth of all classes, but that this right belongs to the Church. Hence the sect makes war upon our public schools; persuades its children to leave them; sets up an opposition school wherever it has a church, and admits that it does this solely for the purpose of indoctrinating the young mind with its peculiar sectarian tenets and observances.[34]

Support for the Union League Club's efforts came from another prominent reform organization, the state Council for Political Reform and its New York City affiliate. Believing that "the dangers which threaten our civil institutions arise largely from political corruption" and that "we ought to unite earnestly in endeavoring to secure honesty, patriotism and virtue in the use of the elective franchise," the council sought to organize local branches where members would help eliminate political chicanery and fraud by participating in local party caucuses and elections. But the council also had a standing Committee on Endowment and Support by the State of Sectarian Schools and Institutions. Its chairman was Dexter A. Hawkins. His April 12, 1870, report to the Albany council meeting was similar to the Union League version, but its tone was more strongly anti-Catholic and its substance more encompassing.[35]

The Council for Political Reform revealed more about its goals and

---

and March 26 (quote), 1870; *Times*, March 2, 31, 1870; Hiram Ketchum (n.p., n.d.) to *Evening Post*, January 14, 17, 1870; and Ketchum (n.p., n.d.) to New York State Legislature in ibid., April 8, 1870. On meeting, *Times*, and *Herald* (quote), March 31, 1870.

34. Ravitch, *Great School Wars*, 93; *Herald*, February 23, 1872. Eight years later, Hawkins's brother, Rush C. Hawkins, joined the opposition to William R. Grace's mayoral candidacy because he feared the Catholic Grace would undermine public education; see *Times*, October 30, 1880; and Rush C. Hawkins (New York, October 30, 1880) to *Times*, October 31, 1880.

35. *Times*, April 13, 1870.

membership in two important public statements. On April 6, 1871, it sponsored a Cooper Union meeting to protest the school-funding controversy and to defend the Americanizing virtues of public education. The council's seventeen-member executive committee included seven men who later were appointed to the Committee of Seventy. Ten other eventual Seventy members were among the many honorary vice-presidents and secretaries of the meeting. Greeley, Bryant, Dodge, and Hawkins also were honored guests and sponsors. In fact, Dodge presided. Speeches were made by George C. Barrett (later of the Seventy), William M. Evarts, Henry Ward Beecher, and the Union League's founder, Henry W. Bellows. Most were temperate; Evarts's was even eloquent. But a common suspicion of Catholic designs and distrust of Catholic education united them all. Barrett called attention to "a vast conspiracy" in government that involved not just the Tweed Ring but all its supporters. Evarts feared his contemporaries might surrender to "the slime of fraud" and to "powerful combinations, stimulated by sordid purposes, and confederated in the bonds of common infamy." Beecher argued that public schools were the great engines of social mobility and that the Irish especially ought to leave their class-bound Catholic schools for the enlightenment of public education. Bellows gave the meeting some statistics and interpreted their meaning. "We have more than 20,000 lewd women and harlots here," he began. "We have about 3,000 grog shops, and 2,000 gambling establishments." Of the "immense number of foreign people here . . . not brought up in our ways of thought," there were "at least 170,000" who were "bound by their connection with a particular creed into a particular box of iron, which is moved about by politicians from one side of the ship to another, and which essentially governs the politics of the city." Bellows asked the audience to remember "that when the majority vote in this city, by an almost fatal necessity it is always against those very principles that lie at the bottom of American freedom and of American institutions."[36]

The council's other major public statement was issued in the form of a July 1871 letter, "To The Citizens of New York." Signed by the council's executive committee, and probably written just after the riot, the letter urged the formation of council branches in the wards. The council's motives were stated so plainly that even the *Herald*

36. *Tribune* (quotes), *Times*, and *Herald*, April 7, 1871.

had to concede that the council was a "Politico-Religious Reform Party." The council explained that "its aim is to organize patriotic citizens, whatever may be their party affinities, into a permanent guardianship over civil interests." Republican institutions were in danger because existing political parties failed to protect them and because "the proper friends of public order" had neglected "to meet the inherent responsibilities of their citizenship. . . . The moneyed, cultured, moral and industrious classes, who are overwhelmingly in the majority, as a rule and habit, have abandoned their posts as citizens and surrendered the care of public affairs into the hands of the vagabond element of society, its idlers and adventurers." The council sought "to secure the elections of a sufficient number of the friends of this movement in the next Legislature of this State to control it."[37]

The council planned an elaborate campaign to gather support. It would sponsor more mass meetings and distribute pamphlets written by "forcible writers" through "the religious and literary press." Moreover, the council said that "measures are in progress to secure the official cooperation of all the clergymen of the State in this branch of work" because the "moral and religious classes are the objects upon which the Council proposes to expend its special efforts, and on which it counts most confidently for its ultimate success." These reformers believed that the Protestant churches especially "possess all the elements and the determining measure of the moral and political forces of the State" and that they were "under the control of influences and agencies that are in full sympathy with the object and methods of the Council. The movement originated with this class, and its management has been principally chosen from it." A small paid staff would handle organizational details. But the council needed many volunteers, and it looked to "the moneyed men and institutions of this city" for financial and moral support in its efforts to protect "our republican institutions, our system of public education, our civil liberties, our religious rights, the peace, if not the existence, of our homes, public morals, . . . and the honor of this city before the world." Others besides the *Herald* understood the council's unstated agenda. To *Star* reader Patrick Farley, the council's platform was "nothing but a political, religious dodge, and there is no question whatever but it has been organized by and with the consent and connivance of the anti-Catholic clergy and laity of New York City

37. *Herald*, September 3, 1871.

for the purpose of arraying the native element of our citizens against the Catholics, and to accomplish what the 12th of July failed to do."[38]

Union League and council members pressed their demands for church and state separation, continued their attacks on alleged Catholic designs to subvert the nation, and elicited much support from others who believed that superstitious Irish Catholics were papal agents who could never be Americanized. When Irish groups urged the school board in 1870 and 1874 to introduce "the study of the Irish language in our schools" because it contained "treasures of poetry and prose unequaled by that of any other land," their petitions were ignored or ridiculed. One board member even suggested "that instruction in language be confined exclusively to the knowledge of English, so as to Americanize our free schools." Yet these petitions and other evidence suggest that many Irish Catholics did not send their children to parish schools. Priests occasionally threatened parents with divine wrath if they enrolled their children in public schools. The *Times* and many citizens viewed the opening of each new parish school as proof of the "Anti-Public School Crusade." For example, schools attached to St. Peter's Church in New York's First Ward and to Brooklyn's St. Paul's parish opened in the fall of 1873. The *Times* claimed some priests planned to name aloud in church those parents who refused to withdraw their children from public schools, took credit for awakening citizens to the dangers of priestly influence, and helped to promote October 1 and October 27 meetings in the two cities to defend common school education.[39]

Many prominent ministers attended the Cooper Union meeting, as did the Committee of Seventy member and school commissioner Albert Klamroth. In his blast at Catholic schools on October 27, Dexter A. Hawkins thundered, "Destroy the common school, and ignorance, poverty, despotism, and bigotry will soon pervade the whole land." The meeting's length prevented Judge William Laimbeer from

38. Ibid.; Patrick H. Farley (New York, September 3, 1871) to *Star*, September 6, 1871.

39. *Times*, February 2, 1870 (Irish petition), and April 2 (board member), 16, 1874. On priests, see, e.g., *Herald*, September 1, 1873, and March 15, 1875; and *Times*, March 6, 1880. On Catholic schools and meeting plans, see *Times*, August 24 (quote), 29, September 8, 9, and October 2, 27, 28, 1873. St. Peter's priest, Father M. J. O'Farrell, was still struggling with his parishioners in 1880. In an interesting interview, the priest admitted he occasionally allowed Catholic children to remain in public schools if their parents wanted them to attend college. O'Farrell explained that workers' children needed a parochial, not a public, education (*Times*, March 6, 1880).

giving his address, but it was published soon after in the *Times.* Laimbeer responded to some Catholic accusations by admitting that public school education was not able to eliminate vice and crime. Yet he asserted "that the licentiousness, crime and pauperism in our community is as nothing compared with the lust, murder, rapine, brigandage and insecurity of life and property pervading most of those countries over whose education the Romish hierarchy holds unlimited sway." Those who sought changes commensurate with Catholic doctrines, including the elimination of Bible reading in public schools, were "a foreign band, representing a foreign policy, having few ideas in harmony with ours, knowing no country, and having no domestic affections or social ties[.] Have they ever obtained political control of a nation," he concluded, "where they have not used their power to subvert its laws and assert the authority of the Church above the State?"[40]

The press even criticized renegade priests like St. Stephen's Edward McGlynn—who championed public education and refused to establish a parish school—for insisting that public schools eliminate Bible reading and religious instruction and that Catholics, like Protestants, be permitted to attend church services in public asylums, orphanages, and prisons. An uproar occurred in 1875 during negotiations between Catholic and public school officials to find ways of alleviating the financial burden on parochial schools. One proposal called for Catholics to send some fifteen thousand children to public schools and to place all parochial buildings and education under school board supervision in return for state aid. The meetings apparently produced no agreements, but even the idea of cooperation infuriated those nativists who believed that devious prelates sought to use their financial crisis as an excuse to establish a foothold in public education. *Times* editorials claimed the issue involved "whether we will submit to see our free schools in any degree subjected to men who profoundly desire the inculcation of . . . false, vicious, and un-American ideas" and warned readers not to underestimate "the immense influences and mideaval [sic] habits of mind among the children of foreign peasantry on American soil." "The fact is," a *Times* subscriber wrote, "the Roman Catholics are endeavoring to undermine our system of Public-schools throughout the country" as the first step to

40. *Times*, October 28, November 8, 1873.

dominating all American life. Other editorials and letters supported this view.[41]

So did Protestant ministers. Calling his April 25, 1875, sermon "Romanism As America's Dangerous Enemy," the Methodist minister M. S. Terry explained that Romanism "is an enemy to the progress of liberty in the nineteenth century; it divorces religion and morality; it fosters and sanctions murder, assassination and outrage." Terry found evidence of such degradation in "the untruthfulness of Irish Catholic servants." The Methodist Oscar Hugo and the Presbyterian David Gregg narrowed their sermons just to the school issue. "Let the religion of our fathers who made the country remain intact," Hugo warned, "and let the Protestant public schools of America be as they always have been—free to all, but managed by people who believe in what we are pleased to term the Protestant creed." Gregg had bitterly denounced Irish Catholics after the 1871 riot. He did so again in 1876 from the same pulpit, accusing Catholics of wanting Bibles removed from schools because they understood that public education was the bulwark of republicanism and American Protestant society. A derogatory *Harper's Weekly* cartoon captured such sentiments and much else. It pictured an Irishman talking to a black child about to enter a schoolhouse. The inscription read:

> "I say, you young Naygur, is that a Thavern?"
> "No; it's a school. Can't you read?"
> "Rade, is it? Hivin save his Riv'rince, do you want to bring me down on a level wid yourself, you young Haythen?"[42]

41. On press criticisms, see *World*, March 31, 1870; *Sun*, April 30 and May 19, 1870; *Times*, July 25 and October 27, 1873; *Herald*, April 2, 3, 1875; Eugene Lawrence, "Hunter's Point—Compulsory Education," *Harper's Weekly* 15 (December 23, 1871): 1197, and "The Bible at Hunter's Point," ibid. 16 (January 16, 1872): 10; and "Ward's Island Chapel," ibid. 12 (July 12, 1873): 595. On 1875 uproar, see *Times*, March 6, 17–19, 22, and April 1, 4–7, 1875; and *Herald*, April 6, 7, 1875. See also George R. Crooks, "The Catholics and the Free Schools," *Harper's Weekly* 20 (January 1, 1876): 10–11. For editorial quotes and the subscriber, see *Times*, April 5 and May 8, 1875; and J.S.P. (New York, April 12, 1875) to *Times*, April 16, 1875. See also editorials in *Times*, March 21, April 10, 22, and May 3, 1875; and *Herald*, March 21, 1875; and letters from various *Herald* readers, March 17, 1875.

42. *Herald*, April 26 (Terry) and May 3 (Hugo), 1875, and January 17, 1876 (Gregg). See also the April 20, 1875, paper delivered by a Reverend Mr. Wheatley to a meeting of Methodist ministers (*Times*, April 21, 1875). Cartoon: *Harper's Weekly* 19 (May 15, 1875): 412.

Frequent attacks on Irish Catholic schools and priests emerged in the press, from Protestant pulpits, and during public meetings. *Times* editorials asked, "How Long Will Protestants Endure?" argued that "the Roman Catholic priesthood plot the overthrow, perversion, or emasculation of the American school system," claimed Catholics sought state aid just to support "criminal" elements, urged "a firm and cordial union of Protestant Christendom" to thwart Rome's ambitions, and asserted in 1880 that "a permanent class of working people" must not be educated by priests whose fidelity to theocracy prevented them from training enlightened voters for a republic.[43]

The most strident nativist assaults appeared in *Harper's Weekly* articles written by Eugene Lawrence between 1871 and 1876. Lawrence blamed Catholics for all the city's ills and barely stopped short of advocating the deportation of all Irish Catholics. Just before the 1871 elections, he reminded voters:

> History must always record that, in the most disastrous moments of the war, the unreflecting Romanists rose to pillage the city, and apparently to deliver it into the hands of the slaveholders; that a succession of riots and disorders has arisen among the ignorant multitude to whom the priests have refused the education of freemen; that the rulers they have placed in offices have committed enormous crimes, and that the utter ruin of the city was only averted by a sudden discovery of their guilt. Such facts are lessons. They show an urgent need of enforcing a thorough system of education upon our foreign population; of teaching them loyalty to the government, the value of honesty, and the duty of gratitude.[44]

Lawrence claimed both that Catholics opposed Grant's reelection in 1872 because the president had established public schools in the South and that they supported Tilden in 1876 because of his favors to the Irish Catholic democracy. "There can in the future be but two parties," he wrote elsewhere, "one the defender of American education, and one eager for its destruction." Arguing again for compulsory education, he asserted, "Our city has been ruled by a class of men

43. *Times*, February 2 ("Protestants"), June 28 ("priesthood"), and November 18 ("criminal"), 1871, October 4, 1873 ("Christendom"), and March 21, 1880.

44. Eugene Lawrence, "The Pope and the Teacher," *Harper's Weekly Supplement* 15 (November 4, 1871): 1042. Similar arguments are in Lawrence, "Jesuit Defeats," ibid. 17 (March 15, 1873): 205–6; and "The Catholic Vote," ibid. 19 (June 26, 1875): 518.

9. The American River Ganges: The priests and the children. Thomas Nast cartoon. *Harper's Weekly*, September 30, 1871.

more infamous than the worst instruments of European despotism. . . . If New York had been thoroughly educated, it would never have fallen into the hands of the profligate and the immoral, or Irish Catholics and foreign priests." "Political Romanism is the chief peril that hangs over our future progress," Lawrence bellowed in still another article. He believed that Irish Catholics were "the bitterest enemies of religious and civil liberty, of education, good order, and progress."[45]

A strong nativist current pervaded all such debates over public funding of education. It was especially evident in the 1875 national controversy surrounding James G. Blaine's proposal for a Constitutional amendment prohibiting public aid to sectarian schools.[46] New York's reformers did not limit their arguments to Constitutional questions or their concerns to hefty tax assessments. The school issue involved fundamental questions about America's future. In the aftermath of a wrenching civil war, and in the midst of a severe depression, reformers and nativists sought to forge a cohesive society based on Protestant-republican values that they believed derived from Revolutionary times. Their vision made no room for conspiratorial agents, be they priests or Irish workers, whom they believed were chained to ignorance, superstition, criminality, idleness, intemperance, and despotism.

More public nativist expressions occurred during the annual celebrations commemorating George Washington's birthday. Nativist

45. On Grant and Tilden, see Eugene Lawrence: "Grant and Education," ibid. 16 (August 3, 1872): 593–94; "Grant, Union, and Education," ibid. (November 9, 1872): 869–70; "Why the Foreign Church Supports Mr. Tilden," ibid. 20 (September 30, 1876): 794–95; "The Destroyers of Our Public Schools," ibid. (October 28, 1876): 874; and "Shall the Roman Catholic Clubs Control the Union?" ibid. (November 14, 1876): 894. For quotations, see Lawrence: "The Demand of Foreign Priests," ibid. 17 (September 27, 1874): 854 ("two parties"); "Compulsory Education in New York," ibid. 19 (January 16, 1875): 58 ("foreign priests"); "Roman Catholic Schools," ibid. (February 6, 1875): 128 ("Politcal Romanism"); and "Jesuits in Politics," ibid. (September 4, 1875): 722 ("bitterest enemies"). See also related Lawrence articles: "Romish Avarice," ibid. 15 (November 18, 1871): 1073–74; "The Papacy in New York," ibid. 19 (October 23, 1875): 863; "Jesuit Intrigues in America," ibid. 21 (January 6, 1877): 10; and "The Jesuits in New York," ibid. (February 24, 1877): 150.

46. See Harold A. Buetow, "Historical Perspectives on New York's 1967 Constitutional Convention and Article XI, Section 3 (The 'Blaine' or 'Know-Nothing' Amendment)," *Catholic Educational Review* 65 (March 1967): 163–67. See also Sister Marie Carolyn Klinkhamer, "The Blaine Amendment of 1875: Private Motives for Political Action," *Catholic Historical Review* 42 (April 1956): 15–49; and Laurence R. Gardner, "The Blaine Amendment of 1876: A Proposal to Extend the Constitution as to Prohibit Indirect Aid to Sectarian Institutions" (Master's thesis, Catholic University of America, 1947).

groups did not participate in 1870 and 1871 festivities on February 22. But the 1871 riot sparked a revival and brought out Orangemen, the APA, and the Order of United American Mechanics (OUAM) every February 22 until 1875, when for unknown reasons the Orangemen and the APA dropped out of the parade, leaving the OUAM to carry the nativist flag for the rest of the decade. The Orangemen continued to hold small parades and picnics on Boyne Day until at least 1874. No incidents marred these events. But the Orangemen decided it would be safer to fly their colors on a more patriotic, "American" holiday by joining other nativist groups on February 22. It was a smart maneuver. They could display American loyalty and champion Protestantism.[47]

How could Irish Catholics legitimately criticize such patriotism? The annual parade of several dozen New York, Brooklyn, and New Jersey nativist contingents in the Washington celebration left Patrick Ford incredulous. "It isn't in the mind of man to conceive of a more glaring contradiction than to imagine Orangemen marching in procession through the streets of New York . . . to celebrate the memory of George Washington," he exploded in 1872. The general had led rebel troops against a successor of William of Orange. Why would Orangemen celebrate that? Ford believed that Orangemen hoped to provoke another riot but failed. He also thought that it would be more appropriate for the "true" Irish to honor Washington's memory. "*They*, like Washington, are perpetual rebels to the same brutal power—the British Government—against which he rebelled. *They* strike at the same detested flag that he struck at." Yet "A Protestant" *Herald* reader later asked why "not a single Catholic organization was represented" in the parade. "A Catholic" quickly replied:

> If "A Protestant" knows anything, he must know there is good reason for Catholics not joining in those processions. They were first instituted during the height of the Know-Nothing furor, and monopolized almost exclusively by the secret Order of United Americans, who proscribed Catholics, and in all probability would not have allowed them, even were they so wanting in self-respect as to march in processions where every other banner was an insult to

47. For coverage, see *Times*, *Tribune*, and *Herald*, February 23, 1870, 1871, and 1872, February 23, 24, 1873, February 23, 1874, and February 23, 1876. See also *Times*, July 13, 1872, July 13, 1873, and February 23, 1876–79.

> their religion. To make those Washington birthday parades unmistakably anti-Catholic, they were joined by the Irish Orangemen. . . . This patriotic body . . . cared about as much for the memory of Washington as they did for the Pope; but being excellent haters of the Catholic Church, made the air resound with their faction tunes . . . which their Orange regalia and no-Popery banners impressed one with the idea that the Father of His Country was a confirmed bigot.[48]

Irish-American perceptions shaped a unique interpretation of the depression years. New York's Irish occasionally found their streets lined with nativist and Orange organizations, but not with gold. City meeting halls often were crowded by reformers who mocked Irish ways and scorned their schools and their patron saint's religion. Yet these same reformers and nativists had helped to cause hard times. The press and the pulpit accused the Irish of undermining republicanism and Christianity. If they lost jobs to the depression, they still were accused of idleness. If they demanded public works or better wages or shorter hours, they were deemed unruly. If they criticized monopoly, attacked usury, and condemned the principle of rent, they were labeled radicals. And ardent Irish-American nationalists were considered disloyal to America.

Many Irish immigrants had heard similar criticisms before they emigrated; and their assessments of American life were framed by a different vision of republicanism than that of their accusers because theirs was derived from experiences in both countries. Currency, tariff, and land questions were viewed through Irish and Irish-American eyes. In 1874, Patrick Ford urged that "democracy" be infused into the Democratic party, and he attacked Tammany's past as "the history of an organized lie. In the past it denied that colored men had any rights which white men were bound to respect," he explained. "Yet Tammany called itself democratic! To-day it practically asserts that Knickerbocker 'respectability' alone should monopolize the chief chair of State, and virtually declares that Irish-Americans ought to put forward no claims to positions of trust and honor." Two years later he blasted American royalists as "the decayed relic of the old Anglo aristocracy of a century ago," who still gathered wealth while oppressing others, "who have all the vices but nothing of the

48. *Irish World*, March 2, 1872; "A Protestant" (n.p., n.d.) to *Herald*, November 17, 1872; "A Catholic" (n.p., n.d.) to ibid., November 24, 1872.

polish which characterizes the profligate aristocracy of European countries, [and] are heartily tired of our simple republican institutions and sigh for a change." Later that year Ford supported neither Hayes nor Tilden but the Greenbacker Peter Cooper. "America is in bondage to a foreign power," he argued. "We are slaves to England's great manufacturing lords. America needs another Declaration of Independence." Farmers and workers were arrayed against "the Aristocracy," "Bondholders," and English commercial agents and shippers who destroyed American jobs.[49]

Early in January 1877, with the election much in doubt, Ford pondered what news the unemployed worker might learn in the *Sun* about election events in Florida and Louisiana. "Well," he bitterly fantasized, "he [the worker] is in hopes that the 'nigger' vote will be counted out. No human being wrapped in a black skin has any right in a voice in the laws made to tax him. That is this white slave's profound conviction. All the arguments which the advocates of any Aristocracy use against *him* he takes at second hand and employs them against his colored neighbor." Workers should more severely question the "pretensions" of a privileged class that sought to achieve absolute power; for once in office, "they will rob you and call it 'taxation,' they will throw you out of work and call it 'retrenchment,' they will grab at the public purse and fill themselves and call it 'salary.'" It was no different in England. Ford blasted the Union League Club in similar terms a week later. The club's purpose was "to import and slavishly imitate the manners of the English aristocracy, deride republican simplicity, bring into contempt democratic institutions, and violate in the most approved style every moral precept and every Christian principle." In March, Ford wrote that these and similar men formed "the very class . . . which longs for the day when the 'English system,' social and political, will be introduced into and will have sway in the United States." They were apologists for British monarchy and defenders of the American "Money Oligarchy." In his Independence Day editorial, Ford incorporated currency, tariff, and land concerns in connecting the nation's problems to conditions that sparked the revolt against England a century before. Believing that "the agricultural class, the manufacturing class, and the commercial class" had objected to "*industrial oppression*" and that all had struggled "for the rights of labor," Ford drew a parallel to the world of his

49. *Irish World*, October 31, 1874, and April 15 and September 30, 1876.

day. "It isn't the bondsman's *body* the slavemaster wants; it is his labor. It isn't the soil the Irish land-robber asks; it is the *products* of the soil" (the products of labor). Ford still had great faith in American liberty. But "mere political freedom is not enough. The fabric of political freedom, unless its foundations are laid deep and firm in industrial freedom, will afford the people but little protection, and must sooner or later tumble in. And industrial freedom means the Land, Manufacturers, and the National Currency." The latter especially had become "the NEW SLAVE POWER," causing enforced idleness for millions of workers.[50]

Ford marked his paper's seventh anniversary on September 1 with an editorial criticizing the monopolistic *Tribune* and *Herald*. He said the papers reflected a dangerous trend in American life:

> The tendency, if not the studied design, of these and such papers is to Anglicize this nation in the worst sense of that word: to make honest labor despised and Industry to appear ungraceful; to inject a pernicious principle into business by diverting enterprise into speculation and speculation into gambling; to sneer at the simple virtues which distinguished the founders of the Republic and which everywhere and at all times should characterize every true republican; and to generate a morbid taste for royalty and king-governed countries.

Ford's views were widely supported. After 1877 his paper carried a permanent column on currency reform and frequent articles on land, labor, the tariff, and industrialization. All placed these issues within an Irish and Irish-American framework, drew lessons from Irish and American history, and expressed concerns about English influence in America. Readers contributed to that dialogue. Thomas Reath wrote that "Democrats and Republicans are doing the work of England in this city as effectively as it could be done in London by forcing the Irish laborers into idleness and consequently into want." A Trenton Greenbacker pointed out that England's monetary policies influenced American practices and caused hard times in both countries. The paper's "Trans-Atlantic" correspondent claimed that the United States had inherited a crippling "Political Gout" from England in spite of the American Revolution. Just as children can inherit their father's gout, "thus it happens that in the third generation

50. Ibid., January 13, 20, March 17, and July 7, 1877.

the old virus breaks out in its malignant symptoms, which nothing can cure but a total change of political habit, a complete and thorough rejection of the use of every principle, axiom and custom and the British system of government."[51]

Ford formalized what he perceived were current Irish sentiments in an August 18, 1877, open letter to state and national officials, and in a succeeding editorial series. Amid the summer's labor strikes, he told legislators that American workers faced European-style depression. "Every patriot, bewildered at the scenes of suffering and disorder about him, asks in wonder: 'Is *this* the Republic of Washington and Jefferson?'" Arguing that lawmakers must deal with crucial currency and monopoly problems, Ford urged them to pay "Bond Lords" in greenbacks, to demonetize gold and silver, to abolish national banks, to promote home industries and abolish usury, to issue a fully redeemable legal tender without interest and not based on gold or silver, to nationalize the mines and railroads, and to increase opportunities to own land. In later editorials, Ford suggested that workers make "Land, Labor, And Money" the basis of an "Industrial Rights' Party." "A just land law will recognize man's birthright—to share in his Father's estate," he explained. "Land means life. Labor in its various forms means the various modes of life. Money means an exchange of labor." But the land question formed the core of his program. "On this solid and universal foundation—the land—must be based all the reforms which we now seek to uprear. Every man born into this world has a natural right to his share in his Heavenly Father's estate." If Americans truly hoped to prevent an "oligarchy," they had to recognize from English and Irish history that money and power all stemmed from land monopolization.[52]

The decade had begun with two bloody riots, the fall of Tweed, a Protestant upper-class reform movement, and depression. Two events in 1879 closed one era and began another: the formation of the Irish National Land League, and the publication of Henry George's *Progress and Poverty*. The Land League was a result of

51. Thomas Reath (New York, February 25, 1876) to ibid., March 4, 1876; Stephen D. Dillaye (Trenton, February 27, 1877) to ibid., March 10, 1877; "Trans-Atlantic," in ibid., October 6, 1877. See also, e.g., "Trans-Atlantic," ibid., May 27, 1876; H. (Jersey City, March 31, 1877) to ibid., April 7, 1877; H. (Jersey City, April 26, 1877) to ibid., May 5, 1877; and Jeremiah J. Driscoll (New York, April 26, 1877) to ibid., May 5, 1877.

52. *Irish World*, August 25 and November 17, 1877, and February 9 and 16, 1878.

near-famine conditions that rocked Ireland in 1879. Formed on October 29 of that year at a Dublin conference of young Irish nationalists and land reformers, the Land League sought land reform legislation, reduced land rents, and freedom for Ireland. The league stirred Irish-American sentiment and financial support as never before. Most important, for New York's Irish workers, it sparked a critique of conditions in Ireland and America that helped to shape Irish and Irish-American nationalist activities and New York City labor affairs in the early 1880s.[53]

Events in New York City also helped to shape these movements. For between 1870 and 1879, the city's Irish learned that liberal reform, nativism, and hard times were systemically related and that land and industrial monopoly challenged labor's capacity to reap rewards commensurate with what they believed were the promises of American republicanism. Concerned throughout his book with the effects of industrial and land monopoly and with the corresponding relationship between "progress and poverty," Henry George wrote that "political liberty, when the equal right to land is denied, becomes, as population increases and invention goes on, merely the liberty to compete for employment at starvation wages." George touched a sensitive Irish nerve. A similar position, formed from the decade's experiences and from events in Ireland, became the core of an Irish-American critique of America that became central to the George mayoral campaign in 1886.[54]

53. Foner, "Class, Ethnicity, and Radicalism"; Brown, *Irish-American Nationalism*; and Gordon, "Irish and Irish-American Thought and Behavior," pt. II.

54. Henry George, *Progress and Poverty* (1879; rpt. New York: Vanguard, 1929), 198.

Appendix A / Killed, Injured, and Arrested in Connection with the 1870 Riot

Information for this appendix was compiled from the 1870 *Tribune*, July 14 and 16: *Sun*, July 13 and 14; *Times*, July 13 and 16; *World*, July 13 and 14; and *Herald*, July 13–15. Because details in these newspapers sometimes differed, I have indicated the more important discrepancies. More complete information is in my "Studies in Irish and Irish-American Thought and Behavior in Gilded Age New York City" (Ph.D. diss., University of Rochester, 1977), app. B.

KILLED

BRADY, CHARLES, age 23 or 24; lived at Fifty-Third Street and Eleventh Avenue; marble polisher. Shot in head or chest while looking for work between Eighth and Ninth avenues at Ninety-second or Ninety-Third Street.

BRADY, JAMES (or MICHAEL), age 14, 15, or 17; lived in a shanty at Sixty-third Street near Eighth Avenue; tool carrier for Boulevard laborers. Either shot while assaulting Orangemen or just an innocent bystander. Coroner attributed death to a skull fracture from a club or stone.

BRADY, PATRICK, age 60. Shot in chest and stomach.

CROWLEY, DANIEL (or BERNARD) B. (or R.), age about 40; born Ireland; lived on Bloomingdale Road near Sixty-eighth or Sixty-Ninth Street; Boulevard laborer. Shot in chest while scaling Elm Park fence.

GARDINER (or GARDNER), JOHN, age 24; emigrated from Ireland 1867; lived at 525 West Thirty-seventh Street. Found with an Orange badge pinned to his clothes; died Bellevue Hospital July 14.

KANE (or KAIN or CAIN), PATRICK, age 31 or 40; emigrated from Ireland 1848; lived either on West Sixty-seventh Street or Eighty-fifth Street between Ninth and Tenth avenues; Boulevard laborer. Skull fracture. Died Bellevue July 13.

KANE (or CAIN), WILLIAM, age 31; emigrated from Ireland 1857; lived at 1495 Third Avenue; quarryman. Stabbed in back in Central Park by Orangeman. Died Bellevue July 13.

WOOD, FRANCIS, age 31; born Ireland; lived at 623 East Ninth Street; member No Surrender Lodge of the APA. Head smashed in Eighth Avenue streetcar at Fifty-eighth Street. Died Bellevue July 13.

INJURED

ADAMS, THOMAS, age 53; born Ireland; lived at 524 West Thirtieth Street; laborer. Slight scalp wounds.

ARNOLD, ROBERT, age 23; lived in Brooklyn. Head and hand wounds on Eighth Avenue streetcar.

BURNETT (or BARNETT or BARRETT), THOMAS, age 30; born Ireland; lived between 131 and 191 West Twenty-eighth Street; baker. Head wounds on Eighth Avenue car near Fifty-ninth Street.

COLLINS, DANIEL. Shot in jaw on Eighth Avenue car; claimed he was innocent bystander.

EAGAN (or EGAN or REAGAN), FRANK, age 26; lived on Tenth Avenue between 129th and 130th streets. Struck on back of head by a club. *Times* report that he died not corroborated.

HERON, JOHN, age 30; Orangeman; emigrated from Ireland 1864; lived on East Seventeenth Street; fireman. Skull fracture, probably in Elm Park.

JOHNSON, JOHN, age 35; born Ireland, lived at 144 Mulberry Street; horseshoer. Found unconscious with bad scalp wound in front of his house July 13.

MURRAY (or MURPHY), THOMAS, age 39; emigrated from Ireland 1848; lived on North Moore Street; teamster. Shot in the face and hit on the head by Orangemen.

NUTT, ROBERT, age 30; Orangeman; emigrated from Ireland 1862; lived in Brooklyn; laborer. Scalp wounds from attacks on Eighth Avenue car at Ninety-second Street and Ninth Avenue.

REYNOLDS, JAMES (or FRANK), age 40; born Ireland. Pistol wound in groin.

ROBERTSON, WILLIAM. Park bandleader. Hit on the head by an instrument (see "A Member of Robertson's Band," n.p., n.d., to *Sun*, July 15).

ROSS, WILLIAM, age 38; lived 710 Seventh Avenue, Brooklyn. Scalp wounds, possible broken jaw, while riding in Eighth Avenue car at Fifty-ninth Street.

SHIELDS (or SHIELS), JOHN, age 40; Orangeman; emigrated from Ireland 1857; lived in Hastings-on-Hudson; shoemaker. Scalp wounds from club or stone at Elm Park.

SMITH, SAMUEL, age 35; Orangeman; emigrated Ireland 1864; lived at 74 or 174 Mulberry Street; sampler. Head cuts, bruises, possible skull fracture at Elm Park.

WRIGHT, JOHN; lived on West Twelfth Street. Gun wound in his arm.

ARRESTED

BOYD, JOHN, age 28; born America to Irish parents; lived at 306 West Twentieth Street; clerk. Threatened to shoot a man. Charged with rioting; jailed when he could not post bond.

DALY, PATRICK. Charged with rioting.

DAWSON, ROBERT, age 30; born Ireland; lived on Fifty-sixth Street near Tenth Avenue; laborer. Disorderly conduct.

HOGENBOOM, STEPHEN K. Fired pistol at John Murphy on the night of July 12. Jailed when he could not post bond.

O'BRIEN, PETER. Rioting.

PATER (or PETERS), JACOB, age 34; born Germany; lived at Eighth Avenue and Seventy-fifth Street. Fired pistol. Released July 13 because judge believed was in park by accident.

Appendix B / Killed, Injured, and Arrested in Connection with the 1871 Riot and a List of Property Damages

Some of the information in this appendix was compiled from the following 1871 newspapers: the *Tribune*, July 14, 15, 17, 18, 20, and 25; *Sun*, July 14, 15, 18, and 20; *Star*, July 14–18; *Times*, July 13–18; *World*, July 14–18 and 20; *Herald*, July 13–18 and 30; and *Irish World*, July 22. Information about police casualties was obtained from the *Second Annual Report of the Police Department of the City of New York: For the Year Ending April 5th, 1872* (New York, 1873). Details about some military casualties come from New York State Adjutant-General's Office, *Annual Report of the Adjutant-General, 1871* (Albany, 1872). Some additional information was obtained from *Wilson's Business Directory of New York City* (New York, 1871) and from the *Ninth United States Census* (1870), *Population Schedules*, second enumeration, for New York City's Twentieth and Sixteenth wards. The names of those listed in the July 24 coroner's report are marked by an asterisk (*). Published in the July 25 *Tribune*, the report did not include all deaths, or even all deaths considered at inquests. The original report is in the Municipal Archives and Records Center. Where possible, I have used the spelling provided by the coroner or census takers. While I have tried to present as accurate an accounting as possible, some irreconcilable details exist and are noted. More complete information, including names of bondsmen, can be found in my "Studies in Irish and Irish-American

Thought and Behavior in Gilded Age New York City" (Ph.D. diss., University of Rochester, 1977), app. C.

CIVILIAN DEATHS

ACKERMAN, PHILIP J. (or L. or M.), age 72; born New York; lived at 262 West Twenty-fifth Street (northeast corner of Eighth Avenue); retired shoe manufacturer. Killed by musket ball that crashed through fourth-floor window into his chest. Daughter later told coroner's inquest Ackerman was killed on rooftop, but *Herald* reporter found body on fourth floor.

ARCHIBALD, ——. Death reported only in *World* (July 14), which stated that the body was taken home by friends.

*BUCKLAND, CHARLES, JR., age 29; born Australia; lived at 590 East Twenty-eighth Street; carman. Shot in abdomen and died July 12.

CLARK, JAMES A., age 44; born New York; lived at 139 East 110th Street; manufacturer of paper collars; member Methodist Episcopal Church; wife and five children. Shot by militia volley at Twenty-sixth Street and Eighth Avenue just after leaving his business. Buried Green-Wood Cemetery July 17.

CULLOUGH, WILLIAM, age 30 or 35; lived in Hudson City. Shot in head.

DONALDSON, JOHN, age 28; lived on Nineteenth Street. Shot in side or heart.

*DOUCE, RICHARD, age 54; black; born Pennsylvania; lived at 102 Greene or Greenwich Street; steward on steamer *Hartford*. Musket ball severed the femoral artery.

*DUGDALE, THOMAS, age 35; born Ireland; lived at 266 West Twenty-fifth Street; Erie Railroad freight depot clerk. Innocent bystander, shot in the left arm and breast in front of Utah House, corner of Twenty-fifth Street and Eighth Avenue. Died at home July 14.

ERSKINE, BENJAMIN FRANKLIN, age 17; born America; lived at 261 West Thirty-ninth Street; clerk. Shot in thigh and knee at Twenty-sixth Street and Eighth Avenue. Died St. Luke's Hospital July 14.

*GARITY, JOSEPH, age 19; lived at 81 Carmine Street. Left home at noon on the twelfth. Shot in heart. Body found at Twenty-fourth Street and Eighth Avenue.

*GILBERT, AUGUSTUS P., age 38; Protestant; born Connecticut; lived in Brooklyn; *Herald* compositor. Shot in back by militia at

Twenty-fourth Street and Eighth Avenue. Died Bellevue Hospital July 14. Buried Cyprus Hills Cemetery July 17.

HANBY, HANNAH CONNOR, age 15; adopted by Irish-born parents; lived at 228 West Nineteenth Street. Shot watching parade. Died Bellevue July 14.

*HANLON, TIMOTHY, age 40; born Ireland; lived at Eleventh Street and First Avenue. Gunshot wound in head or heart.

HARINGTON, ALFRED W. (or M.), age 58; born Canada; lived in Brooklyn; agent. Severe thigh wounds. Died Bellevue July 17. Buried Green-Wood Cemetery.

*HARTUNG, WILLIAM, age 40; deaf-mute; born Germany; lived in Hudson City; cigarmaker. Musket ball in heart as he watched parade.

HAZELTON, ELLEN; lived at 423 West Forty-first Street.

*HINERS, FREDERICK, age 36; born Germany; lived in Brooklyn; worked at Pfiffer's chemical plant in Fulton Street. Gunshot wound in right breast.

*HOLWAY, MORRIS, age 28; born Ireland; lived on Seventy-sixth Street between First and Second avenues; laborer. Gunshot wound in head.

*KELLY (or KELLEY), MICHAEL, age 21; born Ireland; lived at 317 East Thirty-seventh Street; quarryman. Shot in heart. Buried Calvary Cemetery July 16.

KELTENBACH, CHARLES M., age 29; born Germany; lived at 80½ Attorney Street; notary public and commissioner of deeds. On business in area when shot in arms and back by Eighty-fourth Regiment at Twenty-sixth Street. Died at Mount Sinai Hospital July 21.

*KENNEY (or KENNEDY or KINNEY), SARAH, age 30; born Ireland; lived in Brooklyn. Compound skull fracture from bullet or club.

*KERRIGAN, THOMAS, age 21; born Ireland; lived at 339 West Thirty-eighth Street; laborer. Shot in head. *Irish World* (July 22) reported police found empty pistol on body.

LATIMER (or LATTIMERE or LATTIMER), WILLIAM T. (or J.), age about 49; lived at 116 or 166 Dean Street, Brooklyn; stationer. Passing through area when killed by militia barrage on Eighth Avenue. Jaw shot off; wounded in neck and breast. Died Bellevue July 15.

*LAVERY (or LAVENY or SAVERY), JOHN, age 23; born Ireland; lived at 364 Tenth Avenue; laborer. Shot behind right ear.

*LEAHY (or LAHEY), MICHAEL, age 39; born Ireland; lived at 884 or 894 Second Avenue. Shot by guardsmen at Twenty-fourth Street and Eighth Avenue. Died Bellevue July 14 from shock and internal hemorrhaging.

LINNAHAN, ——, MRS. Death reported only in *Sun* (July 14): "one finger on each hand and top of head shot off."

*LOVE, JOSEPH, age 21; lived at 35 Greenwich Street; store clerk. Musket ball in head.

*McCAFFREY (or CAFFERTY, McCAFFERTY, or MCKAFFY), PETER, age 55; born Ireland or Connecticut; lived at 41½ or 147 Washington Street. Musket balls in wrist and abdomen at Twenty-fifth Street and Eighth Avenue. Died Bellevue July 18.

McCLEARY, THOMAS; owned White House Saloon, Brooklyn. Had gone with *Brian Burke* (see "Civilian Injuries") to see parade. Shot in the abdomen. Died July 19.

*McCORMACK (or McCORMICK), MICHAEL, age 55; born Ireland, lived at 381 Sixth Avenue. Musket ball in chest.

*McCORMACK (or McCORMICK), THOMAS, age 17; born England to Irish parents; lived at 309 Ninth Avenue. Returning home from school through Eighth Avenue. Shot in back by militia.

McCUMMINGS, RICHARD, age 55. Gunshot blast in the chest.

McDOUGAL, JAMES, age 34. Chest wound.

*McGRATH, WILLIAM, age 25; born Ireland; lived at 119th Street and Eighth Avenue; coachman. Musket fire shattered left arm; died from "exhaustion" after amputation.

*McMAHON, DENNIS, age 20; born Ireland; lived at 34 East Thirty-fourth Street. Musket ball through hip and abdomen.

McMAHON, JAMES, age 33; born Ireland; lived at 309 Ninth Avenue; blacksmith. Shot in the left temple while in Eighth Avenue.

MADDEN, R. ——, age 19; born Ireland. Body wounds.

MALONEY, ——. Death reported only in *World* (July 14).

*MAUALEAN, PATRICK, age 13; born Ireland; lived at 90 Hay Street. Gunshot wound in back and lungs.

MONAGHAN (or MONOGHAN or MONAHAN), PATRICK, age 20; born Ireland; lived at 88 Henry Street. First spelling taken from later newspaper accounts of the funeral on July 16. Body taken to brother's house at 90 Henry Street. Hence some similarities in names and addresses between MAUALEAN and MONAGHAN (90 Hay Street might be 90 Henry Street), but all papers reported Monaghan was shot through head (not in back).

*MULLEN (or MALLEN), JOHN (or THOMAS), age 24; born Ireland; lived at 502 West 29th Street. Shot in eye.

MULVEY (or MALOY, MUBREY, MULLALY, or MULLABEY), DANIEL, age 23, 28, or 30; born Ireland; lived at 206 East Twenty-sixth Street; laborer. Shot through head or chest while watching parade at Twenty-sixth Street and Eighth Avenue. Buried Calvary Cemetery July 14.

O'SHEA (or O'SHAY), MICHAEL, age 20; born Ireland; lived at 1294 Third Avenue. Shot in head by militia. Died Mount Sinai July 14.

PETTIT, CHARLES H., age 22; born Virginia; lived at 144 Ninth Avenue (corner of Nineteenth Street); butcher. Shot through heart by Eighty-fourth when entering furniture store at Twenty-fifth Street and Eighth Avenue.

*RILEY (or RIELLY or REILLY), JOHN, age 26; born Ireland; lived at 341 East Sixteenth Street; hod carrier. Joined one hundred laborers from construction site and marched to Eighth Avenue. Shot in head. Buried Calvary Cemetery July 14.

*SCOTT, WALTER J., age 30; born Ireland; lived at 156 Hackett Street, Brooklyn. Shot in abdomen and groin on Eighth Avenue.

SHERRY, PETER, age 21; born Ireland; lived at 144 West Nineteenth Street; expressman. Shot in right thigh at Twenty-sixth Street. Died Mount Sinai July 17.

*SHORIEN (or SHUTEN, SHORTEN, or SHORTER), WILLIAM, age 19; born New York; lived at 424 East Fifteenth Street; laborer. Gunshot wound to head.

*SIEGER, CONRAD, age 28; born Germany; lived at 230 Elizabeth Street. Shot in heart.

*SLATTERY (or SLATTERLY or SLATERY), PATRICK, age 46; lived at 277 Rivington Street. Returning from his work when he was shot in wrist and shoulder. Died Bellevue July 13. Buried Calvary Cemetery July 16.

*SPRING, THOMAS J., age 16; born New York; lived at 7 Battery Place; student at Free Academy. Shot in left groin by militia as he entered mother's confectionery shop at 276 or 282 Eighth Avenue. (Shop not listed in census schedules or *Wilson's Directory*.) Bled to death in twenty minutes.

*STANTON, OWEN, age 18; born Ireland; lived at 305 East Twenty-fourth Street. Shot in right thigh by troops at Twenty-fourth Street and Eighth Avenue. Died Bellevue July 19.

*SULLIVAN, TIMOTHY, age 27; born Ireland; lived at 102 Bayard Street; hod carrier. Gunshot wound in head.

TAFF, IVAN. Death reported only in *Irish World* (July 22).

*TIGH, WILLIAM, age 26; born Ireland; lived at 358 West Thirty-sixth Street. Shot in left shoulder and chest on Eighth Avenue.

WARD, JOHN, age 30; born Scotland; lived at 521 West Forty-second Street. Militia ball in abdomen and bladder.

*WASHBURN, GEORGE W., age 26; born Foxboro, Massachusetts; hatter. Musket ball fractured spine.

*WHITESIDE, JOHN A., age 27; b rn Ireland; lived at 207 West Twenty-sixth Street; laborer. Killed b a gunshot wound in chest.

*YORK, MARY A., age 12; lived at 2 4 West Eighteenth Street. At parade with neighbor. Wore orange ibbons or orange scarf. Shot in head by man wearing green ribbon.

*UNKNOWN MAN, age about 30. Gu shot wound in head.

TWO UNKNOWN BODIES. At July 4 coroner's inquest, Thomas S. Brennan, Bellevue's warden, said o bodies remained at hospital morgue.

MILITARY DEATHS

PAIGE (or PAGE), HENRY C., Comp ny K, Ninth Regiment; age 47; Protestant; born England; lived at 14 Eighth Avenue; business manager, James Fisk's Grand Opera Hou e. Pistol ball ripped off part of head while trying to fix musket.

*PRIOR (or PRYOR), WALTER R., pr vate, Company A, Ninth Regiment; age 24; Protestant; lived at 30 Eighth Avenue; Gunshot fractured left leg.

*WYATT, SAMUEL, sergeant, Comp ny F, Ninth Regiment; Protestant; lived at 107 Macdougal Stree ; aged 30; goldsmith. Gunshot wound in the abdomen.

POLICE DEATHS

FORD, HENRY. Twenty-ninth Precinc .

HAMIL, JOHN. First listed as bruised. Official police *Report* indicates death on August 8.

CIVILIAN INJURIES

AHERN, PATRICK; lived on Nineteen h Street. Thigh wound.

AUCKWRIGHT, ——; lived at 42 Sev nth Avenue. Taken with *Lutenberger* (see below) by friends to 238 West Twenty-eighth Street, near Eighth Avenue shooting.

BENTON, JOHN, age 47; born Ireland; lived at 813 Fulton Street. Shot in the back.

BORDEN, JEREMIAH, age 34; lived at Thirty-fourth Street and First Avenue. Scalp wound from club.

BRANNIGAN, JOHN, age 19; born England; lived at 179 First Avenue; stonecutter. Shot in wrist; treated at Bellevue.

BRAZON, JOHN, age 18; lived at 1071 First Avenue. Gunshot wound; treated at Bellevue.

BUNTING, JOHN, age 56; lived in Brooklyn. Wounded in knee.

BURKE, BRIAN; born Ireland; bartender at *Thomas McCleary's* (see "Civilian Deaths") White House Saloon. Serious condition from an undisclosed wound.

CAREY, ELLEN A., age 32; "a respectable Irish woman" (*Tribune* July 15); lived on Eighth Avenue near Fifty-fifth Street. Right leg amputated.

CARR, PETER, age 23; born Ireland; lived on Forty-eighth Street near Sixth Avenue. Shot in breast and arms.

CARR, WILLIAM H. Ninth Regiment shot him in back between Twenty-sixth and Twenty-seventh streets. Slight wound.

CLANCY, WILLIAM, age 29; born Ireland; lived at 279 Delancy Street. Thigh wound; treated at Mount Sinai.

CLARK, PETER, age 23; born Ireland; lived on Fifty-eighth Street between Sixth and Seventh avenues. Militia fire shattered watch into breast. Treated at Mount Sinai.

CLARK, PETER; lived at 10 Ridge Street. Scalp wound.

COLEMAN (or COLMAN), W. P., age 40; born Ireland; lived at 318, 340, or 346 East Eleventh Street. Back wound; treated at Bellevue.

CONNOLLY, BRIDGET; born Ireland.

CONNOLLY, JAMES, age 20; lived on Thirty-fifth Street between Tenth and Eleventh avenues.

COTT (or COE, COLE, or COTE), JOHN, age 30; born England; cotton weaver. Leg wound; treated at Bellevue.

CRUM, JAMES; lived on Twentieth Street; laborer. Shot in breast.

DALTON, MICHAEL; born Ireland. Scalp wound.

DILLON, JAMES, age 14; lived at 324 West Twenty-sixth Street. Found with gunshot wound in shoulder in front of home; treated at Bellevue.

DUNLEAVY, F. Beaten.

ERWIN (or EDWIN), JAMES, age 30; born Ireland. Pistol shot in chest; treated at Bellevue.

FARRELL, CHRISTOPHER; born Ireland. Shot in foot.

FEENEY, JOHN, age 29; born Ireland; lived at 307 Seventh Avenue. Shot in hip.

FIREHOCK (or FIREBOCK, FIREBACH, or FIREHOOK), JAMES W., age 27; lived at 281 Rivington Street. Wounded in hip.

FREEDMAN (or FREEMAN), CONRAD; lived at 209 Avenue C. Beaten at Hibernian Hall.

GRADY, JOHN, age 50; lived in New Jersey. Thigh wound; treated at Mount Sinai.

GUTMAN, JONATHAN; lived at 16 Perry Street. Spent ball in right arm.

HALSEY, EDWARD, a "boy."

HANLEY, PATRICK. Apparently shot in arm.

HANROD, J.; born America. Leg injury; treated at Mount Sinai.

HARVEY, PATRICK, age 40; born Ireland; lived at 246 West Thirtieth Street; laborer. Wounded leg; amputated at Mount Sinai.

HEARN, B. Born Ireland. Treated at police headquarters.

HENDRICK, JOHN, age 26; lived at 578 Court Street, Brooklyn. Shot in hip.

HENRY, JAMES. Face and scalp wounds.

HOCH (or HOCK or KOCK), JOHN, age 52; born Germany; lived at 307 Sixth Street. Wounded in shoulder.

HOWARD, THEODORE (or THOMAS or FREDERICK), age 20; born England; boatman. Leg wound; treated at Mount Sinai.

HUGH, THOMAS; lived on Fifty-sixth Street. Shot in leg.

HUGHES, PATRICK, age 27. Shot in breast, right arm, and left side. *Tribune* (July 15) reporter who visited him at Mount Sinai said he was a "Roman Catholic Irishman" who did not oppose the Orange parade.

HUNTER, ——; lived at 116 Dean Street. Shot in mouth.

HUSSEY, EDWARD G., age 18; born in America (perhaps to Irish parents); lived at 412 West Thirty-seventh Street. Had gone to 264 West Twenty-fourth Street to collect a bill for his mother. Slight thigh wound.

HUSSEY (or HUSEY or HUSSY), FRANK, age 27; lived at 53 Warren Street, Jersey City. Clubbed on head by policeman.

KANE (or CANE), THOMAS, age 18; born England; glassblower. Shot in shoulder and taken to Bellevue.

KELLY, MICHAEL. Perhaps *Michael Kelly* who was killed (see above), but *Times* (July 14), which alone listed this injury, gave address as 114 East Twenty-fourth Street.

KELLY, PATRICK; lived at 119 Bayard Street. Scalp wound.

KIERNEY, JOHN, age 29; born Ireland; lived at 307 Seventh Avenue. Shot in back by musket.

KING, DENIS; Irish born; lived at 73 Columbia Street. Clubbed by policeman.

LANGSTAFF (or LANGSTIFF or LAIGSTATT), HENRY, age 22; born

Germany; lived at 166 Butler Street, Brooklyn; cooper. Hit in knee and elbow by militia. Taken to Bellevue in peddlar's wagon.

LENNON (or LENON or LEMON), JAMES, age 26 or 28; born Ireland; laborer. Shot by troops in left breast and shoulder at Twenty-sixth Street and Eighth Avenue. Recovered at Mount Sinai.

LILLY, PATRICK; born Ireland. Slight injury.

LINDERBACH, PHILLIP, age 21; born New York; lived at 300 West Fortieth Street. Told *Tribune* (July 15) he was shot twice in thigh while standing near Twenty-sixth Street and Eighth Avenue.

LONGWORTH, CHRISTOPHER; born Ireland. Told reporters he was innocent bystander and unsure if shot by troops or onlookers.

LOWREY, JAMES; born Ireland. Face wound.

LUTENBERGER, ——. Taken with *Auckwright* (see above) to 238 West Twenty-Eighth Street but were denied entrance. The 1870 census schedules show an "Elizabeth Lutenberg" at 162 West Twenty-eighth Street—most likely the person identified in the papers as "Lutenberger."

LYNCH, JAMES, age 21 or 24; lived at 229 West Houston Street. Shot in head. Recovered at Mount Sinai.

LYNTON (or LYTON or LYTTON), JASPER (or JOSEPH); Cuban. Leg wound; admitted to Bellevue.

McCORMACK, J. Slight injury.

McCORMACK, THOMAS. Clubbed on head by police near Hibernian Hall and taken to St. Luke's Hospital.

McKENYON, L., age 19; born Ireland. Head injury.

McKINNON, WILLIAM; lived at 428 East Fifteenth Street.

McMAHAN, DENIS, age 30; born Ireland; lived on Eighty-third Street. Head wound; treated at Bellevue.

McMULLEN, JOHN; lived on West Fortieth Street. Cut above eye from club.

MAHONEY, JEREMIAH; lived on Thirty-eighth Street. Shot in head; treated at Bellevue.

MALONEY (or MALONY or MALONE), JEREMIAH (or JERRY), age 17; lived on Eighteenth Street between Eighth and Ninth avenues; laborer. Sixth Regiment musket ball hit face.

MALOY (or MALLOY, MALLOON, or MALLON), TERENCE (or DENNIS or TENNIS), age 31; lived at 248 West Twenty-Eighth Street; cartman. First spelling from census schedules. Maloy said he was between Twenty-fifth and Twenty-sixth Street on his way home from work when he was shot in the cheek.

MANAN, MICHAEL; born Ireland; lived in Yorkville; laborer. Leg injury; treated at Mount Sinai.

MARAN, JAMES; born Ireland. Treated at Mount Sinai.

MATTHEWS (or MATHEWS), JOHN (or JAMES), age 39. Claimed he did not object to the Orange parade. Was in area when he heard firing. Shot by musket in thigh; treated at Bellevue.

MITCHELL, JOHN, age 36; born Dublin; reportedly lived at 248 West Twenty-eighth Street, where *Maloy* (see above) also resided; but census schedules show his address as 238; laborer or carman at Tracy and Russell's brewery in lower Manhattan. Shot in ankle by troops while on his way home from work.

MURPHY, DENNIS; born Ireland; laborer. Shot in back; treated at Mount Sinai.

MURPHY, J. Undisclosed injury; treated at Bellevue.

MURPHY, THOMAS; born Ireland. Breast wound; treated at Mount Sinai.

MURRAY, MARTIN; lived on Fifty-sixth Street. Shot in leg.

NEWPORT, THOMAS, age 32; lived in Brooklyn; laborer. Gunshot wound in arm.

O'BRIEN, JOHN, age 39; born Ireland; lived on East Fortieth Street. Shot in knee; leg perhaps amputated at Bellevue.

O'HARA, PATRICK (or PETER); born Ireland. Leg wound; treated at Bellevue.

O'HERN, PATRICK, age 19; born Ireland. Thigh wound; treated at Bellevue.

O'KEEFE, CORNELIUS, age 25; born Ireland. Slight wound; treated at Bellevue.

PUTNAM, EDWARD (or ADOLPH POTTMAN), age 34; born Germany; lived at Broadway and Erie Street in Jersey City; grainer. Shot in head; admitted to Bellevue.

READ, PATRICK, age 22; lived at 164 or 184 Elizabeth Street. Shot in breast; treated at Mount Sinai.

REARDON, JEREMIAH; lived on Thirty-fourth Street near First Avenue. Cuts on hand and leg; treated at Mount Sinai.

REDMOND, PETER, age 19; born Ireland; lived at Eighty-third Street and Tenth Avenue; laborer. Shot in arm.

REID, ELIZABETH, age 26; servant. Shot in thighs and a hip while watching parade near Twenty-fifth Street and Eighth Avenue.

ROURKE, JOHN; lived at Fifty-fifth Street and Seventh Avenue. Shot in leg; treated at Bellevue.

ROURKE, JOHN J., age 30; born Ireland; lived at 56 Ninth Avenue; conductor. Shot in thigh. Said two dead men fell over him as he lay bleeding on pavement.

SCOTT, JAMES, age 30; born Canada or England; lived at 137 Pine Street. Groin wound; treated at Mount Sinai.

SILVA, GASPAR (or GASPER SILVER or SILVEY), age 24; Cuban. Struck by minnieball while walking with his wife and a friend toward Ninth Avenue in Twenty-fifth Street. Treated at Bellevue.

SNOW, ——; lived on Washington Street. Shot in thigh while riding in an Eighth Avenue streetcar.

STEBBINS, R. Injury treated at police headquarters.

STERN, WILLIAM; born England. Knee wound; treated at Bellevue.

STOCK, C.; born England. Undisclosed wounds.

STOREY, JOHN W. (or WILLIAM STOREY). *World* (July 14) listed a "W. Storey," claimed he was born in England, was wounded in a knee, and was admitted to Bellevue. *Irish World* (July 22) reported that "William Storey" was shot in left leg while riding on Eighth Avenue streetcar between Twenty-seventh and Twenty-eighth streets. Yet *Times* and *World* reported (July 17) that the "Storey" in question was "John W. Storey" of Gideon Orange Lodge. *Times* claimed Storey was waving an orange handkerchief in the procession but stopped when other Orangemen urged him not to provoke an attack. Just then, the militia began firing, and Storey threw up his arms and was struck by a minnieball in an armpit. But on July 19, Gideon Loyal Orange Lodge No. 10 issued a statement denying that an Orangeman had been wounded and that "J. W. Storey" was a member of its organization (see *Times* and *Tribune*, July 20).

TEAMY, M.; born Ireland. Arm wound; treated at Bellevue.

THORN, W. J.; lived at 45 Robinson Street. Clubbed into gutter by three Irishmen near Newsboys' Lodging House in Park Place.

TIERNEY, J.; born Ireland. Hip wound; treated at Bellevue.

WALLACE, THOMAS; born America; lived on 143rd Street. Slight wound.

WARNECK, FRANK; lived at 134 Eighth Avenue; driver for Mitchell's furniture store at 332 Eighth Avenue. Hit in leg by a bullet that came crashing through the store's front window.

WARREN (or WARNER), ROBERT (or WILLIAM), age 11; lived at 331 West Thirty-seventh Street. Shot in shoulder.

UNKNOWN MAN. Mouth wound; treated at Bellevue.

MILITARY INJURIES

Those in the following list who were mentioned in Maj. Gen. Alexander B. Shaler's official report are marked by a double asterisk (**). His report, dated July 19, was printed in the July 22 *World* and *Tribune* and in the New York State Adjutant-General's Office, *Annual Report of the Adjutant-General, 1871* (Albany, 1872).

Sixth Regiment

**ADLER, JULIUS R., lived at 417 Grand Street. Wrist slightly grazed.

BLOOM, LEOPOLD, lived at 463 Broome Street. Sunstroke.

**UNNAMED PRIVATE. Badly bruised leg.

Seventh Regiment

**BEHRINGER, ——; Company B sergeant. Leg wound by stone.

FITZGERALD, LOUIS, colonel; lived at 111 East Thirty-first Street. Slight wound.

**MORGAN, ——, Company I private. Slight scalp wound.

**TOWNSEND, ——, Company G private. Musket ball in neck.

Eighth Regiment

PICKARD, JOSEPH, age 22; born Ireland; painter. Accidently cut on head when bayonet fell from a musket rack.

Ninth Regiment

BRYAN, ——, Company B sergeant. Struck in the side by an onlooker along Eighth Avenue.

**BURNS, DANIEL, Company E Private. Stabbed in back while guarding body of *Henry Paige* (see "Military Deaths") in drugstore.

**BYERS, THOMAS S. (or C. or E.), Company B sergeant. Kicked or struck in the side.

**FISK, JAMES, JR.; lived at 313 West Twenty-third Street. Slightly injured as he tried to find his regiment on Eighth Avenue. "The crowd came for me," he told a reporter. "I was set upon by the mob with stones and brickbats and pitched into the gutter. When I got up my coat was torn off and [I] found I was wounded" (*Sun*, July 15). All other accounts suggest Fisk was thrown from his horse and sprained an ankle.

**GRIFFIN, ——, Company A private. Injured leg.

**SPENCER, BIRD W., Company K captain; lived at 163 West Forty-fourth Street. Struck on head by brick or club.

Twenty-second Regiment

DODGE, ——, Company E private. Hit on head by stone.

EWEN, HAMILTON, Company G; surveyor. Struck on head by brick.

HONEGE (or HONIDGE or HONEDGE), ——, Company I private. Hit on arm by brick.
MILLER (or MULLER), F. B., Company I. Hit by bricks.
MUNDHERK, ——, Company I private. Struck by paving stone.
STEVENS, ——, Company C sergeant. Slight injury.
STYLES, ——, Company A captain. Hit in head by brick or stone.

Eighty-fourth Regiment

**ARCHER, WILLIAM, Company F private. Flesh wound in wrist.
**DOUGLASS, JAMES A., captain. Hit on head by stone.
**JENNIE, WILLIAM, Company I private. Shot in head.

POLICE INJURIES

Amounts awarded by the 1863 Riot Relief Fund are noted at the appropriate entries. Names and amounts were listed in the *Times*, July 21.

BROWN, DENIS, Twenty-ninth Precinct. Convulsions.
BRYANT, ——, Nineteenth Precinct. Shot in hand.
CLANCY, ——, Twenty-second Precinct. Injured in mouth.
CONSTABLE, CHRISTOPHER, Twentieth Precinct. Sunstroke ($350).
COURTNEY, THOMAS, Twenty-second Precinct. Back bruises ($200).
COVERT, GEORGE, Fifteenth Precinct. Sunstroke ($400).
CURTIS, FRANK H., Ninth or Twenty-ninth Precinct. Spent ball struck elbow ($200).
DIXON, WILLIAM, Nineteenth Precinct. Two broken fingers and a bruised hand when clubbed at Hibernian Hall ($300).
DOUGHERTY, MICHAEL (or MICHAEL DOHERTY), Fourth Precinct. Scalp wound.
DOUGHERTY, WILLIAM, First Precinct. Body bruises ($200).
FARBUSH (or FORBUSH), HENRY W., Twenty-second Precinct. Cut knee when thrown from horse ($500).
FINNEGAN, JAMES. Convulsions.
GILGER, EDWARD, Twenty-eighth Precinct. Fell off stagecoach and injured back and arms ($350).
GORMAN, MARTIN, Twenty-seventh Precinct. Stone bruises ($200).
HAVENS, GEORGE H., mounted police sergeant, Thirty-second Precinct. Struck on arm or ear by stones ($525).
HEDDEN, HENRY, captain, Fifteenth Precinct. Nose and eye injuries sustained on Eighth Avenue ($800).

IRVING, WILLIAM, Tenth or Twentieth Precinct. Bruised by paving stone ($200).

JAMES, THOMAS A. (or N.), sergeant, Twentieth Precinct. Bruised by paving stones.

JOYCE, THOMAS C., Thirty-second Precinct. Back bruises from stones and fall from mount ($450).

LEDDEN, WILLIAM J., Sixteenth Precinct. Shot in arm ($525).

McCULLOUGH, WILLIAM H., sergeant, Twentieth Precinct. Knee and leg bruises from brick ($525).

McGRATH, JOHN, patrolman, First Precinct. Bruises ($200).

McKENZIE, ——, Twenty-ninth Precinct. No details ($350).

MAHER, JAMES, Thirteenth Precinct. Heat prostration ($400).

MESCHUTT, FREDERICK A., Fifteenth Precinct. Struck on shoulder by brick ($200).

MURPHY, EDWARD, Twenty-second Precinct. Hit in mouth by stone ($350).

O'CONNOR, JOHN, patrolman, Thirteenth Precinct. Shot in side and badly wounded ($225).

OFFICER NO. 1704, Thirteenth Precinct. Shot in side.

PHILLIPS, LEON (or PATRICK), Nineteenth Precinct. Bayonet wound ($375).

ROBB (or ROFF), WILLIAM H., Thirty-first Precinct. Accidently clubbed on leg by another policeman ($200).

SILLECK (or SELLECK), JOSEPH, First Precinct. Bruises ($200).

WHITCOMB, E. T. (or P.), sergeant, Nineteenth Precinct. Bruised on arms and chest by club ($525).

WILSON, A. S., captain, Thirty-second Precinct. Bruised on back and head by stones ($800).

ARRESTED

Since many cases were dismissed at once, it is likely that police arrested people just to clear the streets. The final disposition of only a few of the following cases could be learned. The only court records I found are in the July 13, 1871, entries of two Second District Police Court Docket Books in the Municipal Archives and Records Center for Justices Hogan and Shandley. Shandley's is labeled *Docket Books*, June 13, 1870–July 16, 1871; Hogan's is *Docket Book*, 1870–71. Names that appeared in these books are marked by a triple asterisk (***). I found no relevant records in New York County Supreme Court's Criminal Branch files and only seven grand jury dismissals in the Municipal Archives. Cases against Thomas Coleman, Thomas O'Neill, and Samuel Sapulen are housed in the Grand Jury Dismissals (1871), Box 9580. Complaints against Bernard McGinnis, Patrick Hogan, John Hayes, and John Henricks are found in Box 105710. Hogan and Shandley usually bailed those who were charged with carrying concealed weapons at five hundred to one thousand dollars and required them to keep the peace for six months to a year. The following information was compiled from the grand jury dismissals, the two docket books, and the *Times*, July 14 and 15; *Herald*, July 15; *Sun*, July 14; and *Tribune*, July 14, 15, 17, 18, and 20; and *World*, July 14 and 15.

***BELLINGTON, SHERWOOD. Disorderly conduct and carrying concealed revolver. Bailed at $500; keep peace six for months.

BLAIR, WILLIAM. Arrested by officer Gilmartin "for frightening women with a pocket knife" (*Tribune*, July 14).

BOWERS, PATRICK. Details unknown. Bailed at $500.

***BOWNEY, ANDREW. Arrested by Third Precinct policeman McDonald for disorderly conduct and carrying loaded revolver. P. T. Carney, 79 Cortlandt Street, posted $500 bond; keep peace for a year.

***CLARK, JOHN W. Disorderly conduct. Bailed at $500; keep peace for six months.

***COLEMAN, THOMAS. Signed "X" to a brief statement affirming that he was a twenty-seven-year-old, Irish-born laborer, of 152 Elizabeth Street. On July 14, officer George Van Buskirk charged Coleman in First District Police Court with carrying a club and urging mob at Hibernian Hall to fight police who had just broken up a large crowd. Coleman admitted he carried the club. Bailed at $2,000; grand jury later refused to indict.

***CONNELL, JOHN. Disorderly conduct. Charges dismissed.

CONNOLLY, FRANK. Unknown charges. Case dismissed.

***CONNOLLY, PATRICK. Disorderly conduct. Case dismissed.

***CONNOR, JOHN. Charged with carrying pistols and trying to incite riot in LaFayette Place. Jailed when he could not post bail. Outcome unknown.

***COX, MICHAEL; lived at 93 Orchard Street. Disorderly conduct. Bailed at $500.

***CROAK, EDWARD. Disorderly conduct for firing into Orange procession. Bailed at $500; keep peace for six months.

***CURTAIN, JOHN; lived in Brooklyn. Disorderly conduct and carrying a revolver. Released on own recognizance.

***DALTON, WILLIAM; lived in Jersey City. Disorderly conduct. Case dismissed.

DARIAN (or DORIAIO), JOHN. Arrested for carrying a trowel. Case dismissed when he explained he was a mason who worked in Cherry Street.

***DEERY (or DEERING), HUGH; lived on 123rd Street. Arrested in Fourth Avenue near Eleventh Street for inciting a crowd to attack parade. Jailed when could not post bond. Outcome unknown.

DEERY (or DIEVEY), JOHN. Carried horse pistol in large crowd in South Street. Bailed at $500.

***DEVINE, WILLIAM; lived at 202 Elizabeth Street. Disorderly conduct and carrying a revolver. Bailed at $500; keep peace for six months.

***DEWEY, JOHN. Rioting. Bailed at $500; keep peace for six months.

***DORMAN, JOHN. Disorderly conduct. Charges dropped.

***DWYER, EDWARD; lived at 212 Elizabeth Street. Arrested at Broadway and Tenth Street with pistol. Chrarged with disorderly conduct and accessory to riot. Bailed at $500.

***DWYER, WILLIAM E. Disorderly conduct. Charges dismissed.

***ENWRIGHT, MICHAEL. Unknown charges. Case dismissed.

***FALON, JOHN. Rioting and carrying a revolver and cartridges. Bailed at $500; keep peace for six months.

***FINLEY, MICHAEL. Unknown charges. Case dismissed.

***FITZHARRIS, THOMAS. Disorderly conduct. Charges dropped.

FLAYES, JOHN. Arrested for possessing a dirk.

FLEURY, JAMES. Rioting. Charges dropped.

***FLYNN, DANIEL H. Waved razor in large crowd and rioting. Bailed at $500.

***FOLLETT, MARTIN. Disorderly conduct. Arrested in Mott Street when Policeman Farley learned that two chambers of Follett's revolver had been fired. Bailed at $500; keep peace for one year.

***FRANTONI, MICHAEL. Disorderly conduct. Bailed at $500; keep peace for six months.

***GALLAGHER, JOHN; lived at 135 Seventh Avenue. Disorderly conduct for firing pistol during night of July 12. Case dismissed.

***GIBNEY, HENRY F. Disorderly conduct for drawing a pistol. Bailed at $500; keep peace for six months.

***GILMARTIN, THOMAS. Rioting in Fourth Street with knife. Bailed at $500; keep peace for six months.

***GREEN, PATRICK. Rioting; found with revolver. Bailed at $500; keep peace for six months.

***HAYES, JOHN, age 45; bricklayer. Disorderly conduct and carrying concealed dirk for trying to rescue prisoner in Bowery Street. Bailed at $2,000; grand jury dismissed the case.

***HENRICKS, JOHN, age 26; lived at 22 Amity Street. Disorderly conduct for carrying foot-long knife on Thirteenth Street. Bailed at $1,000; grand jury dismissed the case.

HENRY, JAMES; New Jersey. Charges unknown. Henry claimed police had beaten him for not keeping up with fellow prisoners.

***HOGAN, PATRICK; laborer. Disorderly conduct for urging a large crowd outside a police station to rescue those inside who had been arrested. Bailed at $100.

***KEELT, FRANCIS. Disorderly conduct. At corner of Twenty-first Street and Fifth Avenue, emerged from large crowd with revolver. Bailed at $1,000.

***KELLAHER, MICHAEL. Unknown charges. Case dismissed.

***KELLY, EDWARD. Rioting and possessing a six-barreled revolver. Bailed at $500.

***KELLY, JOHN. Disorderly conduct. Case dismissed on July 14.

KELLY, MICHAEL. Unknown charges. Case dismissed.

***KELLY, PATRICK. Rioting. Police claimed he threatened to throw stone at Orangemen. Bailed at $500.

KELLY, PATRICK J. The *Times* (July 14) reported he was arrested "in a crowd on Fourth-avenue as the procession was passing. One man shouted: 'Now let us give it to the ______s.' The prisoner thereupon exhibited a pistol, capped and loaded with powder and ball." Bailed at $500; keep peace for six months.

***KELLY, PETER J.; lived on Fifty-second Street. Disorderly conduct.

***KENNEDY, JOHN. Disorderly conduct. Charges dismissed.

KERSHNER (or KERSRER or KERSHAW), GUSTAVUS. Rioting. Dismissed on July 13.

***KILMARTIN, THOMAS; lived in Brooklyn. This was not *Thomas Gilmartin* (see above). Disorderly conduct.

LAHEY, JAMES; lived at 301 Bleecker Street. Intoxicated.

LAMB, EDWARD. Assaulting detective Clapp, who had just arrested someone else, on Prince Street. Bailed at $500 bail.

***LANIHAN, MICHAEL. Carrying loaded revolver. Bailed at $500; keep peace for six months.

***LEEN, THOMAS. Denied charges he carried revolver. Bailed at $500; case later dismissed.

LYNCH, JAMES. Disorderly conduct. Arrested Tenth Street and Sixth Avenue.

***LYNCH, JAMES. Disorderly conduct. Case dismissed July 13.

***LYNCH, THOMAS. Disorderly conduct. Case dismissed.

LYNCH, THOMAS; lived at 61 West Thirty-ninth Street. Carrying concealed weapons at Twenty-third Street and Eighth Avenue.

***McCABE, JOHN. Disorderly conduct for possessing two revolvers or for intoxication and possessing knife. Bailed at $500; keep peace for six months.

McCABE, JOHN. Rioting. Charges dropped.

McCARTHY, JOHN. Charges unknown. Bailed at $500.

***McCARTY, JOHN. Disorderly conduct; concealing knife. Bailed at $500; keep peace for six months.

***McCLINCHEY, ARTHUR; lived in Brooklyn. Disorderly conduct. Charges dismissed.

***McDERMOTT, FRANK. Rioting; possession of revolver. Bailed at $500.

McDONALD, F. Charges unknown. Held for trial.

McDONALD, JAMES; lived in Brooklyn. Rioting.

***McDONALD, THOMAS. Disorderly conduct. Charges dropped.

McGINNIS, BERNARD; *Star* reporter. Possession of billyclub. Bailed at $1,000.

McGOWAN, PATRICK. Disorderly conduct. Charges dropped.

McHUGH, JOHN; lived at 64 West Houston Street. Possessed concealed revolver and ammunition. Bailed at $500.

McHUGH, JOHN (or JAMES B.); lived at 286 West Eleventh Street. Possessed revolver. Bailed at $500.

***MAHONY, CORNELIUS. Disorderly conduct; displaying unnamed weapon; abusive language against police. Bailed at $500.

MALONEY, MICHAEL. Unknown charges. Bailed at $500.

MALVIN, MICHAEL. Carried revolver. Bailed at $500; keep peace for a year.

***MARTIN, BARNEY; lived at 137 Seventh Avenue. Neighbor of *John Gallagher* (see above). Disorderly conduct; fired revolver night of July 12. Charges dropped.

***MERRIGAN, PATRICK. Disorderly conduct. Charges dropped.

***MONTGOMERY, JOHN. Disorderly conduct. Charges dropped.

***NORTON, MICHAEL. Disorderly conduct; had revolver. Bailed at $500; keep peace for six months.

***O'GUIRE, WILLIAM. Disorderly conduct.

***O'MAHONY, PATRICK. Disorderly conduct; carried revolver near Cooper Union. Bailed at $500.

***O'NEILL, EDWARD; lived at 344 West Sixteenth Street. Disorderly conduct; caught with shotgun. Case dismissed.

O'NEILL, THOMAS. A "ringleader." In Second District Police Court, Officer Gillespie charged that "a large disorderly and riotous crowd was collected all around" O'Neill at Twenty-third Street and Fifth Avenue and that O'Neill had "a large revolver concealed and capped." Bailed at $1,000; grand jury dismissed charges.

***ORST, FREDERICK. Unknown charges. Case dismissed.

PLUNKETT, JOSEPH; lived at 452 West Nineteenth Street. Disorderly conduct; carrying revolver. Bailed at $500.

***POWERS, PATRICK. Rioting; carrying loaded revolver. Arrested Twenty-seventh Street and Eighth Avenue. Bailed at $500; keep peace for six months.

***RADIGAN, PATRICK, age 41; born Ireland; lived at 154 West Eighteenth Street; laborer. Disorderly conduct; fired pistol at night. Charges dropped.

***REGAN, THOMAS. Disorderly conduct. Bailed at $500.

***REICHER, GUSTAVUS. Disorderly conduct. Charges dropped.

***RIESTER, GEORGE. Rioting. Charges dropped.

RIORDAN, MICHAEL. Disorderly conduct. Charges dismissed.

***ROACH, JAMES. Disorderly conduct. Charges dismissed.

***RUSSELL, FRANK; lived at 298 First Avenue. Disorderly conduct. Charges dropped.

RYAN, THOMAS; lived at 468 Greenwich Street. Disorderly conduct; carried weapons on Fifth Avenue. Bailed at $500.

***RYAN, THOMAS; lived at 161 West Thirty-ninth Street. Carried revolver. Bailed at $500.

***SAPULEN, SAMUEL. In Officer Charles Heidelberg's affidavit: "Denied to officer he had a weapon—but when searched found a club or billy in the inside pocket of his vest." Bailed at $1,000 but freed on August 11 when grand jury dismissed case.

SERRES (or SECRES), WASHINGTON. Disorderly conduct. Charges dismissed.

SHAW, MICHAEL; lived at 741 Sixth Avenue. Disorderly conduct.

SHAW, PATRICK. Unknown charges. Case dismissed.

***TOBIN, WILLIAM. Disorderly conduct. Charges dismissed.

TOYLET, MARTIN. Carried loaded revolver.

***TUCKER, WILLIAM. Disorderly conduct. Case dismissed.

***WALLACE, THOMAS. Rioting at Fourteenth Street and Broadway. Had cartridges and percussion caps, was bleeding from a fight. Bailed at $500; keep peace for six months.

WALSH, JAMES. Disorderly conduct. Bailed at $1,000.

***WARD, JAMES. Unknown charges. Case dismissed.

WARD, MICHAEL; lived at 145 East Thirty-second Street. Intoxication.

DAMAGE TO PROPERTY

This list is compiled from the July 15 *World* and *Tribune* and the July 16 *Times*. Twenty-one merchants and one resident along Eighth Avenue claimed damages to property. Most said they would sue the city for damages, but no record could be found of such action. The total amount came to $4,011.

ABELS, JOSEPH. Lager beer saloon, 300 Eighth Avenue. Claimed Ninth Regiment troop firing caused $2 damages.

ANDREWS, G. N. Druggist, 278 Eighth Avenue. Claimed some people who sought safety in store stole fifteen bottle of perfume valued at $2 each. Militia fire damaged shop. Loss: $500.

ANDREWS, J. Apothecary shop, corner of Twenty-fourth Street. Broken windows, bottles, and goods; several militia bullets lodged in back wall. Loss: $1,000.

ANGWIN, JOSEPH (or ANGUIN). Tea and coffee shop, 282 Eighth Avenue. Damage when crowds took refuge from militia fire. Loss: $50.

BRUCE AND QUINTON. Plumbers, 286 Eighth Avenue. Damage to stock and windows; minié balls lodged in walls. Loss: $200.

COHEN, JACOB. Cigar store, 288 Eighth Avenue. Loss: $100.

COLLINS, LAWRENCE. Butcher shop, 290 Eighth Avenue. People broke glass and crockery rushing into store to escape firing. Loss: $40.

CREGAN, DANIEL. Liquor store, 278 Eighth Avenue. Stones broke windows, shelves, demijohns, liquor casks. Loss: $300.

CROGAN, JACOB. Cigar dealer. Claimed people stole cigars; damage to doors and windows. Loss: $800.

GANZ, EMANUAL. Cigar store, 328 Eighth Avenue. Two panes of glass broken.

GASWEEN, JACOB. Bookstore, 306 Eighth Avenue. Damage from militia fire. Loss: $25.

ISAAC, MORRIS. Merchant tailor, 318 Eighth Avenue. People broke down door seeking shelter. Loss: $50.

KOEHLER, JOHN. Tinsmith, 284½ Eighth Avenue. Militia fired fourteen shots into awning. Loss: $13.

LIDDLE, D. Confectioner, 302 Eighth Avenue. Claimed people breaking into his shop stole candles. Loss: $150.

McDONALD, WILLIAM J. Jeweler, 282 Eighth Avenue. Said musket ball killed man in front of store then broke clocks in show window. Loss: $50.

MEAGHER, PATRICK J. Used furniture store, 286 Eighth Avenue. Claimed men destroyed mirrors and furniture in cellar. Loss: $130.

O'SHEA, PATRICK. Oyster house, 308 Eighth Avenue. Damage from muskets. Loss: $300.

ROACH, F. W. Produce store. People escaping musket fire broke two panes of glass. Loss: $5.

SCHINKEL, ADOLPH. Bakery, 324 Eighth Avenue. Damage to showcase and pane of glass. Loss: $50.

SHAW, E. A. Basement restaurant, 250 Eighth Avenue. Loss of business: $20.

TOPLITZ, I. Downtown merchant whose private residence at 264 West Twenty-fourth Street was damaged by military. Loss: $56.

WHITE, JOSEPH. Hardware store, 312 Eighth Avenue. Musket fire damage: $100. Crowd damage: $50. Loss from theft: $10.

Appendix C / Sources of Biographical Information on Selected Committee of Seventy Members

Babcock, Samuel D.

Bigelow, John. *Retrospections of an Active Life.* Vol. 5. Garden City, N.Y.: Doubleday, Page, 1913. P. 281.
Mandlebaum, Seymour J. *Boss Tweed's New York.* New York: Wiley, 1965. P. 81.
Ratner, Sidney, ed. *New Light on the History of Great American Fortunes: American Millionaires of 1892 and 1902.* New York: Kelley, 1953. P. 60.
Unger, Irwin. *The Greenback Era: A Social and Political History of American Finance, 1865–1879.* Princeton: Princeton University Press, 1964. Pp. 154n, 288, 288n, 289.

Bailey Isaac H.

Manning, James Hilton. *Century of American Savings Banks: New York Volume.* New York: B. F. Buck, 1917. Pp. 173–74.

Ballin, Eugene

Ratner. *Great American Fortunes.* P. 61.
Times, June 24, 1885.

Barlow, Francis C.

Alexander, De Alva Stanwood. *A Political History of the State of New York.* Vol. 3. New York: Holt, 1909. Pp. 130, 135, 174, 264, 275, 307.

Barrows, Chester L. *William M. Evarts: Lawyer, Diplomat, Statesman.* Chapel Hill: University of North Carolina Press, 194. Pp. 193, 250.
Bowen, Croswell. *The Elegant Oakey.* New York: Oxford University Press, 1956. Pp. 157–66.
Flick, Alexander C. *Samuel Jones Tilden: A Study in Political Sagacity.* New York: Dodd, Mead, 1939. Pp. 226, 252, 344–47.
Times, January 12, 1896.
Who Was Who in America: Historical Volume, 1607–1896. Rev. ed. Chicago: Marquis, 1967. P. 109.

Barrett, George C.

Callow, Alexander B. *The Tweed Ring.* New York: Oxford University Press, 1965. Pp. 206, 278.
"Judge Barrett." *Harper's Weekly,* April 12, 1890. P. 273.
Times, June 8, 1906.

Brown, James M.

Browne, Junius Henry. *The Great Metropolis: A Mirror of New York.* Hartford, Conn.: American Publishing, 1869. P. 542.
Who Was Who. P. 146.

Bundy, Jonas M.

Times, September 10, 1891.
Who Was Who. P. 153.

Choate, Joseph Hodges

Martin, Edward S. *The Life of Joseph Hodges Choate: New Englander, New Yorker, Lawyer, Ambassador.* New York: Scribner's, 1917.

Clews, Henry

Clews, Henry. *Henry Clews: Fifty Years on Wall Street.* New York: Irving, 1908.

Detmold, Christian E.

Who Was Who. P. 216.

Dix, John A.

Dix, Morgan, comp. *Memoirs of John Adam Dix.* 2 vols. New York: Harper, 1883.
Strong, George Templeton. *The Diary of George Templeton Strong.* Vol. 4, *The Post-War Years, 1865–1875.* Allan Nevins and Milton H. Thomas, eds. New York: Macmillan, 1952. Pp. 50–51 passim.

Who Was Who. P. 220.

Eaton, Dorman B.

Times, December 24, 1889.

Emott, James

Barrows. *Willam M. Evarts.* Pp. 183–84.
Strong. *Diary.* Vol. 4. P. 273.
Times, September 12, 1884.
Who Was Who. P. 249.

Evarts, William M.

Barrows. *William M. Evarts.*

Foley, John

Edwards, Richard, ed. *New York's Great Industries.* 1884. Rpt. New York: Arno, 1973. Pp. 152–53.
Herald, September 18 and October 12, 1872.
Lynch, Denis Tilden. *"Boss" Tweed: The Story of a Grim Generation.* New York: Garden City Books, Blue Ribbon, 1927. P. 374.

Green, John C.

Albion, Robert A. *The Rise of New York Port, 1815–1860.* New York: Scribner's, 1939. P. 199.
Ratner. *Great American Fortunes.* P. 67.
Who Was Who. P. 286.

Havemeyer, William F.

Furer, Howard B. *William Frederick Havemeyer: A Political Biography.* New York: American Press, 1965.
Manning. *Century of American Savings Banks.* P. 199.
Ratner. *Great American Fortunes.* P. 67.
Who Was Who. P. 309.

Hoe, Robert

Ratner. *Great American Fortunes.* P. 69.
Times, September 14, 1884.

Iselin, Adrian

Ratner. *Great American Fortunes.* P. 69.
Times, March 20, 1905.

James, D. Willis

Ratner. *Great American Fortunes*. P. 70.
Times, September 14, 1907.

Kennedy, Robert Lennox

Ratner. *Great American Fortunes*. P. 71.
Strong. *Diary*. Vol. 4. Pp. 100, 187, 478, 482.

Krackowitzer, Ernest

Times, September 25, 1875.

Ledwith, Thomas A.

Herald, November 29, 1871.
Strong. *Diary*. Vol. 4. P. 397.

Moulton, Severn D.

Herald, November 29, 1871.
Times, April 20, 1878.

Neilson, William H.

Times, May 27, 1882.

Nicoll, Henry

Strong. *Diary*. Vol. 4. P. 549.
Who Was Who. P. 450.

O'Donohue, Joseph J.

Herald, May 2, 1875.
Ratner. *Great American Fortunes*. P. 75.
Times, June 26, 1897.

Phelps, Royal

Ratner. *Great American Fortunes*. P. 75.

Pierrepont, Edwards

Barrows. *William M. Evarts*. Pp. 10, 102–3, 184, 223, 238, 324, 328, 393.

Potter, Howard

Herald, December 29, 1875.

Radde, William

Times, May 20, 1884.

Roosevelt, Robert B.

Katz, Irving. *August Belmont: A Political Biography*. New York: Columbia University Press, 1968. P. 137n.
Ratner. *Great American Fortunes*. Pp. 76–77.
Times, June 15, 1906.

Ruggles, Samuel B.

Thompson, D. B. Brinton. *Ruggles of New York: A Life of Samuel B. Ruggles*. New York: Columbia University Press, 1946.
Who Was Who. P. 528.

Salomon, Edward

Herald, December 29, 1875.

Schultz, Jackson S.

Browne. *Great Metropolis*. P. 670.
Ratner. *Great American Fortunes*. P. 81.
Times, May 3, 1885.

Spaulding, Henry F.

Ratner. *Great American Fortunes*. P. 80.

Spofford, Paul A.

Albion. *Rise of New York Port*. P. 127.
Weed, Harriet A., ed. *The Life of Thurlow Weed*. Vol. 1, *Autobiography of Thurlow Weed*. 1883. Rpt. New York: Da Capo, 1970. P. 502.
——. *The Life of Thurlow Weed*. Vol. 2, *Memoir of Thurlow Weed*. 1884. Rpt. New York: Da Capo, 1970. P. 339.

Stebbins, Henry G.

Barrows. *Willaim M. Evarts*. P. 328.
Mandlebaum. *Boss Tweed's New York*. P. 81.
Times, December 10, 1881.
Who Was Who. P. 574.

Sterne, Simon

Barrows. *William M. Evarts*. Pp. 194–95.
Bernstein, Iver. *The New York City Draft Riots: Their Significance for American Society and Politics in the Age of the Civil War*. New York: Oxford University Press, 1990. Pp. 219–20.

Herald, December 29, 1875.
Times, September 23, 1901.

Stewart, John A.

Mandlebaum. *Boss Tweed's New York*. P. 81.

Sturges, Jonathan

Ratner. *Great American Fortunes*. P. 79.
Sharkey, Robert P. *Money, Class and Party: An Economic Study of Civil War and Reconstruction*. Baltimore: Johns Hopkins University Press, 1959. Pp. 172–73, 173n, 273.
Times, November 30, 1874.

Tilden, Samuel J.

Bigelow, John. *The Life of Samuel J. Tilden*. New York: Harper and Row, 1895.
Flick. *Samuel Jones Tilden*.

Varian, George W.

Times, February 2, 1875.

Vermilye, William R.

Mandlebaum. *Boss Tweed's New York*. P. 81.

Index

Library of Congress Cataloging-in-Publication Data

Gordon, Michael A. (Michael Allen), 1941–

The Orange riots : Irish political violence in New York City, 1870 and 1871 / Michael A. Gordon.

p. cm.

Includes bibliographical references (p.) and index.

ISBN 0-8014-2754-1 (cloth : alk. paper). — ISBN 0-8014-8034-5 (paper : alk. paper)

1. Irish Americans—New York (N.Y.)—History—19th century. 2. Riots—New York (N.Y.)—History—19th century. 3. New York (N.Y.)—History—1865–1898. 4. New York (N.Y.)—Ethnic relations. I. Title.

F.128.9.I6G67 1993

974.7'10049162—dc20 93-9847